Repent ye; for the Kingdom of Heaven is at hand.

Matthew 3:2 KJV

I will arise and go to my father, and will say unto him, Father, I have sinned against heaven, and before thee, and am no more worthy to be called thy son.

Luke 15:18, 19 KJV

But let a man examine himself, and so let him eat of that bread, and drink of that cup. For he that eateth and drinketh unworthily, eateth and drinketh damnation to himself, not discerning the Lord's body.

1 Corinthians 11:28, 29 KJV

Religion is not simply as is generally supposed an inherently virtuous human quest for God. It is merely a final battleground between God and man's self-esteem.

Reinhold Niebuhr,
The Nature and Destiny of Man, vol. 1: 200

Christ Carrying the Cross, by Hieronymus Bosch

Worship as Repentance

LUTHERAN LITURGICAL TRADITIONS
AND CATHOLIC CONSENSUS

Walter Sundberg

WILLIAM B. EERDMANS PUBLISHING COMPANY

GRAND RAPIDS, MICHIGAN / CAMBRIDGE, U.K.

© 2012 Walter Sundberg

Published 2012 by
Wm. B. Eerdmans Publishing Co.
2140 Oak Industrial Drive N.E., Grand Rapids, Michigan 49505 /
P.O. Box 163, Cambridge CB3 9PU U.K.
www.eerdmans.com

Printed in the United States of America

18 17 16 15 14 13 12   7 6 5 4 3 2 1

Library of Congress Cataloging-in-Publication Data

Sundberg, Walter.
Worship as repentance: Lutheran liturgical traditions and catholic consensus /
Walter Sundberg.
p.   cm.
ISBN 978-0-8028-6732-2 (pbk.: alk. paper)
1. Lutheran Church — Liturgy. 2. Liturgics. 3. Public worship —
History of doctrines. I. Title.

BX8067.A1S86 2012

264′.041 — dc23

2011049261

Material quoted in Appendices II and III is from *Service Book and Hymnal* copyright ©
1958 Service Book and Hymnal admin. Augsburg Fortress Publishers. Reproduced by
permission. All rights reserved.

Except where otherwise noted, Scripture quotations are from the New Revised Standard
Version of the Bible (NSRV), copyright © 1999 by the Division of Christian Education of
the National Council of Churches in the U.S.A., and used by permission.

Contents

Contents

Preface

"Well, now, and that was a beautiful thing to see. I've known it again and again. The devil resists until the last moment and then the Grace of God is too much for him."[1] We are in the last pages of Evelyn Waugh's (1903-66) *Brideshead Revisited*. It is the 1930s in Great Britain. Lord Marchmain, whose magnificent estate is named "Brideshead," has just passed away after living a life that had little to commend it. He converted from Anglicanism to Catholicism so he could marry Teresa Flyte, who became the Marchioness of Marchmain and the mother of his four children. He abandoned her and his Christian faith to live in Italy for many years with a foreign woman named Cara.

His oldest son, the Earl of Brideshead or "Bridey," is a religious prig, his other son, Sebastian, a dissolute alcoholic. At the end of the novel, his eldest daughter Julia is on the way to divorce; her present lover, Charles Ryder, is also divorcing. Charles in his youth had taken up sexually with Sebastian. Charles is the novel's narrator. There is finally the youngest daughter, Cordelia. She is fragile; who wouldn't be after watching the spectacle of her elders, both parents and siblings? She is very religious and a good person.

Lady Marchmain preceded her long absent husband in death. She was also religious, but extremely bitter. After her death, Lord Marchmain returned to Brideshead, coming home to die. Death takes a while to do its work. As long as he could speak, Lord Marchmain wanted no priest or last rites to attend his final moments.

1. Evelyn Waugh, *Brideshead Revisited* (reprint, New York: Everyman's Library, 1993) 306.

The end inevitably comes. Marchmain is in bed. Julia the eldest daughter, her lover Charles, the mistress Cara — all of them, by standards of respectability, walking wrecks — are in the room. When Marchmain is too weak to protest, Julia sends for the priest to perform the Catholic sacrament of extreme unction. Julia and Cara are kneeling. "'Now,' said the priest, 'I know you are sorry for all the sins of your life, aren't you? Make a sign, if you can.'"[2] Charles Ryder, our narrator, is moved. Although he has had a lifelong disdain for Christianity, he cares about Julia, who wishes with all her heart that her father will die reconciled to the Church.

Caring for the woman he loves, however, is not all that is happening to Charles. There is something else going on inside him that has nothing to do with his love; indeed, it is the enemy of the love affair between Charles and Julia. Before the day is over, Julia will separate from Charles and he will not protest. That something is the Catholic faith: the Catholic faith as sheer fact, represented at the end of the novel by the ritual of last rites. At the hour of Lord Marchmain's death, all things in the novel come under examination. Christianity in the form of Tridentine Catholicism, conveyed by the liturgy of extreme unction, is pushing its way into the confused and failed life of Charles. It is also focusing in a new way the life of Julia. This momentous, sacred, forbidding, desire-denying event is taking place as the genial, stumbling, priest goes about his duty.

To his own surprise, Charles prays for a sign of faith. Into the room, through the mouth of the priest, come the words of ancient Latin; the medieval rite, *unctio extrema,* done word for word, unchanged, accommodating nobody. From somewhere inside his diminished, dying self, Lord Marchmain finds the will to make the sign of the cross. Weak, flat on his back, *in extremis,* he repents. He is forgiven.

"When the intensity of the religious attitude finds proper expression in art," observes the literary critic T. E. Hulme (1883-1917), whose artistic sensibility shaped the generation of English writers that included Waugh, "[it] springs not from a delight in life but from a feeling for certain absolute values, which are entirely independent of vital things." Thus it is characterized by "disgust with the trivial and accidental characteristics of living shapes, the searching after an

2. *Brideshead Revisited,* 305.

austerity, a monumental stability and permanence, a perfection and rigidity."[3]

When the priest says of Lord Marchmain's passing that "it is a beautiful thing," he is giving expression to this religious attitude. This beauty is of a certain type: a beauty that appears at the conjunction between time and eternity where time is understood as a world of degradation and eternity as the realm of perfection. The death of Lord Marchmain is a beautiful thing if one accepts a fallen world, subject to the devil, deserving of judgment, where people waste their lives and find no ultimate satisfaction. Into this world comes the promise of release, the offer of the grace of God. To receive this grace requires one thing and one thing only: repentance. To teach this central fact of Christian faith, to give it unerring, objective expression is the purpose of Catholic worship in *Brideshead Revisited:* worship as practiced unchanged for centuries, worship as repentance. When the church worships in this way it demonstrates the dogmatic principle *Ecclesia semper eadem:* the church is always the same.

Protestants, no matter how steeped in the doctrine of justification, can give no better witness to unmerited grace than the fierce and conservative Roman Catholic Evelyn Waugh does in this, his greatest novel. Protestants speak in the same way about sin and forgiveness. Martin Luther (1483-1546) in one of his pivotal essays, the "Exposition of Psalm 90" (1534), describes the ultimate saving event as Waugh understands it. Commenting on verse 8 of Psalm 90 ("You have set our iniquities before you, our secret sins in the light of your countenance"), Luther writes:

> This is the climax of the drama which God enacts with us. His intention is that we play our part in full awareness of our sins and of death. Yet it is not an evil thing . . . to have this awareness, to complain about our miseries, and to conclude that there is nothing within us but damnation. Indeed, one should complain and sigh this way. One should try to arrange and govern one's life in accordance with such sighing. Then it will happen that one becomes aware of salvation.[4]

---

3. T. E. Hulme, *Speculations: Essays on Humanism and the Philosophy of Art,* ed. Herbert Read (London: Routledge & Kegan Paul, 1924) 9.

4. *LW* 13:116.

For Luther this is the *Urerlebnis* or "primal experience" of the wrath of God that prepares the individual for the coming of grace. The primal experience undergirds Luther's entire theology.[5] It has shaped Lutheran worship for centuries, leaving its mark in liturgical forms such as the "exhortation to communicants" that sternly calls believers to turn from sin and make amendment of life and the conditional absolution, common in the public order of confession, that places as much emphasis on the binding of sins as their loosing in the exercise of the office of the keys.

On the matter of repentance as the center of worship, the cloud of witnesses can be multiplied. Like Roman Catholicism and Lutheranism, Anglicanism is committed to the preservation of liturgical tradition. In the *Book of Common Prayer* (1662 edition), the Order for Morning Prayer opens with a selection of evocative verses from Scripture that calls worshipers to turn from their sins and repent.[6] It then announces the purpose of worship:

5. See Werner Elert, *The Structure of Lutheranism,* tr. Walter A. Hansen (St. Louis: Concordia Publishing House, 1962) 17-28.

6. When the wicked man turneth away from his wickedness that he hath committed, and doeth that which is lawful and right, he shall save his soul alive. *Ezek.* xviii.27.

I acknowledge my transgressions, and my sin is ever before me. *Psalm* li.3.

Hide thy face from my sins, and blot out all mine iniquities. *Psalm* li.9.

The sacrifices of God are a broken spirit: a broken and a contrite heart, O God, thou wilt not despise. *Psalm* li.17.

Rend your heart, and not your garments, and turn unto the Lord your God: for he is gracious and merciful, slow to anger, and of great kindness, and repenteth him of the evil. *Joel* ii.13.

To the Lord our God belong mercies and forgivenesses, though we have rebelled against him; neither have we obeyed the voice of the Lord our God, to walk in his laws which he set before us. *Daniel* ix.9, 10.

O Lord, correct me, but with judgment; not in thine anger, lest thou bring me to nothing. *Jer.* x.24. *Psalm* vi.1.

Repent ye; for the Kingdom of Heaven is at hand. *St. Matt.* iii.2.

I will arise and go to my father, and will say unto him, Father, I have sinned against heaven, and before thee, and am no more worthy to be called thy son. *St. Luke* xv.18, 19.

Enter not into judgment with thy servant, O Lord; for in thy sight shall no man living be justified. *Psalm* cxliii.2.

If we say that we have no sin, we deceive ourselves, and the truth is not in us; but if we confess our sins, God is faithful and just to forgive us our sins, and to cleanse us from all unrighteousness. 1 *St. John* i.8, 9.

Book of Common Prayer (London: W. M. Collins Sons, 1968) 49-50.

Dearly beloved brethren, the Scripture moveth us, in sundry places, to acknowledge and confess our manifold sins and wickedness; and that we should not dissemble nor cloak them before the face of Almighty God our heavenly Father; but confess them with an humble, lowly, penitent, and obedient heart; to the end that we may obtain forgiveness of the same, by his infinite goodness and mercy. And although we ought, at all times, humbly to acknowledge our sins before God; yet ought we chiefly so to do, when we assemble and meet together to render thanks for the great benefits that we have received at his hands, to set forth his most worthy praise, to hear his most holy Word, and to ask those things which are requisite and necessary, as well for the body as the soul. Wherefore I pray and beseech you, as many as are here present, to accompany me with a pure heart, and humble voice, unto the throne of the heavenly grace. . . .[7]

This is language for the ages. It is stately and classic. It is meant for repetition, week after week, year after year. It goes deep into the soul. No matter what one's religious tradition, the *Book of Common Prayer* does not fail to move its reader or the penitent believer in the pew.

Worship as repentance is an ecumenical matter because it is the center of Christian identity.

Or is it?

It has become common nowadays in the church to conceive of worship essentially as a celebration of God's love. This love is declared to be inclusive and unconditional. Confession of sins is deemphasized. Embracing the self as it is, without struggle or soul-searching, appears to be the order of the day. Current Lutheran practice exemplifies this trend. In the official hymnal of the Evangelical Lutheran Church in America, *Evangelical Lutheran Worship,* the congregation preparing for Holy Communion is given the option to use an order for confession and forgiveness or instead to employ a newly contrived liturgical piece entitled, "Thanksgiving for Baptism." In the latter, there is no explicit confession of sins. The presiding minister simply declares to the assembled worshipers that "in the waters of baptism we are clothed in mercy and forgiveness." As water is poured into the font, the minister gives thanks to God on behalf of the people for being claimed by God "as

---

7. *Book of Common Prayer,* 50.

daughters and sons," made "heirs," and renewed in "forgiveness, grace, and love."[8] In the alternative public order for confession and absolution, there is no expression whatsoever given to the binding key, no instruction that repentance must be earnest and true, or that belief is the condition for receiving forgiveness.[9] It would appear that simply saying the words printed in the book is enough; grace is delivered *ex opere operato:* that is, by means of the action of worship in the words being spoken.

That confession is dispensable at Holy Communion is also part of the liturgical rubrics for the previous official hymnal of the ELCA which had been approved by two of its predecessor bodies, The American Lutheran Church and the Lutheran Church of America: the *Lutheran Book of Worship*. In 1978, when the hymnal appeared, optional confession was something new in Lutheran worship. The *Manual on the Liturgy*, a companion to the hymnal, published the following year, provided a confident rationale for the new practice:

> The brief order for Confession and Forgiveness is used, when desired, before Holy Communion begins. It is, however, not theologically or liturgically necessary that a congregational act of confession precede every celebration of the Holy Communion. The confession was not originally part of the Eucharist and only developed in the Middle Ages with the increasing emphasis on sin and unworthiness, and then as a part of the priest's personal preparation for mass. At the Reformation the confession was given to the entire congregation.[10]

Apparently, being worried about repentance is a "Middle Ages thing."

The *Manual on the Liturgy* gets neither the history nor the theology right. This is because it is a product of the so-called "liturgical renewal movement." In this school of thought, which arose in the late nineteenth century, blossomed in the first half of the twentieth century, and dominates liturgical scholarship today, it is common to treat repentance as an element in "the liturgy," a supposed ideal form of worship practice based on the Roman mass in its Tridentine form. In this

---

8. *Evangelical Lutheran Worship* (Minneapolis: Augsburg Fortress, 2006) 97.

9. *Evangelical Lutheran Worship*, 96.

10. Philip H. Pfatteicher and Carlos R. Messerli, *Manual on the Liturgy: Lutheran Book of Worship* (Minneapolis: Augsburg Publishing House, 1979) 195-96.

way of treating the subject, repentance is examined in relation to that section of the mass known as the *Confiteor*, a general confession of sin found at the beginning of the Roman rite and dating to the eleventh century. To understand repentance in the history of worship, the liturgical scholar, beholden to the method of the liturgical renewal movement, need do nothing more than to trace the origin and development of the *Confiteor* in Western liturgical practice. This leads to the claim that confession of sins in a service of Holy Communion is a medieval development that influenced early Protestant worship. When imposed as necessary, confession leads to a legalistic distortion of true Christian worship, creating a gloomy "penitential piety" that engenders "guilt consciousness" on believers, preventing them from understanding communion as "celebration." What is needed is a true "eucharistic piety" which is (supposedly) the original understanding of worship in the early church as a celebration of grace and unity with God through participation in the Lord's Supper.[11] This method of liturgical study leads to a misreading of the history of the church. It engenders a superficial liturgical theology that undercuts a proper understanding of sin and grace.

It is the purpose of this book to demonstrate that repentance is the heart of worship. The call to repentance is grounded in Scripture. Jesus commands that we repent before the presence of the Kingdom of God (Mark 1:15). St. Paul demands that we examine ourselves before eating the bread and drinking the wine (1 Corinthians 11:28). These biblical imperatives undergirded the eschatological consciousness of the early church. They shaped the sacramentality of the Middle Ages. They were central to the reform of worship initiated by Luther in the sixteenth century, which has determined the identity of Lutheran worship in the centuries that followed. Christian worship as repentance forms Christian identity across time and across denominational boundaries. It has created a catholic consensus in the West as to the fundamental purpose of worship and has engendered a variety of liturgical forms and rites such as the discipline of penance, extreme unction, the order for confession and absolution, the *Confiteor* of the mass, and even, as we shall see, the camp meeting of revivalist Protestantism based on the Re-

---

11. This is the argument of one of the most notable proponents of "eucharistic piety," Wolfhart Pannenberg. See *Christian Spirituality* (Philadelphia: The Westminster Press, 1983) 13-49.

formed practice of "fencing the table." It is an understanding that needs to be renewed and preserved today, lest liturgical worship lose weight and gravity.

The following study seeks to tell the story of worship as repentance with particular focus on Lutheran theology and liturgical practice, especially the development of orders for confession and absolution. But it investigates these orders in the larger context of penitential discipline as practiced by all Christians in the West. Thus the study is meant not just for Lutheran readers, but also for the general reader interested in the theology and history of worship.

I am indebted to four works of superb scholarship that have guided me in the understanding of penitential piety in the early church, the Middle Ages, and the Reformation: Oscar Daniel Watkins (1848-1926), *A History of Penance*[12] is the primary source in the English language on the historical theology, practice, and discipline of penance in both West and East. All who write about this subject are dependent on his voluminous and prodigious research. Misconceptions about the discipline of confession and forgiveness in the early church in the West, the Middle Ages, and the Reformation abound, especially in the liturgical renewal movement. Watkins's work, along with Thomas N. Tentler, *Sin and Confession on the Eve of the Reformation,*[13] and Ronald K. Rittgers, *The Reformation of the Keys: Confession, Conscience, and Authority in Sixteenth-Century Germany,*[14] helped me sort through the thicket. Above all, I am thankful for the work of Oliver K. Olson, Lutheran scholar and teacher, now retired from Marquette University, for articulating and defending, often against great odds, an interpretation of liturgy grounded in the principles of the Reformation, most recently in *Reclaiming the Lutheran Liturgical Heritage.*[15] This book is an effort to build on his work.

12. 2 vols.; New York: Burt Franklin, 1961, originally published in 1920.
13. Princeton: Princeton University Press, 1977.
14. Cambridge: Harvard University Press, 2004.
15. Minneapolis: Reclaim Resources, 2007.

Acknowledgments

My thanks to Pastor Mark Luther Johnson of St. Paul Lutheran
Church in Springfield, Minnesota, for encouraging me to examine Lutheran worship traditions, especially confession and absolution; to Pastor Dan Baker of First Lutheran Church, Albert Lea, Minnesota, and
Executive Director of Reclaim Resources, along with the Board of Di-
rectors of Reclaim for encouragement and financial support; to Professors Gracia Grindal and Roy Harrisville of Luther Seminary for essential help along the way; to the faculty and Board of Luther Seminary
for the privilege of sabbatical leave to write the book; to the Faculty
Secretary of Luther Seminary, Victoria Smith, for preparing the index;
above all to Professor Oliver K. Olson, scholar, teacher, and mentor, to
whom this book is dedicated.

Abbreviations

ANF   Alexander Roberts and James Donaldson, eds., *The Ante-Nicene Fathers.* 10 vols. Buffalo: Christian Literature Publishing, 1885-97.

BC   Theodore G. Tappert, *The Book of Concord.* Philadelphia: Fortress Press, 1959.

EKO   Emil Sehling *et al.,* eds., *Die evangelische Kirchenordnungen des XVI Jahrhunderts.* 19 vols. Leipzig and Tübingen: O. K. Reisland and J. C. B. Mohr [Paul Siebeck], 1902-.

LW   Martin Luther, *Luther's Works, American Edition,* ed. Helmut T. Lehmann, *et al.* 55 vols. Philadelphia: Fortress Press and St. Louis: Concordia Publishing House, 1955-86.

NPNF   Philip Schaff and Henry Wace, eds., *Nicene and Post-Nicene Fathers.* 14 vols. Reprint, Peabody: Hendrickson, 1994.

TRE   Gerhard Müller, Gerhard Krause, *et al.,* eds., *Theologische Realenzyklopädie.* 36 vols. Berlin and New York: Verlag Walter de Gruyter, 1977-2004.

Introduction

Controversy over Liturgical Practice

Some years ago, presiding at the weekly service of Holy Communion in the Luther Seminary chapel held on Wednesdays, I opened with the customary order for the confession of sins. When it came time to pronounce the absolution, I said the following:

> Almighty God, our heavenly Father, hath had mercy upon us, and for the sake of the sufferings, death, and resurrection of his dear Son, Jesus Christ our Lord, forgiveth us all our sins. As a Minister of the Church of Christ, and by his authority, I therefore declare unto you who do truly repent and believe in him, the entire forgiveness of all your sins: in the name of the Father, and of the Son, and of the Holy Ghost. Amen.
>
> On the other hand, by the same authority, I declare unto the impenitent and unbelieving, that so long as they continue in their impenitence, God hath not forgiven their sins, and will assuredly visit their iniquities upon them, if they turn not from their evil ways, and come to true repentance and faith in Christ, ere the day of grace be ended.

The stately old-fashioned prose of this absolution got the attention of the assembled worshipers immediately. People were not used to the archaic language. When I came to the second paragraph with its warning of judgment, all became quiet in the sanctuary. Faculty and stu-

I

dents appeared somewhat in shock. Trained as they were in matters liturgical, they knew that I was carrying out what is called in the tradition "the office of the keys," the binding and loosing of sins. But to hear the binding key pronounced so explicitly was something most of them had never experienced in an actual worship setting. Malcolm Muggeridge (1903-90), the English journalist and satirist (and adult Christian convert), once said in a television interview that the purpose of his life was "to find the perfect dead cat to heave into the lap of the complacent." It appeared that morning in chapel that I had found just such a cat. A number of people in attendance thought I was performing a stunt, others that I was being "un-Lutheran." After the service I had a steady stream of visitors to my office. No one mentioned the sermon I had preached; everyone wanted to talk to me about the conditional absolution I had pronounced.

For the record, I was interested neither in performing a stunt nor in doing something foreign to the Lutheran liturgical tradition. The conditional absolution I employed in the communion service has deep roots in Lutheran practice. I took it from the old *Service Book and Hymnal* which had been in use from 1958 to 1978 in the Lutheran Church in America, the American Lutheran Church, and their predecessor bodies. This absolution appears in the "The Order for Public Confession" meant for what was called in the worship book "a specially appointed preparatory service" such as might be scheduled during Holy Week or when confession precedes the administration of the Sacrament of the Altar by a day.[1] This same absolution, word for word, can be found in the orders for public confession in both the *Common Service Book and Hymnal* (1917) authorized by the General Synod, the General Council, and the United Synod in the South, all of which joined to form the United Lutheran Church in America in 1918. The Common Service, which goes back to 1888, is the historic anchor for liturgical practice in American Lutheranism in the twentieth century. It may also be found, again word for word, in *The Hymnal and Order of Service* (1925) of the Augustana Synod.[2] In both of these older worship books, the sugges-

1. *Service Book and Hymnal* (Minneapolis and Philadelphia: Augsburg Publishing House and Board of Publication Lutheran Church in America, 1958) 249-52. See Appendix II below. A different conditional absolution appears in "A Brief Order for Public Confession" in the *Service Book and Hymnal*, 247-48. See Appendix III.

2. *Common Service Book and Hymnal of the Lutheran Church* (Philadelphia and Columbia: The Lutheran Publication Society, The General Council Publication Board, the Lu-

tion is made that the order for public confession may be used on Sunday morning as a preface to the communion service.

As a church historian and seminary teacher, I have always understood the daily chapel service at Luther Seminary not only as a time to worship but also as an occasion to learn about the church and its historic practices. If there is any corporate act of the church in which memory and tradition are to be self-consciously preserved and passed on, it is the formal liturgy. In this case, however, something that was once part of the liturgy had been cut off and cast aside. When I employed it that Wednesday morning, it carried the shock of something new, strange, and, since it pronounced judgment, suspicious.

Why should something that was once part of the Lutheran liturgy, something carefully preserved, something considered by communal decision of the church to be essential to the discipline of the church's practice of Holy Communion, be allowed to disappear?

In *All Is Forgiven: The Secular Message in American Protestantism,* sociologist Marsha G. Witten argues that in contemporary American society, with its strong secular profile, there is but a "small social space left for sacred things."[3] The temptation for the preacher is to modify and accommodate Christian faith to the dominant values of the culture in order to make religious practice more marketable. Such things as the quest for individual fulfillment, the therapeutic mindset, moral relativism, and tolerance — all of which have a profound influence on our lives — work their way into the preaching and teaching of the church. When this happens, the inherited tradition is subject to reevaluation: "The transcendent, majestic, awesome God of Luther and Calvin — whose image informed early Protestant visions of the relationship between human beings and the divine — [undergoes] a softening of demeanor. . . ."[4] Witten illustrates this with the personal example of experiencing a stark contrast in religious sensibility. She was listening to a performance of *St. Matthew's Passion* by Johann Sebastian Bach (1685-1750) broadcast on the radio on a Good Friday afternoon. This profound work of Western culture portrays the pathos of events of the Pas-

theran Board of Publication, 1917) 267-68; *The Hymnal and Order of Service* (Rock Island: Augustana Book Concern, 1925) 727-28.

3. Marsha G. Witten, *All Is Forgiven: The Secular Message in American Protestantism* (Princeton: Princeton University Press, 1993) 5.

4. Witten, *All Is Forgiven,* 53.

sion of Christ and calls the believer to identify with the suffering of Jesus. That same afternoon the mail brought to Witten's door a flyer from a local church, advertising the benefits of the congregation in these upbeat terms:

- Enjoy exciting music with a contemporary flavor
- Hear positive, practical messages which uplift you each week
     How to feel good about yourself
     How to overcome depression
     How to have a full and successful life
     Learning to handle your money without it handling you
     The secrets of successful family living
     How to overcome stress
- Trust your children to the care of dedicated nursery workers
     WHY NOT GET A LIFT INSTEAD OF A LETDOWN THIS SUNDAY?[5]

Witten reports that she was immediately struck by the dissimilarity between the words and music of Bach and the come-ons of a local American parish seeking to appeal to harried suburbanites. What do the blandishments of this advertising flyer have to do with the plaintive first aria in the *St. Matthew's Passion* for alto voice:

Grief and remorse
Rend the sinful heart in two
That the tears of my eyes
Be an acceptable gift
To Thee, faithful Jesus.[6]

Although not a Christian herself (her study is all the more valuable for being the observations of an outsider), Witten knew that these two experiences of "church" have nothing in common.

Perhaps Witten's comparison is not exactly fair. We certainly accept Bach's compositions as great art. His music transcends time. But can we accept the austere worship tradition that he assumed and out of

---

5. Witten, *All Is Forgiven*, 3-4.
6. *Buß und Reu*
     Knirscht das Sündenherz entzwei
     Daß die Tropfen meiner Zähren
     Angenehme Spezerei
     Treuer Jesu, dir gebären.

which he worked? Is it not this austere tradition that is in question and is often used as a foil for the contemporary church seeking to be relevant? The sad fact is that when a liturgical practice of the past confronts the mainline church with the stark literalness and severity of the original faith, it is often deemed too uncomfortable to deal with and therefore is removed.

While I pondered these questions at the time, I did not pursue them as a matter for study and reflection. I might have left the entire episode in the past if it were not for a much more recent experience along the same lines. I serve on the advisory board for the *Reclaim* hymnal project, an effort among Lutheran teachers, pastors, and lay people to develop an independent worship resource securely grounded in the Lutheran liturgical tradition of worship and singing. A small introductory edition of the hymnal was published in 2006 to acquaint congregations with the project and to solicit response. Nothing in this introductory edition caused more controversy than the two formulations for absolution and the exhortation to communicants found in the sample worship service. Especially problematic in the view of many respondents was the second option for absolution in the proposed communion service:

> Almighty God, our heavenly Father, has had mercy on you, and has given his only Son to die for you, and for his sake forgives you all your sins. To all who believe in Jesus Christ he gives the power to become children of God, and bestows on you his Holy Spirit. On the other hand, I declare to the impenitent and unbelieving, that so long as you continue in your impenitence, God has not forgiven your sins, and will surely visit your iniquities upon you if you do not turn from your sinful ways and come to repentance and faith in Christ before the day of grace is ended. Amen.[7]

This formulation of the absolution met the same negative reaction that I experienced years before when I recited the conditional absolution from the *Service Book and Hymnal* in chapel at Luther Seminary. I was asked by the editorial board of the *Reclaim Lutheran Hymnal* to make a defense. In attempting to explain the absolution, I became ensnared in a number of debates over whether this formulation was legitimately

7. *Reclaim: Lutheran Hymnal for Church and Home, Introductory Edition* (Minneapolis: Bronze Bow Publishing, 2006) 19.

part of the Lutheran tradition. The charges were various: that what one finds in this general absolution is an assault on authentic Lutheran identity because it proclaims conditional forgiveness instead of unconditional; that it represents a confusion of law and gospel; that it displays the wrong ordering of law and gospel, since the absolution ends on a word of judgment. I replied that the formulation in the introductory edition of the *Reclaim Lutheran Hymnal* is a variant of the absolution in the public order for confession that may be found in historic worship books of American Lutheranism and that it draws upon precedents that go back to Luther and the early Reformation. This answer appeared to make no difference to the critics. Motivated by abstract theological principles and, as we shall see, a strain of Lutheran theology that goes back to the Nuremberg reformer Andreas Osiander (1498-1552), the critics were simply indifferent to this history and tradition.

This more recent controversy, unlike the earlier one, led me to investigate the matter with more formal research, the results of which I presented as a paper at the *Reclaim* worship conference in June 2007: "Reclaiming Absolution: Conflict over Confession and Absolution in the Lutheran Liturgical Tradition." The following text is an expansion of that presentation. It also draws on two further public lectures: one given in June 2008 at the second *Reclaim* conference and entitled "Does a Theology of Worship Matter?" and the other given in June 2009, "Worship as Repentance." In these three lectures, I attempted to set the historical record straight. My basic argument was as follows:

> The use of a conditional absolution in a liturgical order of public confession is a time-honored practice in Lutheranism.
> It is a legitimate and effective exercise of the discipline of the office of the keys.
> It is closely related to other common practices of Lutheran churches in the past such as the exhortation to communicants, private confession, and the distinction between administration of Holy Communion and reception.

There is no doubt that these practices have been abandoned in contemporary mainline American Lutheranism as represented in the Evangelical Lutheran Church in America. The criticism I experienced at Luther Seminary and in relation to the *Reclaim Lutheran Hymnal* represents widespread opinion. This opinion has developed over decades and represents serious and sincere theological reflection. Thus, in attempting to explain the Lutheran liturgical tradition of worship as repentance, especially on the matter of confession and absolution, with special attention to the place of the binding key in the declaration of forgiveness, I realize that I may not convince critics already set in their opinion. Proposing the return of the binding key to Lutheran liturgy may be arguing a lost cause in many quarters of the church. What I will not accept is that practices such as the conditional absolution are being dismissed out of hand and treated with contempt. It is simply wrong to call such practices "un-Lutheran." On the contrary, they are very much Lutheran in their identity. They have much to teach us about Lutheran theology, confession, and liturgical tradition. More important, they have much to teach us about that most elemental act of Christian worship: the confession of sins. They thus deserve attention and respect. And they should be embraced anew.

Lutheran Identity

To claim that study of these liturgical practices can teach us about Lutheran identity raises the question of what Lutheran identity is. It is difficult to make broad claims about the persistent identity of any historic institution or movement such as a church. Social entities are complex phenomena in which competing factions vie for dominance and control. They change over time. This change can be a gradual evolution or an abrupt break with the past. The Christian church is not exempt from these forces, even though it has, on occasion, claimed to be. But this does not mean that institutions or movements lack commonalities, enduring behaviors, and fundamental principles which represent their enduring character. To say that there is something called "Lutheranism" is to claim that there is a continuity and consistency of thought and practice in an important branch of the Christian church that may be discerned and described, despite the fact that change, fragmentation, and debate beset the church in each generation.

Werner Elert (1885-1954) gave much thought to this matter. Lutheran identity, he said, cannot be located in a single theologian, even Luther himself, or a particular school such as the "orthodox" or the "pietist," or a single dogmatic principle such as "law and gospel." This identity — or as Elert called it, the "morphology" — of the Lutheran tradition is an intricate affair that involves not only the investigation of Luther, the confessions, and the important figures of academic theology, but also the record of communal texts (liturgical formulations, church ordinances, government regulations), politics, and culture that are a window on the social identity and piety of the Lutheran church at any given time and place. To be sure, this complex record of material changes over time but also displays consistent themes and actions.[8]

The practice of worship as repentance is well suited to contribute to the understanding of the "morphology" of Lutheranism for three reasons. First, it not only entails consideration of theological debates but also attends to those often neglected communal texts that reflect the corporate will and consensus or conventional opinion of the church at a particular time. Liturgical texts, church ordinances, legal regulations, and the like are a goldmine of information that reflect the efforts not only of individuals but of committees, church agencies, and in Europe, government authorities. They speak the voice of the church as a whole because they reflect the conventional, shared opinion of an age. Second, the subject of worship as repentance entails theological reflection on central matters of dogmatics, matters that relate to daily life in the church: repentance and forgiveness, ministerial authority, the office of the keys, Christian obedience and discipleship, and the Lord's Supper. All of these have been at the heart of Lutheran theological interest. Third, worship as repentance, especially the liturgical matter of confession and absolution, has been the cause of a number of significant theological controversies.

In light of these observations, the book is organized in the following way. Chapter I will consider confession and absolution, particularly the binding key of judgment, in relation to the purpose of liturgical worship broadly understood. It will be argued that St. Paul's exhortation to examine oneself (1 Corinthians 11:28) — that most sobering of biblical injunctions — stands at the very heart of liturgical practice and has broad implications for worship and sacramental practice. To worship God, to stand before God *(coram Deo)* as God is known in and through the Lord Jesus Christ, is rightly done only by those "who do truly repent and believe in him." This purpose of worship is to be carried out week after week, season after season, year after year in a person's life.

---

8. *Morphologie des Luthertums,* 2 vols. (Munich: Beck, 1931); first volume translated as *The Structure of Lutheranism* (Saint Louis: Concordia, 1962).

Thus, liturgical worship practices repentance in what might be called "blessed repetition." This blessed repetition of worship as repentance plays itself out in two types of ecclesiastical morphology defined a century ago by Ernst Troeltsch (1865-1923) and now the common coin of religious sociologists: the "church type" and the "sect type." The church type emphasizes the role of the Christian community as an established institution of society and culture that seeks to be all-inclusive in its proclamation of grace as assurance of salvation. The loosing of sins, not the binding of sins, is the focus of worship. The church type is the common form of European territorial churches and their American counterparts: Roman Catholic, Episcopal, and Lutheran to name three prominent examples. The sect type emphasizes faith as conversion, asserting that the normal beginning of genuine Christian life is spiritual transformation. Transformation entails making explicit commitment to Christ and taking responsibility for one's life in moral terms. The sect type does not shy away from the exercise of the binding key. Discipline is basic to its identity. The sect type is the historic ecclesiastical form of Anabaptists, Puritans, Pietists, and other dissenters in Europe. In America it commonly identifies evangelical denominations such as Southern Baptist and Pentecostal. Lutherans in their history have had a stake in both the church type, as officially established in territorial churches, and the sect type, as exemplified by Pietism. Lutherans across the centuries have debated the merits of each. This debate has consequences for understanding St. Paul's command to examine oneself, which is the call to confession of sins.

Chapter II will seek to gain further perspective on the purpose of worship by considering the experience of the early church. Early Christian worship, especially in the West, was characterized by a dominant eschatological consciousness of the impending judgment of God in the final days. Christians of the time feared falling into sin after receiving the gift of the Holy Spirit in baptism as "unforgiveable" (Matthew 12:31), as "the sin unto death" (1 John 5:16), as a falling away that makes it impossible to be "restored again to repentance" (Hebrews 6:4-6), and so they made stringent demands on sinners, especially those who had committed apostasy, adultery, or bloodletting. It was believed that the church must measure up to "holiness," one of the essential "marks" of the church defined in the Nicene Creed. Holiness, it was believed and taught, should characterize the common, everyday life of authentic believers. The demand to be holy, however, placed the church in a predicament concerning participation in sacramental life. Who is truly holy? Is anyone holy enough? "Leaders of the early Church," observes Ronald K. Rittgers, "were much more confident in using the binding key than the loosing one."[9] For centuries the common discipline in the Western church taught that repentance for post-baptismal sins could only be made once in a lifetime. This repentance was enacted in a dramatic, public ritual. Harsh rules for penance no doubt meant theological and pastoral difficulties for proclaiming the grace of the gospel. But it also meant that ancient liturgical worship had both an urgency and integrity that later ages abandoned. The early church stands in the sect-type tradition and does so intensely.

Against the measure of the early church, both the Middle Ages and the Reformation, which are the subject of chapter III, represent a certain laxity in discipline, but also a liberation of the sacramental life. Change in Western teaching regarding repentance and forgiveness for post-baptismal sins begins with Irish monks who ministered to the church in the Dark Ages when civilization in the West hung by a thread. These remarkable figures, St. Patrick (c. 387–c. 460) and St. Columba (c. 521-597) among them, revived the faith among Christians decimated by war and plague and evangelized pagan tribes of northern Europe. They brought with them an insight into the gospel that had eluded the church in the West: penance is a gift that, as it were, "keeps on giving," a repeatable event in the life of a Christian, done in private between penitent and priest, giving room for spiritual comfort and pastoral care. The imperative to examine oneself, they declared, could be carried out again and again, thus becoming part of the pattern of Christian life. It is the Irish who introduced "blessed repetition" to the liturgical practice of confession and forgiveness.

The medieval church and the Lutheran reformers, each in their own way, embraced this blessed repetition of confession and forgiveness. Each sought to proclaim the assurance of grace to the masses that made up Christendom. This is the church type coming to birth, seeking to ameliorate the demand to be holy. In doing so however, both the medieval Roman Church and the reformers sought to discipline the faithful in order to insure that the examination of oneself would not be taken for granted; thus the centrality of penance in the theology of

9. Ronald K. Rittgers, *The Reformation of the Keys: Confession, Conscience, and Authority in Sixteenth-Century Germany* (Cambridge: Harvard University Press, 2004) 29.

both Catholicism and Protestantism at the time. In this regard, the purpose of Christian worship, according to the Lutheran theological tradition, is not only to comfort believers with the promise of the gospel, but also to confront them with the command to self-examination. An enormous amount of theological energy in early Lutheranism was expended on the articulation of the binding key in the liturgical form of conditional absolution.

The debate over confession and absolution led to significant controversies during and after the Reformation. The first that I have chosen is the debate over the legitimacy of public confession and absolution versus private confession in the important Lutheran center of Nuremberg in the 1520s and early 1530s. This is discussed in chapter III. In chapter IV three further controversies are examined. One is the so-called *Berliner Beichtstuhlstreit* (1696-1698), or conflict over the confessional which came to a close when Friedrich III (1657-1713, later Friedrich I of Prussia) ended mandatory private confession as a requirement for receiving communion. Another controversy is the debate over confession and absolution between Samuel Simon Schmucker (1799-1873) and William (Wilhelm) Julius Mann (1819-1892) in nineteenth-century American Lutheranism. The last is the debate over unconditional absolution that embroiled Norwegian Lutheran immigrants in the Midwest from the time of the Civil War until the beginning of the twentieth century. In chapter IV, the debate between Schmucker and Mann will be given the most attention because it has the most to do with the direction of Lutheran worship practice as American Lutheranism entered the twentieth century.

Attending to the argument on confession and absolution, especially as it is pursued by theologians, pastors, and administrators in the church who cared deeply about the matter, is to enter into the identity of Lutheran worship forging itself across time and, by the end of the nineteenth century, reaching widespread consensus on the liturgical form of an order for public confession in the Common Service (1888).

As will be argued in chapter V, this consensus served Lutherans well for the first six decades of the twentieth century, helping to shape a morphology that made Lutheranism a formidable and robust tradition in American Protestantism. In the decade and a half following World War II, Lutheranism prospered as it grew in numbers and found a distinct voice in American culture. The heritage of the Common Service contributed to both the success and distinctiveness of American Lutheranism.

A sea change in Lutheran worship practice took hold beginning in the 1960s and gathering force thereafter. This is the change in understanding between worship as repentance and worship as ritual participation in the divine, the former now denigrated as "penitential piety" and shunned, the latter touted as "eucharistic piety," the true, ecumenical vision of worship. Eucharistic piety motivates and informs the *Lutheran Book of Worship* (1978) and *Evangelical Lutheran Worship* (2006). It also influences the *Service Book and Hymnal* (1958) to an extent, but not on the matter of confession and absolution.

Worship as ritual participation in the divine is a theological understanding that emerges out of the liturgical renewal movement in Roman Catholicism, a movement that has deep roots in German Romanticism and Idealism. Chapter V will trace these roots and profile the movement. It will also offer criticism. So-called "penitential piety" — worship as repentance — is not to be shunned, but embraced as the ground and identity of Christian worship.

CHAPTER I

Worship as Repentance

Blessed Repetition

The instructor placed a felt-tip marker on the seat for each student in the class.[1] She taught ESL — English as a Second Language. She was working this day with church volunteers who had signed up to help Hmong immigrants, pilgrims to a new land in the Central Valley of California. "With the marker," the teacher said, "write the number 44 on the palm of your left hand and the number 66 on the palm of your right." She explained: "To learn a language so that a person can navigate his way through the world, each word must be repeated a minimum of between 44 and 66 times before it is implanted in the brain. To teach people even the rudiments of a new tongue is laborious. Dear volunteers: you will need great patience."

Think of it: to repeat between 44 and 66 times each word, with which to build a sentence, to make an observation, to ask directions. So much effort to find our way in the world among earthly things, to live in this mortal realm.

What is the number of repetitions needed to learn things divine? To find our way in the spiritual realm? Seventy times seven? Forty years wandering in the wilderness? Or shall we just say with the Psalmist: "The days of our life are seventy years, or perhaps eighty, if we are strong; even then their span is only toil and trouble; they are soon

---

1. The following story was told to me by Rev. Karen Deutscher of Fresno, California. It recounts the experience of volunteers from Grace Lutheran Church of Fresno in 1984.

gone, and we fly away" (Psalm 90:1). It takes enormous effort just to stumble and mumble in halting speech on the path that leads through this vale of tears to God.

This effort we must make. We are called to witness to Christ. And we cannot witness if we are inarticulate, unable to traffic in the visible and invisible and make the connection between them. Scripture admonishes: "Always be ready to make your defense to anyone who demands from you an accounting for the hope that is in you" (1 Peter 3:15), and "Do your best to present yourself to God as one approved by him, a worker who has no need to be ashamed, rightly explaining the word of truth" (2 Timothy 2:15). To witness to our hope in Christ, to explain forthrightly what we believe to be true and not be ashamed in doing it, is a mandate for each Christian.

To fulfill this mandate, we must be prepared and nourished in worship. For preparation, St. Paul commands us to examine ourselves, and to do so repeatedly, in the presence of holy things, bread and wine that are body and blood of the Lord, to take stock of ourselves and what we do. For nourishment we receive the Lord's Supper. By means of the Supper, God forgives us, feeds us, and strengthens us. But this is not merely for our own benefit. Receiving the Supper leads to witness: "For as often as you eat this bread and drink the cup, you proclaim the Lord's death until he comes" (1 Corinthians 11:26).

As St. Paul makes clear, preparation means everything. Self-examination is the hinge to the entire process of becoming Christian in and through worship. And it is especially difficult because it is fraught with eternal consequence:

> Whoever, therefore, eats the bread or drinks the cup of the Lord in an unworthy manner will be answerable for the body and blood of the Lord. Examine yourselves, and only then eat of the bread and drink of the cup. For all who eat and drink without discerning the body, eat and drink judgment against themselves. For this reason many of you are weak and ill, and some have died. But if we judged ourselves, we would not be judged. But when we are judged by the Lord, we are disciplined so that we may not be condemned along with the world. (vv. 27-29)

To learn the language of the spiritual realm means peeling away layers of illusion and pretension and bringing to light what we want to keep

in the dark. We resist doing this. Even if our personal sins do not particularly bother us, we do not wish to dwell on them. We certainly do
not want to disclose them for fear of being caught, embarrassed, and
thus made ashamed. To search the self takes great courage; which is a
rare thing. "I do not know the man so bold," writes the poet Emily
Dickinson (1830-1886), "He dare in lonely Place/That awful stranger
Consciousness/Deliberately face."[2] God calls us to face ourselves and
will not abide our excuses to avoid examination. We are warned repeatedly by the offices of the church, especially the power of the keys, not to
shirk our duty but instead truly to repent "ere the day of grace be
ended."[3]

Whatever its faults and misuses over the centuries — and they have
been legion — liturgical worship, at its best, has this purpose: *to call
Christians to repentance; to warn them to be under no illusion as to who they
are and how far they fall short when they stand before God and holy things; to
teach them to worship God in humility; to feed them the Bread of Life; to make
them ready to give testimony to Christ in word and deed.* To do these things
in worship is to learn the language of the divine realm and participate
in the realities it discloses.

Where is the grace of God in this austere conception of liturgy and
its purpose? Grace resides in the repetition. Liturgical worship assumes
the weakness and frailty of Christian believers. It takes for granted that
the Christian will ever mumble and stumble on the path to God; that
she will never be instantly and permanently converted; that he will fall
away; that Christians must ask for forgiveness again and again. Repetition there must be. This repetition is blessed by God. It is grounded in
the promise that Christ will not give up on us; he will carry us through
the valley of the shadow of death and protect us from all enemies.

Imagine that on the palms of the hands of our Lord are not only the
bloody wounds made by ancient spikes, but a fabulous pair of numbers,
known only to him, numbers far in excess of the 44 or 66 repetitions it
takes to learn a new word in the mundane world. Whatever those sacred
numbers may be, they are in their essence the loving repetitions that our
patient divine teacher will make for each of us in worship, guiding us

2. Emily Dickinson, untitled poem; first line "I never hear that one is dead." See
Cynthia Griffin Wolff, *Emily Dickinson* (New York: Da Capo Press, 1988) 467.
3. *Service Book and Hymnal* (Minneapolis and Philadelphia: Augsburg Publishing
House and Board of Publication Lutheran Church in America, 1958) 252.

along, we the faltering immigrants in the spiritual realm seeking to learn the language of a new land. It is the grace of God that Christ gives himself to us in the language of worship each time believers gather. His liturgical self-giving is an aspect of the Incarnation. It represents one of the forms that his divine presence takes in the Body of Christ, a means by which we in the church know that God loves us.

It also fulfills a deep-seated human desire. The Jewish theologian Martin Buber (1878-1965) once observed: "Man desires to have God; he desires to have God continually in space and time. He is loath to be satisfied with the inexpressible confirmation of the meaning; he wants to see it spread out as something that one can take out and handle again and again — a continuum unbroken in space and time that insures life for him at every point and moment."[4] Human beings take great comfort in being allowed to locate the eternal in the midst of their lives. This is a primary purpose of religious art and imagery. It is why people take care that the architecture of a church inspires and enhances the landscape of town and village and that the decoration of the church suggests holy things and aids the visible part of devotion. The Sabbath rest, coming every seventh day, rounds off the week and anchors it in a higher purpose to start the next. The liturgy disciplines worship with a familiar regularity and declares the presence of God. This is an essential part of the blessed repetition of liturgical practice and enhances its effect.

The regularity of liturgical practice is meant to convey the assurance of Christ. It influences the morphology of the church, grounding it in the core conviction that salvation is a matter of grace alone. Grace means assurance of salvation. This theological principle is deep in the heart of Lutheranism, but also undergirds the tradition of liturgical churches represented by the Roman Church, Orthodoxy, and the Anglican Communion. As the German scholar Ernst Troeltsch (1865-1923) recognized at the beginning of the last century, the doctrine of grace as assurance molds the self-understanding of the Christian in a particular way. It encourages the Christian to interpret salvation as:

something finished, certain and sure, a pure gift of God, independent of the ego, of all one's struggles and subjective efforts, and

4. Martin Buber, *I and Thou*, tr. Walter Kaufmann (New York: Charles Scribner's Sons, 1970) 161-62.

only has to be appropriated by faith; the soul then absorbs the great principle of an objective Divine creative energy, which effects everything in and through the individual, while it is itself quite independent of the individual.[5]

Familiarity Breeds Contempt

This fundamental conviction brings with it a potential danger to faith. It can tempt the Christian to take Christ for granted, to treat salvation as a matter of ritual formula done by rote. This is the central problem facing what Troeltsch calls the "church type." The church type is that political form the church takes when, grounded in the doctrine of grace as assurance, it conceives itself as a divinely sanctioned institution in society, "endowed with grace and salvation as the result of the work of redemption."[6] A church viewed in this way tends to understand itself as part of the establishment, accommodating itself to the dominant cultural elite. Membership in the church is usually defined as sacramental incorporation through infant baptism. To identify a Christian by baptism avoids the thorny issue of what makes for a "true" Christian. It downplays conversion and individual commitment. Persons are assumed to be Christians as a matter of course, "once baptized, always saved" as the saying goes. Church membership is treated like citizenship in the state: both are understood as a matter of birthright. The church type "is able to receive the masses, and to adjust itself to the world, because, to a certain extent, it can afford to ignore the need for subjective holiness for the sake of the objective treasures of grace and of redemption."[7]

Acceptance of "the masses" encourages the church type to adopt an inclusive principle of witness, to be tolerant and nonjudgmental, offering the grace of God as a pure gift that requires no merit to receive it. This is generally considered a good way for the church to be, especially in a modern democratic culture that prizes tolerance above all other virtues. But it is not without problems. By ignoring "the need for sub-

5. Ernst Troeltsch, *The Social Teachings of the Christian Churches*, tr. Olive Wyon (New York: Harper Torchbooks, 1960) 2:481. The original German edition was published in 1911.

6. Troeltsch, *Social Teachings*, 2:993.

7. Troeltsch, *Social Teachings*, 2:993.

jective holiness" the church type is in danger of creating a permissive environment in which members feel little or no obligation to adhere to strict standards of belief and conduct. A church with lax membership is a church without core beliefs. The imperatives of Scripture are avoided or ignored. The fundamental biblical claim about Christ — "There is salvation in no one else, for there is no other name under heaven given among mortals by which we must be saved" (Acts 4:12) — is disputed or even denied. Mission, evangelism, and the nurturing of the faith are enervated; confession and absolution are not taken seriously. Liturgical worship, so central to the life of the church type, appears a flaccid exercise, a faux language that talks the talk while avoiding walking the walk. The repetition of worship forms, instead of being a blessing, becomes a curse. Faith is neither increased nor ratified. The church that makes lofty claims to possess "the objective treasures of grace and of redemption" ends up without any treasure at all. This is the church in decline, a familiar situation to many of us, so familiar that for many the church type breeds nothing but contempt.

The most famous purveyor of this contempt was the Danish philosopher and theologian Søren Kierkegaard (1813-1855). Kierkegaard decried the tendency to accommodation to which the church type is prone because it encourages a class of conventional or superficial Christians who are tempted by "a secular mentality" that "wants to have the name of being Christian but wants to become Christian as cheaply as possible."[8] This is an evasion of the divine will. It is an illusion of the laity encouraged by the clergy whose proclamation of unconditional grace is motivated less by creed than out of concern to keep their jobs. The clergy want to make faith as comfortable as possible. They do not want to rock the boat. Thus they absolve parishioners of responsibility to make a decision for faith. The church type (or "church theory" as Kierkegaard calls it) assumes that everyone is a Christian already, membership being guaranteed by the prestige of a historic institution, enduring across time, that possesses orthodox creeds and confessions, divinely mandated liturgy, and above all, the sacrament of infant baptism conceived "as something magical to hold on to" that replaces the responsibility of personal faith.[9] Kierkegaard

8. Søren Kierkegaard, *For Self-Examination,* ed. and tr. Howard V. Hong and Edna H. Hong (Princeton: Princeton University Press, 1990) 16.

9. Søren Kierkegaard, *Concluding Unscientific Postscript to Philosophical Fragments,* ed.

satirizes this as "a Danish idea." His specific object of derision is the Lutheran high churchman Nikolai Grundtvig (1783-1872).[10] But what he is after generally is the conventionality of nominal faith that characterizes the European territorial church. The church type has its defenders: usually church bureaucrats and academics representing a "high church" party that claims the prestige of ecclesiastical tradition. Kierkegaard has little patience with this line of argument. He interprets it as little more than romanticism, trafficking in sentimentality and nostalgia, an exercise in "sheer estheticism."[11] This is "a Christianity from which the terror has been removed."[12] No doubt it offers an appealing cultural vision of religion as a blend of sacramental theology, piety, and patriotism. But its driving force is to reduce Christianity to the lowest common denominator of the immature. This may be Christendom but it is not Christianity. It denies the true purpose of the faith. Kierkegaard is scathing in his attack, focusing on membership in the church type through sacramental incorporation:

> The interest of Christianity, what it wants is — true Christians.
>
> The egoism of the priesthood, both for pecuniary advantage and for the sake of power, stands in relation to — many Christians.
>
> "And that's very easily done, it's nothing at all: let's get hold of the children, then each child is given a drop of water on the head — then he is a Christian. If a portion of them don't even get their drop, it comes to the same thing, if only they imagine they got it, and imagine consequently that they are Christians. So in a very short time we have more Christians than there are herring in the herring season."[13]

The confusion of Christianity and Christendom in the church type or church theory can have tragic consequences. The prime example is the German territorial church in the 1930s which refused to face up to the threat posed by the Nazi ascendancy. Dietrich Bonhoeffer (1906-

---

and tr. Howard V. Hong and Edna H. Hong (Princeton: Princeton University Press, 1982) 1:44.

10. Kierkegaard, *Concluding Unscientific Postscript,* 1:36.

11. Kierkegaard, *Concluding Unscientific Postscript,* 1:608.

12. Kierkegaard, *Concluding Unscientific Postscript,* 1:122.

13. Søren Kierkegaard, *Attack upon "Christendom,"* tr. Walter Lowrie (Princeton: Princeton University Press, 1968) 147.

1945) accused this church of idolatry and false witness. The territorial church had disguised its apostasy by proclaiming "cheap grace":

> Cheap grace is the deadly enemy of our Church. . . . Cheap grace means grace sold on the market. . . . The sacraments, the forgiveness of sin, and the consolations of religion are thrown away at cut prices. Grace is represented as the Church's inexhaustible treasury, from which she showers blessings with generous hands, without asking questions or fixing limits. Grace without price; grace without cost! . . . Cheap grace means grace as a doctrine, a principle, a system. . . . The Church which holds the correct doctrine of grace has, it is supposed, *ipso facto* a part in that grace. In such a Church the world finds a cheap covering for its sins; no contrition is required, still less any real desire to be delivered from sin.[14]

Because of this distorted version of the doctrine of grace as assurance, the German territorial church could not follow Christ and bear "the cost of discipleship."

Kierkegaard and Bonhoeffer directed their criticism and contempt of the church type to the ways in which it falsely proclaims the gospel. Each spoke to the specific social and political circumstances of his day. Their arguments are intensely theological and still hold today. More recent criticism of the church type, however, has focused attention less on false teaching than on the ineffectiveness of witness. The church type is declining in membership, to such a degree and for so long that this decline appears to be sociologically inevitable. The lesson seems to be this: If nothing is required of faith, why practice the faith at all? We see this weakness in both American and European Protestantism. In America mainline denominations have lost members steadily for over a generation. Since 1965 the Episcopal Church has lost roughly 35% of its membership, the Presbyterian Church USA 45%, the United Methodist Church 25%, the Evangelical Lutheran Church in America and its predecessor bodies 20%, with the rate of decrease intensifying in the first decade of the twenty-first century. The old territorial churches of Europe present an even more frightening picture. Not only is there a decline in church attendance, but also neglect and rejection of Christian ritual. Rites of passage that have accompanied the lives of generations

---

14. Dietrich Bonhoeffer, *The Cost of Discipleship*, tr. R. H. Fuller, rev. Irmgard Booth (New York: Macmillan, 1963) 45-46 (published in German in 1937).

of Christian believers across centuries are disappearing. In a symposium on secularization in Europe, the following was reported (and this is just a sample): The proportion of babies receiving Catholic baptism in France, for example, fell from 91% to 51% between 1958 and 1990. In the same period, the percentage of those married in Catholic weddings fell from 79% to 51%. In the late 1950s, approximately 40% of females in Great Britain were confirmed in the Church of England. Between 1961 and 1974, female confirmation fell to 19.6%. At the present time, the Church of England faces what one scholar calls a "recruitment catastrophe" as less than 20% of those baptized enter into full communion.[15] This is the church type at its worst. The church has ignored what Troeltsch calls "the need for subjective holiness" in order "to receive the masses," and the masses have turned away. Here the liturgical and sacramental practice of the church is denied by being ignored; indeed, it is in danger of being forgotten.

We can no longer afford to speak of the liturgy as "the product and possession of the universal church" that "enshrines the faith and experience of every age and continent," representing "the objective, the universal, and the eternal rather than the individualistic and the temporal."[16] Such rhetoric rings hollow in a postmodern world suspicious of any attempt to create a meta-narrative where one size fits all. To try to do so is a futile exercise. It may itself be an indication of just how weak we have become. J. Edward Carothers (1908-2000), for many years chief executive of home missions for the United Methodist Church, goes so far as to posit an inverse relationship between certain superficial aspects of formal worship and the mission of the gospel as he bemoans the decline of mainline Protestantism in America:

> A sure sign of paralysis [for a denomination] is when leadership begins to make more and more of ritual, tradition, finery of symbols, and special attractions. It seems there may be some relationship between the increased splendor of vestments in the chancel and . . . declining power. . . . It would be extreme to say that when heavy pectoral crosses adorn the vestments of the clergy there is functional decline in passionate dedication to justice, mercy, and good

---

15. See Hugh McLeod and Werner Ustorf, eds., *The Decline of Christendom in Western Europe, 1750-2000* (Cambridge: Cambridge University Press, 2003).

16. Luther D. Reed, *The Lutheran Liturgy* (Philadelphia: Fortress, 1947) 21, 23.

faith, but the ancient prophets took a dim view of too much emphasis on finery.[17]

The predicament facing denominations that represent a church-type morphology, which holds liturgy and sacraments in high regard, is of crisis proportions. What is to be done? Perhaps we need to think anew about the purpose of the liturgy as handed down and how that purpose is fulfilled. We defined that purpose as follows: *to call Christians to repentance; to warn them to be under no illusion as to who they are and how far they fall short when they stand before God and holy things; to teach them to worship God in humility; to feed them the Bread of Life; to make them ready to give testimony to Christ in word and deed.* If the morphology of the church type fails to fulfill this purpose, or at least has demonstrated serious weakness in fulfilling it, is there another form of Christian existence to take it up and carry it forward, especially under the peculiar conditions of modernity?

The Sectarian Tradition

According to Søren Kierkegaard there is. Against the superficialities of the church type, Kierkegaard asserted "true Christianity." True Christianity is not to be found in an institution or a ritual, but in making a personal decision of faith. To speak of "personal decision" is to employ a common term of Christian evangelicals. It calls to mind revival preachers exhorting people to come forward on the sawdust trail to the altar and pledge their lives to Jesus. But Kierkegaard places the idea of personal decision in a universal, intellectual perspective of unusual theological weight by calling it "the Socratic secret" of Christian faith. Socrates (469-399 BC) is honored as a hero of Western thought because he taught the critical principle: "the unexamined life is not worth living."[18] With great courage and integrity, he chose death at the hands of the state rather than give up this principle. All people who desire to be truly human are called to the same principle and, if necessary, the same

17. J. Edward Carothers, *The Paralysis of Mainstream Protestant Leadership* (Nashville: Abingdon Press, 1990) 80.

18. *The Dialogues of Plato,* tr. Benjamin Jowett, in Robert Maynard Hutchins, ed., *Great Books of the Western World* (Chicago: Encyclopedia Britannica, Inc., 1952) 7:210 (*Apology* 38a).

sacrifice. Above all, obedience to this principle is the duty of Christians. This is because Christ died at the hands of the state for the same principle as Socrates. The difference is that Christ invested the principle with a power of forgiveness and the promise of salvation that Socrates, a mere mortal, did not know. The ministry and passion of Christ reveal that the critical principle of the examined life is nothing less than the command of God, a duty incumbent upon all those made in the divine image.

In drawing a parallel between Socrates and Christ, Kierkegaard draws on ancient tradition. In the second century, the apologist Justin Martyr (100-165 AD) argued that Socrates was actually a Christian because he defended "true reason" and was willing to die for it.[19] In this he mirrors the will of Christ who is Reason itself *(logos)*. Justin made this claim while living and witnessing in Rome, the city where, as the Roman historian Tacitus (c. 55–c. 120 AD) described it, "all things hideous and shameful from every part of the world meet and become popular."[20] Christ embodies the will of the Creator, who invests the universe with a moral identity and chooses those who obey his will: "[God] accepts only those who imitate the good things which are his — temperance and righteousness and love of mankind, and whatever else truly belongs to God. . . ."[21] Degradation and decadence are the enemies of the divine. They are demons. Against them Justin makes this courageous witness, calling human beings to rise above corruption and give their allegiance to God:

> We have also been taught that in the beginning He in his goodness formed all things that are for the sake of men out of unformed matter, and if they show themselves by their actions worthy of His plan, we have learned that they will be counted worthy of dwelling with Him, reigning together and made free from corruption and suffering. For as He made us in the beginning when we were not, so we hold that those who choose what is pleasing to Him will, because of that choice, be counted worthy of incorruption and of fellowship [with Him]. We did not bring ourselves into being — but as

19. Cyril C. Richardson, *Early Christian Fathers* (New York: Touchstone, 1996) 244 (*First Apology* 5).

20. *Annals* 15.44.4, quoted in J. Stevenson, *A New Eusebius: Documents Illustrating the History of the Church to AD 337*, rev. W. H. C. Frend (Cambridge: SPCK, 1987) 2.

21. Richardson, *Early Christian Fathers*, 247 (*First Apology* 10).

to following after the things that are dear to God, choosing them by the rational powers which he has given us — this is a matter of conviction and leads to faith.[22]

Kierkegaard stands in this same noble tradition. Like Justin, he calls humanity to the challenge of following God. The decision of faith as the exercise of the principle of critical thought, and ultimately the seeking of good, entails a painful examination of oneself and a "subjective transformation" of one's entire way of being in the world.[23] Only in self-examination can a Christian realize personal existence, become what God intended: an individual moral self. The majority of people do not reach individual personhood. Most people spend their lives avoiding serious decisions. Instead of seeking commitments, they drift along on the surface of life seeking momentary pleasure and diversions, conforming to the wishes of others, refusing to take responsibility, living as an anonymous member of the crowd. In the end such a life becomes an increasingly panicky flight from boredom and is bound to end in decadence and despair. In order to become a true self, one must face the predicament of one's existence. This is a risky and unattractive business. It is the polar opposite of nominal church membership: "remember that the higher the religious is taken, the more rigorous it becomes, but it does not necessarily follow that you are able to bear it."[24] True faith entails taking on an alien consciousness, becoming a stranger in the world, embracing a life of striving that is the essence of what it means to be human: "continued striving is the consciousness of being an existing individual."[25] This is not easy to do, especially in a secular age. Most people, even in the church, reject the strenuous imposition of commands. They refuse to acknowledge that in order to belong to God they must change. They desire faith to be a passive assurance, the simple possession of a comforting, non-threatening truth. True faith can be no such thing. Rather, it is like "a true love affair": a "restless thing" that grips one's very being and constantly tosses one about.[26] True faith de-

---

22. Richardson, *Early Christian Fathers,* 247 (*First Apology* 10).

23. Kierkegaard, *Concluding Unscientific Postscript,* 1:38; *Self-Examination,* 10-11. On what follows see also, Søren Kierkegaard, *Stages on Life's Way,* ed. and tr. Howard V. Hong and Edna H. Hong (Princeton: Princeton University Press, 1988).

24. Kierkegaard, *Self-Examination,* 11.

25. Kierkegaard, *Concluding Unscientific Postscript,* 1:122.

26. Kierkegaard, *Self-Examination,* 21.

mands examination of the self, an examination that begins with the hearing and reading of Scripture.

Dietrich Bonhoeffer picks up this Kierkegaardian theme in order to confront complacent German Christians on the eve of the Second World War. "Through the call of Jesus," he writes, "men become individuals." This means "they are compelled to decide, and that decision can only be made by themselves." This is the work of Christ "who makes them individuals by calling them. Every man is called separately, and must follow alone." Bonhoeffer bases his demand directly on a hard saying of Scripture which he exposits without equivocation: "Whoever comes to me and does not hate father and mother, wife and children, brothers and sisters, yes, and even life itself, cannot be my disciple" (Luke 14:26).[27] Bonhoeffer matched his words with his deeds. In 1933 he helped found the Confessing Church, which was subject to suspicion and persecution by the authorities. He himself became a martyr less than a month before the war in Europe ended in 1945.

To speak of Christians as "individuals" and place emphasis on the "decision" of faith as Kierkegaard and Bonhoeffer do is to enter into a different morphology of the church with distinctive theological assumptions of its own. Troeltsch calls this "the sect type" of Christian organization. "The sect," says Troeltsch,

> is a voluntary society, composed of strict and definite Christian believers bound to each other by the fact that all have experienced "the new birth." These believers live apart from the world, are limited to small groups, emphasize the law instead of grace, and in varying degrees within their own circle set up the Christian order, based on love; all this is done in preparation for and expectation of the coming Kingdom of God.[28]

There is a lot in this word "sect." To be sectarian is to belong to a religious subgroup out of sync with the dominant religious power. Sectarians can trace their roots back to the earliest Christians. The Jews of the Temple (the church type of its day) labeled Christians a sect when they first appeared, a designation that St. Paul acknowledges as he defends Christianity before the Roman governor Felix: "But this I admit to you, that according to the Way, which they call a sect, I worship the

27. Bonhoeffer, *Cost of Discipleship*, 105.
28. Troeltsch, *Social Teachings*, 2:993.

God of our ancestors, believing everything laid down according to the law or written in the prophets" (Acts 24:14). Sectarians are forever profaning the Temple in defense of what they perceive as the true, original faith. They are often judged as heretical. (Indeed, the Greek word for "sect" is *haerēsis* — from which we get the word "heresy.") Dogmatic in belief, strict in behavior, refusing to accommodate to state and culture, sectarian Christians have been a significant force in church history. They include groups such as the Montanists and Donatists in the early church, the radical reformers of the sixteenth century (e.g., Anabaptists, Mennonites), Puritans, Pietists, and Baptists of the seventeenth century, Methodists in the eighteenth century, and Pentecostals in the nineteenth and twentieth centuries. Sectarians may take the form of separate denominations or appear as unruly subgroups within territorial churches and mainline denominations.

The meta-doctrine of sectarianism is the teaching that the normal beginning of genuine Christian life is spiritual transformation, what Troeltsch calls, following the terminology of the Bible and Lutheran Pietism, "the new birth." The particular theological orientation that underlies this meta-doctrine may differ among various sects. Some, like the old Puritans, draw on the scholastic Protestant distinction between "historical" and "saving" faith; others emphasize an Arminian anthropology of free choice; still others speak of regeneration through an "anointing" of the Holy Spirit. Whatever the basis, the fundamental sectarian impulse is to preach adult conversion. The sect type consistently challenges the culture at large and Christians of the church type to take responsibility for their lives in practical, moral terms. Generally speaking, sectarians are suspicious of government interference in the life of the church, the conventionality of ritual worship, the objectification of the sacraments, especially the elevation of infant baptism as a guarantee of salvation, and the hierarchical organization of the clergy. Sectarians have a strong rebellious streak which leads them to look askance at any form of conventional Christianity.

Kierkegaard and Bonhoeffer (both Lutheran by birth) self-consciously took up the sectarian impulse in their theologies to combat the failures of the church type of their day. Under the impact of secularization, especially in Europe after the Second World War, other prominent theologians have found themselves reassessing classic sectarian themes as the church has become more and more marginalized culturally. Karl Barth (1886-1968), for example, argued against infant baptism as a detriment to the integrity of the church's evangelical witness. Sacramental incorporation, he recognized, is the cornerstone of the church type. Against this "custom," Barth asserted that what the church needs is a "mature" membership engaged in mission, able to explain and defend its faith, and not determined by "undiscriminating generosity" and content with the maintenance of the way things are. "How can [the church] be credible to the rest of the world so long as it persists in thinking it can pacify its concern for recruitment of personnel [by infant baptism] which is neither responsible to God, to its own message, nor to those who live either externally or internally *extra muros* [outside the walls]?"[29]

Like Barth, the Roman Catholic theologian Karl Rahner (1904-1984) recognized that traditional Christendom under a church-type organization is inadequate to the challenge of secularization. What then should the churches do, especially those like the Roman Church, which had so much invested in Christendom and was largely responsible for its formation and endurance? Rahner's proposal comes in the form of a prediction of what "the Church" will find itself having to do in the future in order to survive: "The theology of the future will, in a more direct sense than hitherto, be a missionary theology. . . . For in the future the Church will no longer be held up by traditions that are unquestioningly accepted in secular society, or regarded as an integral element of that society. The community Church will be transformed into a Church made up of those who believe as a matter of personal conviction and individual decision."[30] "Personal conviction" and "individual decision": these are the hallmarks of the sectarian impulse to adult conversion.

In America the sect type has been the dominant form of Christian social organization from colonial times to the present. Those churches most identified with sectarianism in Europe — evangelical denominations such as Baptists and Pentecostals — have prospered in the American religious environment, having a large hand in shaping it, while churches that trace their roots to territorial churches and the church type, such as the Episcopalians and Lutherans, have traveled a rocky path, at least since the 1960s. Why this is so has been the

29. Karl Barth, *Church Dogmatics* 4/4, tr. G. W. Bromiley (Edinburgh: T. & T. Clark, 1969) xi.

30. Karl Rahner, "Possible Courses for a Theology of the Future," *Theological Investigations,* tr. David Bourke (New York: Seabury, 1975) 13:40 (essay first published in 1970).

primary question for religious sociologists since the landmark study by Dean Kelley, *Why Conservative Churches Are Growing*, appeared in 1972. Kelley, a Methodist pastor and officer in the National Council of Churches, argued that sectarians or evangelicals (as they are commonly labeled in this country) are more successful because they are better able to carry out the indispensable function of religion: to explain the meaning of life in ultimate terms for their members, especially in times of crisis such as illness and death.[31] Evangelicals have been able to capture the imagination of ordinary people and provide them with a concrete understanding of the transcendent in daily existence. They inculcate temperance, frugality, a passion for holiness, the sanctity of family life, and self-examination. Above all, their commitment to doctrinal strictness delivers intact across the generations the fundamental truth of salvation through Christ alone, a teaching that is held to in spite of the alluring blandishments of worldly culture. Theirs is a theology meant to capture the common person and to do so by being a counter-cultural force. Surveying the history of the American religious environment with its unmistakable pattern of church-type decline and sect-type success, not just in the last half century but across two centuries, with evangelicals as their focus, sociologists Roger Finke and Rodney Stark assert: "The churching of America was accomplished by aggressive churches committed to vivid otherworldliness."[32]

This otherworldliness brings with it a pronounced style of worship which, at least at first glance, appears much different from those churches committed to formal liturgy. It is a style that makes a self-conscious effort to retain a simple, direct, eschatological orientation, confirming Troeltsch's classic description of the sect doing all things "in preparation for and expectation of the coming Kingdom of God."[33] This eschatological orientation is depicted dramatically by Donald E. Miller, a professor of religion at the University of Southern California, in *Reinventing American Protestantism*. Miller, a self-confessed liberal Protestant Episcopalian, studies three successful sectarian church movements in California: Calvary Chapel, Hope Chapel, and the Vineyard. At

31. Dean M. Kelley, *Why Conservative Churches Are Growing* (New York: Harper & Row, 1972) 43.

32. Roger Finke and Rodney Stark, *The Churching of America 1776-2005: Winners and Losers in Our Religious Economy*, 2nd ed. (New Brunswick: Rutgers University Press, 2005) 1.

33. Troeltsch, *Social Teachings*, 2:993.

the time of the book's publication over a decade ago, these three churches had spawned nearly 1400 congregations in the United States and abroad. Part of the power of Miller's book is that it represents "a personal pilgrimage" for its author. Miller did not expect to find what he found. Whereas he had thought for most of his adult life that the problem of the church was the rational one of the dissonance between faith and modern knowledge, he learned anew the old truth that "the heart has its reasons that reason does not know." At Hermosa Beach in Southern California one Sunday afternoon, Miller watched seventy new members give testimony and receive baptism in an extended worship service that was anything but an exercise in conventional Christianity: "Several cited drugs or divorce as the precipitating factor that brought them to Hope Chapel. Others talked about a general feeling of emptiness and commented on the family warmth they found the very first time they came to Hope Chapel." For Miller this scene disclosed the purpose of true worship going back to the very origin of the church: "As they were talking, I flashed back to another baptismal scene . . . when John baptized people in the river Jordan and I began to wonder if those first century converts might have said something similar to the seventy people I had just heard give witness."[34]

What Miller describes is liturgical practice as a countercultural force in society, a confrontation of American secular culture at its very center: Southern California, where the "meta-narrative" of Christendom broke down a long time ago — if it was ever present! He is also asserting that in this most impermanent of social environments it is sectarians who are preserving the essence of the Christian tradition going back to the River Jordan when John the Baptist prepared the way. Their liturgy may not conform to the usual models found in denominational hymnbooks, but they know the authentic purpose of liturgy.

The Samaritan Woman

The argument of this chapter — that the sectarian impulse is a most vital witness to the fundamental purpose of worship as repentance — goes against the grain of much conventional thought. The usual argu-

34. Donald E. Miller, *Reinventing American Protestantism: Christianity in the New Millennium* (Berkeley: University of California Press, 1997) 38.

ment is that sectarians dismiss the liturgical traditions of the church "as merely formal or external manifestations of religion that [go] only skin deep."[35] In doing so they court a dangerous subjectivism that places the treasures of faith at the mercy of individual will and emotion. There is no doubt that this is a real danger. But there is potential danger in every position. There is no Christian theology or morphology that cannot be distorted and have ill effect. On this earth, we see through a mirror darkly (1 Corinthians 13:12). If, however, worship is to help the ingathering of believers to learn by repetition the language of the divine realm so that they may worship God properly, give testimony to Christ in word and deed, and be under no illusion as to who they are and how far they fall short when they stand before God and holy things, then the mere performance of ritual is not enough. True worship seeks the heart; its purpose seeks to change us.

What does the Scripture say? One cannot help but think of that great scene from the Gospel of John, Jesus with the Samaritan woman. This woman who has no mark of holiness about her, a Samaritan whose inherited faith of tradition does her no good because it is heretical in its denial of the First Commandment, this woman who should not be seen talking to a man, let alone a Jew in public — this woman asks this unconventional figure standing before her, who dares to speak to her, this dangerous individual to religious authorities because he is a prophet, a question about the external form of true religion:

> The woman said to him, "Sir, I see that you are a prophet. Our ancestors worshiped on this mountain, but you say that the place where people must worship is in Jerusalem." Jesus said to her, "Woman, believe me, the hour is coming when you will worship the Father neither on this mountain nor in Jerusalem. You worship what you do not know; we worship what we know, for salvation is from the Jews. But the hour is coming, and is now here, when the true worshipers will worship the Father in spirit and truth, for the Father seeks such as these to worship him. God is spirit, and those who worship him must worship in spirit and truth." (John 4:19-24)

True faith is not in Jerusalem or in Rome. It is not guaranteed through ordained ministry and the sanctioned worship book. But it is seen and

35. D. G. Hart, *The Lost Soul of American Protestantism* (Lanham, MD: Rowman & Littlefield, 2002) xxiii.

heard when the unlettered, divorced Samaritan woman (or the former druggie on the sands of Hermosa Beach) gives her testimony to the people:

> Many Samaritans from that city believed in him because of the woman's testimony, "He told me everything I have ever done." So when the Samaritans came to him, they asked him to stay with them; and he stayed there two days. And many more believed because of his word. They said to the woman, "It is no longer because of what you said that we believe, for we have heard for ourselves, and we know that this is truly the Savior of the world." (vv. 39-42)

The last verse is especially important. What is this "we have heard for ourselves" if not the knowledge of those who have come to the decision of faith, who have undergone "a subjective transformation of their entire way of being in the world" (Kierkegaard), who "become individuals through the call of Jesus" (Bonhoeffer), who reflect "mature" membership (Barth), who believe "as a matter of personal conviction" (Rahner). Kierkegaard, Bonhoeffer, Barth, and Rahner: two Lutherans, a Reformed, and a Roman Catholic sensitive to the sectarian impulse and desirous that the true purpose of worship be fulfilled.

CHAPTER II

The Witness of the Early Church

"As they were talking," writes Donald E. Miller of new members of Hope Chapel giving testimony before being baptized, "I flashed back to another baptismal scene . . . when John baptized people in the river Jordan and I began to wonder if those first century converts might have said something similar to the seventy people I had just heard give witness."[1] Miller's reference to John the Baptist is not only germane to the event he witnessed but also suggestive of an approach for an understanding of worship as repentance. In this "post-Christendom" age of contemporary Europe and America, it may behoove us to take our theological bearings from the worship practice of the church in the earliest period of its existence, the "pre-Christendom" age, when all Christians were sectarians, outsiders to the dominant culture. We may not readily identify with these ancient Christians. They were marginalized in ways that most contemporary Christians do not experience. There was a simplicity and directness to their worship that centered on an effort to lift up the imperatives of Scripture and the judgment of God. This gave their worship forms a disruptive quality that may seem strange to us, but may also help us see the matter of liturgy afresh. What is certainly clear is that these ancient Christians witnessed unambiguously to what I defined in the first chapter as the central purpose of liturgical worship. To state that purpose once again: *to call Christians to self-examination; to warn them to be under no illusion as to who they are and*

---

1. Donald E. Miller, *Reinventing American Protestantism: Christianity in the New Millennium* (Berkeley: University of California Press, 1997) 38.

how far they fall short when they stand before God and holy things; to teach them to worship God in humility; to feed them the Bread of Life; to make them ready to give testimony to Christ in word and deed.

Superstition

This purpose is at work in the earliest account of Christian worship that we have from an outside observer — and all the more valuable for that — a Roman governor, Pliny the Younger (c. 61-113), writing early in the second century to the Emperor Trajan (53-117). Pliny was at the time governor *(propraetor)* of the Roman province of Bithynia, located on the southern shore of the Black Sea in Asia Minor (what is today modern Turkey). In ancient times, this province had a significant Christian colony that developed apart from Paul's missionary work (Acts 16:7), but which is addressed in 1 Peter as part of the "exiles of the Dispersion" (1:1). This group was under suspicion and suffered persecution. Pliny calls their religion a "superstition" *(superstitio),* a term of derision meaning, in the view of the Romans, an antisocial belief grounded in the primitive fear of the gods that encouraged extreme behavior — what we might call a sect or cult.[2] The proper religious attitude, according to the Romans, was "piety" *(pietas),* what we today might call "civil religion." Its purpose was to uplift the populace by providing its adherents with an ordered, rational understanding of the meaning of life and the means to call on divine favor to fulfill what all human beings hope for and desire: happiness, fulfillment, and success for self, family, and tribe or country. True religion was enlightened, pluralistic, showing respect for the past, patriotic in honoring the Roman emperor, concerned with moral training in the conventions of society. As long as the emperor was given allegiance, people were free to worship their gods. To have many gods was just fine; human beings are all different. But in the end all people want the same things; all religions have a common root and goal under the aegis of Roman authority.

In this framework of understanding, the early Christians did not fit. They were exclusive in their belief, not inclusive. They followed the command of their Lord: "I am the way, and the truth, and the life. No

2. See Robert L. Wilken, *The Christians as the Romans Saw Them* (New Haven and London: Yale University Press, 1984) 48-67.

one comes to the Father except through me" (John 14:6). The Christians were treated with suspicion by the general populace. Accusations of sedition and impiety were made to the governor; lists of Christian suspects drawn up and submitted to Roman authorities. Pliny writes to the emperor to tell him how he has dealt with the problem:

> I interrogated them whether they were Christians; if they confessed it I repeated the question twice again, adding the threat of capital punishment; if they still persevered, I ordered them to be executed. For whatever the nature of their creed might be, I could at least feel no doubt that contumacy and inflexible obstinacy deserved chastisement.[3]

The result of his investigation, which was carried on "with the assistance of torture, from two female slaves, who were styled *deaconesses,*" revealed no more than what Pliny labels with contempt a "depraved and excessive superstition"[4] whose identity, he tells the emperor, is disclosed in their practice of worship:

> . . . the whole of their guilt, or their error, was that they were in the habit of meeting on a certain fixed day before it was light, when they sang in alternate verses a hymn to Christ, as to a god, and bound themselves by solemn oath, not to any wicked deeds, but never to commit any fraud, theft or adultery, never to falsify their word, nor deny a trust when they should be called upon to deliver it up; after which it was their custom to separate, and then reassemble to partake of food — but food of an ordinary and innocent kind.[5]

This brief description is the most detailed witness we have to earliest Christian worship practice from an outside source. It allows us to see our ancient forebears gathered together in secret, perhaps in some cave or ravine, calling on Christ in a hymn, repeating in each other's presence the Ten Commandments. The commandments taught them to walk the path to God in a world that belongs to the devil; to commit themselves to one another in trust, lest under persecution they betray

3. Pliny, *Letters,* tr. William Melmoth; rev. W. M. L. Hutchinson (Cambridge: Harvard University Press, 1961) 2:401-03.
4. Pliny, *Letters,* 2:403.
5. Pliny, *Letters,* 2:403-05.

their brothers and sisters in the faith; and then to share bread and wine. These early Christians lived under mortal threat, surrounded by enemies ready to betray them. They could only depend on each other. In this context, worship and ethical behavior were united. The purpose of worship was to strengthen the resolve of believers and forge bonds of solidarity and mutual discipline with one another so that all members could endure attack. They knew that the Light had come into the world; they also knew that the world loved darkness and hated the Light (John 3:19).

From this same period, another Christian source, the *Didache* or "Teaching," gives a similar witness. Worship and ethics are joined as early Christians praise Christ and pledge themselves to one another. The *Didache* opens by reciting Jesus' commandments in their application to Christian witness. This it calls "the way of life." Turning against the commandments is "the way of death." True Christianity is choosing the right way to live, which is pleasing to God, and rejecting the way that incurs divine wrath. The instructions are specific and blunt. They grate on the ear of the modern liberal Christian shaped by the tolerant canons of the mainline church. At the same time, they are eerily prophetic of troubling aspects of today's society and the contemporary church. For example, "The Second Commandment of the Teaching: Do not commit murder; do not commit adultery; do not corrupt boys; do not fornicate; do not steal; do not practice magic; do not go in for sorcery; do not murder a child by abortion or kill a new-born infant. . . ."[6]

The simple and direct descriptions of worship practice in the early church, evident in documents such as Pliny's letter or the *Didache* and emphasizing the ethical response of believers, were given a provocative analysis by the great church historian of the late nineteenth and early twentieth century, Adolf von Harnack (1851-1930). Harnack argued that the ritual described in these early sources is so bare-boned, so devoid of self-conscious theological speculation, that it had little if any role in the development of the church's doctrinal tradition. "The history of dogma in the first three centuries," declares Harnack, "is not reflected in their liturgy."[7] What evidence we have of liturgical practice shows lit-

---

6. Cyril C. Richardson, *Early Christian Fathers* (New York: Touchstone, 1996) 172 (*Didache* 2.2-3).

7. Adolph Harnack, *History of Dogma,* tr. Neil Buchanan from the 3rd ed. (New York: Dover, 1961 [1894]) 1:334.

urgy to be intellectually unreflective. Worship was moral in intent, oriented toward behavior and action.

This is by no means a criticism. In Harnack's view "dogma" is "a work of the Greek Spirit on the soil of the Gospel."[8] It is abstract and philosophical and often alienating to the experience of faith among common people: "Dogmatic Christianity . . . is always intellectual Christianity, and therefore there is always the danger here that as knowledge it may supplant religious faith, or connect it with a doctrine of religion, instead of with God and a living experience."[9] "The Gospel," says Harnack, "entered the world as an apocalyptic, eschatological message not only in its form, but also in its content."[10] This engendered a type of faith that was vibrant, where "the essence of the matter is a personal life which awakens life around it as the fire of one torch kindles another."[11] The mission of Christ was born in white-hot conviction of the risen Christ, his righteous Kingdom, and his imminent return "like a thief in the night" (1 Thessalonians 5:2). Early Christians prayed *Maranatha*, "Our Lord come" (1 Corinthians 16:22; *Didache* 10.6). Believers were warned in no uncertain terms to hold to the faith and not fall away:

> Let us hold fast to the confession of our hope without wavering, for he who has promised is faithful. And let us consider how to provoke one another to love and good deeds, not neglecting to meet together, as is the habit of some, but encouraging one another, and all the more as you see the Day approaching. For if we willfully persist in sin after having received the knowledge of the truth, there no longer remains a sacrifice for sins, but a fearful prospect of judgment, and a fury of fire that will consume the adversaries. (Hebrews 10:23-27)

Early worship practices complemented these convictions. They witness to an ethical preoccupation on the part of the communities of faith that employed them. They were characterized by simple, direct, forms whose purpose was to lead people to a kingdom that was not of this world (John 18:36).

8. Harnack, *History of Dogma,* 1:17.
9. Harnack, *History of Dogma,* 1:16.
10. Harnack, *History of Dogma,* 1:58.
11. Harnack, *History of Dogma,* 1:71.

Scholars of later generations have built upon Harnack's insights, if not always acknowledging him as a source. G. W. H. Lampe (1912-1980), followed by J. N. D. Kelly (1909-1997), argue that the liturgical practice of the sacraments was of decisive importance for retaining in a vivid, conscious way the eschatological orientation of Christian believers — that is, the expectation of the Lord's return — even as the church found itself having to carry on day after day with the business of living in the world and the temptations of conventional life, what the scholars call institutionalization and routinization. "In Baptism," writes Lampe, "the faithful receive the guarantee of the promised inheritance; they are sealed for the final redemption of soul and body at the *Parousia* [i.e., the Second Coming of Christ]."[12] Through baptism, the faithful cate-chumen received the promise of resurrection through Christ by means of potent symbolic enactment. The Christian was seen to die and rise again, to die and rise with Christ and enter the life of the Spirit.

Baptism

This understanding is affirmed by what we know of the baptismal practice of the early church.[13] The baptismal ritual accented an escha-tological viewpoint. In a stark work, *The Apostolic Tradition,* also known as the *Canons of Hyppolytus,* we have preserved an austere and dramatic description of what is purported to be the approved ritual of baptism at Eastertide with its attendant instructions. The origins of this work are obscure. But it is a window on earliest Christian practice, which at the time of its writing may have already been changing. The work treats this practice as a divinely directed mandate to be preserved. This is its value. It "illuminates the half-Judaic past already vanishing when it was written." Thus, "it affords us a glimpse of the upper reaches of the great stream of Christian liturgical tradition."[14] The instructions con-cerning baptism in the work include the following:

12. G. W. H. Lampe, "Early Patristic Eschatology," *Scottish Journal of Theology Occasional Papers No. 2* (Edinburgh: Oliver and Boyd, 1953) 22; J. N. D. Kelly, *Early Christian Doctrines* (New York: Harper and Row, 1960) 459ff.

13. See A. Hammann, "Baptism," in Angelo Di Berardino, ed. *Encyclopedia of the Early Church,* tr. Adrian Walford (New York: Oxford University Press, 1992) 1:108.

14. Gregory Dix, ed., *The Treatise on the Apostolic Tradition of St. Hippolytus of Rome,* rev. Henry Chadwick (London: SPCK, 1968) 1.

And when they are chosen who are set apart to receive baptism . . . let their life . . . be examined, whether they lived piously . . . while catechumens . . . , whether "they honoured the widows" . . . , whether they visited the sick, whether they have fulfilled every good work.[15]

These chosen catechumens were to have a hand of blessing laid on them each day until their baptism. They were also to undergo exorcism each day. As the baptism drew near, the bishop himself was to perform exorcism on "each one of them, that he may be certain that he is purified."[16] There was a preparatory fast, vigil, and confession. The conferring of baptism was to take place at dawn on Easter Sunday after the all-night Easter vigil. The "chosen" were to disrobe. Little children were first, then the men, and last the women "who shall [all] have loosed their hair and laid aside the gold ornaments . . . [which they might be wearing]. Let no one go down to the water having any alien object . . . with them."[17]

An essential part of the ancient order of baptism was the renunciation of the devil; this is baptism as exorcism. It recalls the experience of the Lord. John baptized Jesus in eschatological anticipation of the New Age. To usher in this New Age there had to be battle, spiritual warfare, with the powers of darkness. Thus we read in the Gospels that after his baptism by John, Jesus is led by the Spirit into the wilderness to face the devil, whom he must renounce. Satan tempts Christ with the prospect of fulfilling desires that all human beings crave (Matthew 4:3-9): the satisfaction of hunger ("turn these stones into bread"), the testing of God to elicit proof of divine love ("throw yourself down, for it is written, 'He will give his angels charge of you'"), and the promise of earthly power and prestige ("All these things I will give you if you will fall down and worship me"). Satan is no haphazard force, but is organized for destruction. He cannot be underestimated. In Satan's temptations regarding material satisfaction, security from harm, and political power the tragic history of humanity unfolds. In the words of the Russian novelist Fyodor Dostoevsky (1821-1881): "the whole subsequent history of mankind is, as it were, brought together into one whole, and foretold, and in them are united all the unsolved historical contradic-

---

15. *Apostolic Tradition of St. Hippolytus*, 30-31.
16. *Apostolic Tradition of St. Hippolytus*, 31.
17. *Apostolic Tradition of St. Hippolytus*, 33.

tions of human nature."[18] Jesus resists these temptations and re-nounces Satan: "Jesus said to him, 'Away with you, Satan! For it is writ-ten, 'Worship the Lord your God, and serve only him'" (v. 10).

The New Testament teaches that Satan returned to do battle with Je-sus and continues to infect the world lost in darkness. His powers are enormous. As one historian puts it, "The figure of Satan in the New Testament is comprehensible only when it is seen as the counterpart, or counterprinciple, of Christ." To fail to recognize this is to do "violence to the essence of Christianity."[19] The devil is prince of the world, space, and time (John 12:31; 14:30; 16:11; Ephesians 2:1; 1 Corinthians 2:6; 1 John 5:9). He is the lord of matter and flesh (Ephesians 2:3). Satan seeks to pervert humanity as tempter (1 Thessalonians 3:5), liar, and murderer (John 8:44), a cause of illness and death (Luke 13:16; Hebrews 2:14), a power behind the storm (Mark 4:39). He attacks by possession (Mark 5:7-8). He can enter a person's heart (Luke 22:3). He is the master of sor-cery and idolatry (Acts 13:8-10). Above all, he works to obstruct the mis-sion of Christ: "In their case the god of this world has blinded the minds of the unbelievers, to keep them from seeing the light of the gos-pel of the glory of Christ, who is the likeness of God" (2 Corinthians 4:4); "For we wanted to come to you — certainly I, Paul, wanted to again and again — but Satan blocked our way" (1 Thessalonians 2:18). Against Satan and his infernal host, Christians are engaged in spiritual warfare: "For our struggle is not against enemies of blood and flesh, but against the rulers, against the authorities, against the cosmic powers of this present darkness, against the spiritual forces of evil in the heavenly places" (Ephesians 6:12).

Early Christians accepted spiritual warfare as the crucible in which their faith and witness were put to the test. They understood themselves to be called to resist the devil and renounce him as Jesus did in the wil-derness. In the battle against evil the believer reaped the reward of salva-tion. This is why Ignatius of Antioch (c. 35 or 50–between 98 and 117 AD) in a famous passage from his *Letter to the Romans* declares that he is eager to enter the *arena* and sacrifice his life for his faith. The *arena*, where

---

18. Fyodor Dostoevsky, *The Brothers Karamazov*, tr. Constance Garnett, rev. Ralph E. Matlaw (New York: W. W. Norton, 1976) 233. For a theological analysis of the tempta-tions, see Diogenes Allen, *Between Two Worlds* (Atlanta: John Knox, 1977), rev. ed. under the title *Temptation* (Cambridge, MA.: Cowley, 1986).

19. Jeffrey Burton Russell, *The Devil: Perceptions of Evil from Antiquity to Primitive Chris-tianity* (Ithaca and London: Cornell University Press, 1977) 222.

Christian martyrs died for the sport of the masses, was the sand-strewn field of combat in the amphitheater that not only provided entertainment for the masses, but also symbolized the centrality of warfare in Roman culture. To Christians the *arena* epitomized the true nature of the world. Satan is powerful in the *arena*. He blocks the way to Christ. In his letter Ignatius proclaims that he is willing to take up the challenge of the *arena* to gain Christ: "Come fire, cross, battling with wild beasts, wrenching of bones, mangling of limbs, crushing my whole body, cruel tortures of the devil — only let me get to Jesus Christ!"[20]

Spiritual warfare against the devil is the context of early baptismal orders, with renunciation of Satan a central feature. The first explicit testimony to the use of a definite formula regarding renunciation comes from Tertullian (c. 160–c. 220): "When entering the water, we make profession of the Christian faith in the words of its rule; we bear public testimony that we have renounced the devil, his pomp, and his angels."[21] In *The Apostolic Tradition,* the catechumen turns to the West, where the sun sets (symbolic of the kingdom of darkness), and says: "I renounce . . . thee, Satan . . . , and all thy service and all thy works."[22] The believer is brought starkly before the decision of faith. He or she then turns to the East, where the sun rises (symbolic of the Son who is the Light of the world), submits and consents to the Father, Son, and Holy Spirit, beseeching God: *"Grant me to do all Thy wills* [sic] *without blame."*[23]

We have images and iconography from the early church showing baptized believers washed with a jet of water or having water poured on them. They could enter a pool up to the waist, or experience full immersion in a cistern, or at least immersion of the head three times. Afterward they were given a meal of milk and honey as a foretaste of the Promised Land (Exodus 3:8). Baptisms were celebrated at Easter and Pentecost by the bishop; later, baptisms were also done during other feasts such as Christmas and Epiphany.

The water of baptism calls to mind dramatic stories of the Bible that accent the theological and existential context of spiritual warfare which define the sacrament. Water can mean rejection: God using the waters of chaos to drown humanity when he could not abide their re-

20. Richardson, *Early Christian Fathers,* 105 (*Letter to the Romans* 5.3).
21. ANF 3:81 (*De spectaculus* iv).
22. *Apostolic Tradition of St. Hippolytus,* 34.
23. *Apostolic Tradition of St. Hippolytus,* 35.

bellion and sin and "was sorry he made humankind on the earth" (Genesis 6:6), Pharaoh drowning Hebrew boys in the Nile to rid Egypt of the Jews (Exodus 1:22), God destroying the army of Pharaoh in the Red Sea (Exodus 14:28). But water can also point to rescue: Noah, his family, and the animals of the earth sail on the flood in the ark of salvation (Genesis 6:18-21), which prefigures baptism (1 Peter 3:20); and Jochebed sends her infant son Moses into the waters of the Nile, the very same river used to drown the Hebrew boys, to be rescued by no one less than Pharaoh's daughter (Exodus 2:6).

The resonance of these images of rejection and rescue was profound in ancient society. In the harsh world of the Roman Empire physical birth did not mean the right to life. The *patria potestas* (power of a father) in Roman law was a power of life and death that extended over fetus and infant. Since the waters of baptism at this fundamental physical level signify rescue and not rejection, it is no wonder that in the *Didache* early Christians declare that "they do not murder a child by abortion or kill a new-born infant."[24] At a spiritual level, the dialectic of rejection and rescue play out in the life of the believer, who stands before God and follows Jesus. The waters of baptism mean the rejection of sin and the old self, and they symbolize the Passion of Christ. We are baptized into the death of Christ so that we die to sin (Romans 6:2-3). Christ is the "living water" who has the power to reject the waters of the abyss that bring death and out of those waters rescue his disciples (Mark 4:41).

Lampe sees these ancient baptismal practices, grounded as they are in vivid biblical imagery, preserving the literalism or fundamentalism of the common folk.[25] Kelly writes that through the liturgical practice of the sacraments, "in early centuries, as indeed in other epochs, wherever religion was alive and healthy, the primitive conviction of enjoying already the benefits of the age to come was kept vividly before the believer's consciousness."[26] Symbolic ritual was in service to the conviction of faith. It placed the believer before the holiness of God, reminding him or her of the last things and the age to come, requiring the believer to make witness in repentance to judgment and grace, death and life.

---

24. Richardson, *Early Christian Fathers*, 172 (*Didache* 2.2-3).
25. Lampe, "Early Patristic Eschatology," 25.
26. Kelly, *Early Christian Doctrines*, 461.

The Lord's Supper

The early liturgy of the Lord's Supper also retained vital eschatological symbolism for the early church and its common folk. It called to mind the heavenly banquet that brings about the deliverance and ingathering of Judah: "On this mountain the LORD of hosts will make for all peoples a feast of rich food, a feast of well-aged wines, of rich food filled with marrow, of well-aged wines strained clear" (Isaiah 25:6).[27] Through the Lord's Supper the faithful were incorporated into Christ in such a way that they were able to enjoy, while still on earth, a foretaste of the supernatural life. It was the New Covenant forecast in Jeremiah ("I will put my law within them, and I will write it on their hearts; and I will be their God, and they shall be my people," Jeremiah 31:33) and fulfilled in the blood of the Suffering Servant, who was "wounded for our transgressions" (Isaiah 53:5). From early on, the Lord's Supper was central to the church in its life of worship: the Lord is truly present in the signs of bread and wine. The Supper was thus an experiential complex which even more than the spoken word itself enabled the church to retain its sense of the epiphany of God. "Here the Church," writes Hans Küng, "is truly itself because it is wholly with its Lord."[28]

As the church grew larger and became more successful, it sought to accommodate itself to the world. The eschatological rigor of early liturgical practice, especially the Lord's Supper, began to cause problems for the self-understanding of the Christian community, which, in turn, generated theological debate. Tensions arose between those who wished the church to be exclusive and disciplined and those who wanted it to be more inclusive and flexible and for whom "pastoral considerations were making the old rigorism difficult to maintain."[29] This tension turned into a battle over the identity of the church that was played out, at least in part, in arguments over the sacraments. "The doctrine of the church and the doctrine of the sacraments were corollaries," writes Jaroslav Pelikan (1923-2006), "for both described the divinely instituted means through which grace was communicated." The church and sacraments were both understood to be "holy." With regard

---

27. Kelly, *Early Christian Doctrines*, 461f.

28. Hans Küng, *The Church*, tr. Rosaleen and Ray Ockenden (New York: Sheed and Ward, 1967) 223.

29. Kelly, *Early Christian Doctrines*, 199.

to the church, "The term 'holy' applied with special force."[30] "Holy" was the "stock epithet" of the church insofar as it expressed "the conviction that it is God's chosen people and is indwelt by His Spirit."[31] Of the four classic marks of the church *(notae Ecclesiae)* developed in the early creedal tradition and given final form at the Second Ecumenical Council of Constantinople (381) — "one, holy, catholic, apostolic" — holiness holds pride of place as the earliest to emerge in the corporate creedal language of the church. "It is used already in the New Testament. . . . [It] appeared in more creeds and in earlier creeds than did any of the others."[32]

In general, there was no debate that the church should be holy. It is the Body of Christ, his Bride. The church is holy because Christ is present in it. A favorite image of the church was the apocryphal figure of Susanna, who would rather have risked death than dishonor. The church was the earthly Eden regained, from which the apostate sinner was excluded. And when the early fathers spoke this way, they envisioned nothing less than the empirical, visible society of the church: the martyred Apostles, especially Peter and Paul, the Christians who suffered torture and death at the hands of the Roman governor Pliny, the great bishops Ignatius of Antioch and Polycarp of Smyrna (c. 69–c. 155), and the many thousands who would undergo periodic persecution in the Roman Empire until the beginning of the fourth century. The reputation of authentic Christians in the ancient world was that they would rather die than deny the Lord.

This literal understanding of the holiness of the church as grounded in the actual self-sacrificing behavior of men and women was given particular expression in the practice of the sacraments. The instructions in the *Didache* regarding participation in the Lord's Supper are clear and blunt: "You must not let anyone eat or drink of your Eucharist except those baptized in the Lord's name. For in reference to this, the Lord said, 'Do not give what is sacred to dogs' [Matthew 7:6]."[33] There is added this injunction: "If anyone is holy, let him come. If not, let him repent."[34] To be a member of the church, to participate in its

---

30. Jaroslav Pelikan, *The Emergence of the Catholic Tradition (100-600)* (Chicago: University of Chicago Press, 1971) 156.

31. Kelly, *Early Christian Doctrines*, 190.

32. Pelikan, *Emergence*, 156.

33. Richardson, *Early Christian Fathers*, 175 *(Didache 9.5)*.

34. Richardson, *Early Christian Fathers*, 176 *(Didache 10.6)*.

sacramental life, meant that one was called to be "holy." This is the ancient church as sect: living apart from the world, strict in demands, its members loyal to each other and doing all "in preparation for and expectation of the coming Kingdom of God."[35]

But how was the church to understand repentance as it found itself living with the delay of the *parousia,* that is, the return of Christ? The church had to go on with the business of living in a messy and complicated world where believers stumble, fall away, and return, and then fall away again. The *Didache* calls for repentance at the Lord's Supper. It also declares that only the baptized can attend the Lord's Table.[36] But, as already noted, the author of Hebrews bars the way to forgiveness for the baptized who have sinned, that is, "those who have once been enlightened, and have tasted the heavenly gift, and have shared in the Holy Spirit" (Hebrews 6:4). At baptism the Holy Spirit is bestowed. To sin against the Spirit after baptism was interpreted as the unforgivable sin (Matthew 12:32). Likewise 1 John refuses the aid of prayer to one who has committed "sin unto death" (1 John 5:16, KJV). Does this mean that there are limits to repentance or a category of persons, namely the baptized, for which repentance has no effect? Then what does repentance mean in the *Didache?* And for what sins is repentance valid? To the woman who had committed adultery and was to be stoned, Jesus showed compassion, but he also commanded her to "sin no more" (John 8:11). Does this mean there is only once chance to repent?

Penance

Our knowledge is "bafflingly meager"[37] about how the church worked out the problem of sin and repentance after baptism in its early discipline and liturgy. But the result was the practice of "penance," that is, a process of repentance that leads to forgiveness for post-baptismal sins. It worked this way: the church's power to forgive the repentant person was ultimately grounded in Christ, the Lord of the church, who receives his authority from God. This is made clear in the Gospel of Mark

---

35. Ernst Troeltsch, *The Social Teachings of the Christian Churches,* tr. Olive Wyon (New York: Harper Torchbooks, 1960) 2:993.

36. Richardson, *Early Christian Fathers,* 175 (*Didache* 9.5).

37. Kelly, *Early Christian Doctrines,* 198.

when Jesus says to the paralytic at Capernaum, "Son, your sins are forgiven" (Mark 2:5). The scribes recoiled at this, charging Jesus with sacrilege: "Why does this fellow speak in this way? It is blasphemy! Who can forgive sins but God alone?" (v. 7). Jesus rebukes them and stakes his claim to divine power by the demonstration of miracle:

> [Jesus] said to them, "Why do you raise such questions in your hearts? Which is easier, to say to the paralytic, 'Your sins are forgiven,' or to say, 'Stand up and take your mat and walk'? But so that you may know that the Son of Man has authority on earth to forgive sins" — he said to the paralytic — "I say to you, stand up, take your mat and go to your home." And he stood up, and immediately took the mat and went out before all of them; so that they were all amazed and glorified God, saying, "We have never seen anything like this!" (vv. 8-12)

Jesus passes this authority to forgive sins on to the church, promising "the keys to the kingdom of heaven" first to Peter (Matthew 16:18-19), then to the disciples: "If you forgive the sins of any, they are forgiven them; if you retain the sins of any, they are retained" (John 20:23; cf. Matthew 18:15-20).

The church, then, has the legitimate right to forgive sins in the name of Christ. The question for the early church, however, was this: How is this power to forgive sins (later known as "the office of the keys") to be exercised toward those who have committed serious sins, such as apostasy, adultery, and bloodshed, that threaten the holiness of the church? Is there a limit to forgiveness?

The earliest reference to this problem that we have is in the second-century document *The Shepherd of Hermas*. The work is purported to be by "Hermas," a former slave who is in dialogue with an angel from heaven who appears in the form of a shepherd to give instruction. It consists of visions, mandates, and precepts. Among the mandates is the command that a husband must take back an adulterous wife if she repents. Adultery certainly qualifies as a most serious sin. But the command is that the wife be given a second chance. The dialogue turns to repentance and its relation to baptism:

> And [Hermas] said to him, "I should like to continue my questions."
> "Speak on," said [the Shepherd]. And I said, "I heard, sir, some

45

teachers maintain that there is no other repentance than that which takes place, when we descended into the water and received remission of our former sins." He said to me, "That was sound doctrine which you heard; for that is really the case. For he who has received remission of his sins ought not to sin any more, but to live in purity. Since, however, you inquire diligently into all things, I will point this also out to you, not as giving occasion for error to those who are to believe, or have lately believed, in the Lord. For those who have now believed, and those who are to believe have not repentance for their sins; but they have remission of their previous sins. For to those who have been called before these days, the Lord has set repentance. For the Lord, knowing the heart, and foreknowing all things, knew the weakness of men and the manifold wiles of the devil, that he would inflict some evil on the servants of God, and would act wickedly towards them. The Lord, therefore, being merciful, has had mercy on the work of His hand, and has set repentance for them; and He has entrusted to me power over this repentance. And therefore I say to you, that if any one is tempted by the devil, and sins after that great and holy calling in which the Lord has called His people to everlasting life, he has opportunity to repent but once. But if he should sin frequently after this, and then repent, to such a man his repentance will be of no avail; for with difficulty will he live."[38]

The sinner, after baptism, has one chance to repent and receive divine forgiveness just as the adulterous wife has one chance to repent and receive forgiveness from her husband.

The Latin theologian Tertullian takes up this same subject of a second repentance in the early part of the third century. Strict in discipline — he would later join a rigorist Christian sect, the Montanists — Tertullian finds it hard to admit that there is even possibility of forgiveness after the commitment of baptism for fear that he is "pointing to a yet further space for sinning." But the custom is in place and so he declares the rule: "God foreseeing, although the gate of forgiveness has been shut and fastened up with the bar of baptism, has permitted *it* still to stand somewhat open. In the vestibule He has stationed the second repentance. . . ." The second chance is the last chance: "now *once for all*, because now for the second time; but never more. . . ."[39] For "this

38. ANF 2:22 (*Mandates* 4.3).
39. ANF 3:662-63 (*On Penitence* 7).

second and only (remaining) repentance" the process of probation is "laborious." There must be "prostration and humiliation" in demeanor especially with regard to dress and food. The penitent is:

> to lie in sackcloth and ashes, to cover his body in mourning, to lay his spirit low in sorrows, to exchange for severe treatment the sins which he has committed; moreover, to know no food and drink but such as is plain, — not for the stomach's sake, to wit, but the soul's; for the most part, however, to feed prayers on fastings, to groan, to weep and make outcries unto the Lord your God; to bow before the feet of the presbyters [the pastors], and kneel to God's dear ones; to enjoin on all the brethren to be ambassadors to bear his deprecatory supplication (before God).[40]

In this understanding, strictness of discipline is meant to preserve the church as, in the words of Hippolytus of Rome (c. 170–c. 236), "the holy assembly of those who live in accordance with righteousness."[41]

The liturgical practice of the early church allowed a single repentance for post-baptismal sins of a serious nature, no more. "Nowhere in the West can the status of the penitent be twice assumed in a human life."[42] Penance can never be taken for granted. The very knowledge that it exists can be dangerous to the believer striving to remain faithful to baptism. St. Jerome (c. 347-420) warns the Roman virgin Demetrias (c. 398-460) in his letter of advice as she dedicates her life to virginity and service to Christ: "let us know nothing of penitence, lest the thought of it lead us into sin. It is a plank for those who have had the misfortune to be shipwrecked; but an inviolate virgin may hope to save the ship itself. For it is one thing to look for what you have cast away, and another to keep what you have never lost." He reminds her of the Apostle Paul's struggle for obedience: "Even the apostle kept under his body and brought it into subjection, lest having preached to others he might himself become a castaway."[43] For the penitent who had been "shipwrecked" and needed the "plank" of penance in order to receive

---

40. *ANF* 3:664 (*On Penitence* 9).

41. *Exposition of Daniel* 1.17.7, quoted and tr. Pelikan, *The Emergence of the Catholic Tradition,* 157.

42. Oscar Daniel Watkins, *A History of Penance,* 2 vols. (New York: Burt Franklin, 1961) 1:481.

43. *NPNF* 6:266 (*Epistle* 130.9).

the Lord's Supper, the liturgical process for this single repentance was arduous. Usually the penitent confessed sins in private, but not always. Those who committed grave offenses were often made to confess in public. Grave sins included apostasy, adultery, and acts of violence, but were not limited to these. The tradition of cataloging sins emerges early. A famous list is the *emphatheis logismoi* or "emotional desires" defined by the desert father Evagrius of Pontus (345-399). The *logismoi* are the raw material that demons inhabit and employ to ensnare the believer: gluttony, pride, lust, avarice, despair, anger, vanity, and *acedia,* which is a kind of aimless discontent or dissatisfaction with one's place in life. Through John Cassian (360-435), among others, this catalogue passed over to the West and became, under Pope Gregory I (540-604), the "seven deadly sins": pride, avarice, gluttony, extravagance, despair, wrath, and envy. There is also a well-known and quite elaborate list of sins in St. Augustine's *Confessions:* ambition, cruelty, wantonness, sloth, lust, wasteful spending, avarice, envy, anger, and self-pity.[44] These lists are notable for pointing to common failings, not criminal acts; they encompass the familiar weaknesses and destructive behavior to which all people are prone. In the moral theology of the Roman church, if one commits any of these sins and does so intentionally and without remorse, he or she is committing mortal sin.

While confession of sins could be private, reconciliation had to be public. The church required penitents to submit themselves at a public function presided over by the bishop. This often took place during Lent or on Good Friday. Penitents had to stand apart from the congregation during worship. They were, by the standards of the day, the elderly. The young who had fallen were excluded from the penitential process for fear that they had too many years left in their lives to be ensnared by the devil and fall again, and thus face the horror of the "unforgivable sin," for which there is no remedy.

Harsh liturgical practices such as these show that "leaders of the early Church were much more confident in using the binding key than the loosing one." The eschatological note of judgment that determined the liturgy of the early church animated its faith and made it a dynamic,

---

44. St. Augustine, *Confessions,* tr. Vernon J. Bourke (Washington, D.C.: Catholic University Press, 1953) 43-44 (2.6.13). On Evagrius of Pontus see Jeffery Burton Russell, *Satan: The Early Christian Tradition* (Ithaca: Cornell University Press, 1981) 177-85; Diogenes Allen, *Spiritual Theology* (Cambridge: Cowley Publications, 1997) 65-78.

countercultural force in the world, a *superstitio*. Fear of being unworthy to receive communion was a paramount concern. This fear shaped the morphology of the Christian community as it gathered around the Lord's Table. As late as 589, the idea that the chronic sinner could come to the Table was forbidden by the Third Council of Toledo.[45]

Seeds of Change

But there was another position developing that began, however slowly and haltingly, to call this understanding of holiness into question. The view represented by Tertullian and Hippolytus found an adversary in Pope Callistus (d. 223), who, it appears, exercised the office of the keys toward sinners who committed sexual indiscretions in such a way as to be accused by his opponents of laxity in discipline. What exactly he did to raise the ire of his rigorist opponents remains unclear. More important is how he is remembered in the history of doctrine. Callistus has become in the dogmatic memory of the Western church a symbol of progressivism who offered a more open and tolerant definition of the membership of the church. Instead of the gathering of the righteous, the church is, according to Callistus, a *corpus permixtum,* a mixed body of saints and sinners. This definition, said Callistus, is congruent with the Bible. Scripture discloses the true nature of the church by prefiguring it in the ancient ark that carried both clean and unclean animals (Genesis 7:2-3, 8) through the Flood. It is symbolized in the parable of the wheat and the tares (Matthew 13:24-30) that mingle together until the final judgment. In the view of historians of doctrine, views such as these indicate a change in church teaching. The church is no longer to be thought of as *"de facto* holy" or "consisting exclusively of actually good men and women."[46] Instead, the holiness of the church should be understood as grounded in the act of forgiveness.[47]

If there was change in church teaching, it did not come quickly. Its full significance took generations to appear. Perhaps in keeping with the parable of the wheat and the tares the idea of the church as a

---

45. Ronald K. Rittgers, *The Reformation of the Keys: Confession, Conscience, and Authority in Sixteenth-Century Germany* (Cambridge: Harvard University Press, 2004) 29.

46. Kelly, *Early Christian Doctrines,* 410.

47. Pelikan, *Emergence,* 158.

"mixed body" should best be thought of as working like a seed planted. Its meaning for the later history of the church is that it was powerful enough to find root, to grow, and to begin to bear fruit, helping the church interpret difficult challenges. A generation after Pope Callistus, Cyprian (d. 258), bishop of Carthage, used a more tolerant conception of the church to justify his exercise of the "loosing" key of mercy to re-admit to membership those who had committed apostasy during the persecution of Emperor Decius (201-251). The same idea came into play during the lengthy Donatist controversy, which began in 311 and raged in North Africa for over a century. In this doctrinal conflict, the issue of holiness focused on the righteousness and integrity of the clergy. The argument was that, while it may be fitting to speak of the laity as a mixed body of saints and sinners, it is wrong to conceive the priest-hood in this way. For the church to be holy its clergy must be holy. This issue arose because a faction of church leaders in North Africa, which would come to be called the Donatists, rejected a candidate chosen by Rome to be the new bishop of Carthage, Caecillian, on the grounds that his consecrator, Felix of Aptunga, had been a *traditor* during the persecution under Emperor Diocletian (244-311). During this persecu-tion, Diocletian forbade Christians the possession of the Scriptures. A *traditor* in the church was an individual who obeyed the emperor's edict by handing over the Scriptures to the authorities, thus betraying the faith. According to the Donatists (named after Donatus, their candi-date for bishop), a priest who committed such an act was unholy and the sacraments he administered invalid.

The Donatist schism was a long and bloody struggle that involved not only doctrine and discipline, but also an incipient nationalism on the part of native North African Christians who resented rule from far-off Rome. The Donatists lost both the theological debate and the polit-ical struggle. Holiness was no longer a requirement for the clergy in or-der for them to be able to perform sacramental acts. Instead, the mark of holiness was claimed to be inherent in the sacraments themselves. The sacraments are valid because God promises to work through them. This means that the church is holy because God makes it holy. Holi-ness does not depend on the behavior of Christians, laity or clergy.

St. Augustine (354-430) is the great architect of this position in the West, building on Pope Callistus, Cyprian, and Optatus (fl. c. 370), bishop of Milevus in Numidia (North Africa). The earthly institution of the church, the "visible church" in Augustine's phrase, includes both sinners and the just. They live together, commingled generation after generation, until the Lord returns in glory. The church is the agent of redemption because God gives to it the means of redemption, not because its members conform to strict standards. This understanding points to a "fundamental principle . . . that our Lord Jesus Christ has appointed to a 'light yoke' and an 'easy burden,' as he declares in the Gospel [Matthew 11:30]." The Lord "has bound his people under the new dispensation together in fellowship by sacraments, which in number are very few, in observance most easy. . . ."[48] Thus there is this rule for participation in the Lord's Supper: "If [a person's sins] are not so great as to bring him justly under sentence of excommunication, he ought not to withdraw himself from the daily use of the Lord's body for the healing of his soul."[49]

The redefinition of the church as a "mixed body" would eventually have enormous consequences. It would become nothing less than the theological foundation for the morphology of the "church type." But that took time. The tolerant re-conception of the church met with liturgical resistance. It is one thing to say that the church is made up of saints and sinners; it is another thing entirely to absolve actual sinners when they fall away. St. Augustine exemplifies this. Although willing to embrace a concept of the visible church of saints and sinners, Augustine made an essential concession to the rigorist position of his opponents, the Donatists. He confessed in effect that "Christ's Bride must be 'without spot or wrinkle' here and now."[50] The "invisible church" of the truly faithful is the essential church, the true church, hidden from the eyes of the world. The outward fellowship of the institutional church is stained by the unrepentant, the damned. In Augustine's chilling words:

> . . . few share in the inheritance of God, while many partake in its outward signs; that few are united in holiness of life, and in the gift of love shed abroad in our hearts by the Holy Spirit who is given to us, which is a hidden spring that no stranger can approach; and that many join in the solemnity of the sacrament, which he that

48. *NPNF* 1:300 (*Epistle* 54.1).

49. *NPNF* 1:301. Augustine cites this rule as a quotation from "another." It would take on a life of its own in Gratian's *Decretum* (twelfth century), ascribed to St. Hilary of Poitiers (d. 368).

50. Kelly, *Early Christian Doctrines*, 415.

eats and drinks unworthily eats and drinks judgment to himself, while he who neglects to eat it shall not have life in him, [John 6:54] and so shall never reach eternal life. . . . [T]he good are called few as compared with the multitude of the evil, but that as scattered over the world there are very many growing among the tares, and mixed with the chaff, till the day of harvest and of purging.[51]

One can imagine Hippolytus or Tertullian expressing these same puritanical sentiments. The church is wheat, not tares. "Do not give what is sacred unto dogs" (Matthew 7:6). But there is a difference. Augustine is more fiercely eschatological than many of his predecessors or contemporaries. Eschatological awareness makes him more humble, less moralistic. The true church belongs to the divine future, not to the human present. Who the good and saved are is not given to us to know or judge, at least not with any confidence or self-righteousness. As Kelly rightly remarks: "many even of those who to all appearances belong to 'the invisible fellowship of love' may not possess the grace of perseverance, and are therefore destined to fall away; while many others who at present may be heretics or schismatics, or lead disordered lives or even are unconverted pagans, may be predestined to the fullness of grace."[52] At any time and at any place, God can break into human life like a thief in the night. When he does this he can be full of surprises. God can choose a Samaritan traveling on the road from Jerusalem to Jericho, a Samaritan woman with a checkered past, a Roman centurion who lives by the sword, or a Saul who persecutes the faithful to be his servant. Belonging to the righteous may not be a matter of strict moral rules and a single chance to repent. Instead the imperative to examine the self and repent may be a constant process through which God shapes us, a blessed repetition of binding and loosing in which we travel the path to God and learn the language of the spiritual realm.

Augustine had personal reasons to know this. A decade after his conversion, he wrote the *Confessions* (c. 397–c. 401), which many consider to be the first recognizably "modern" autobiography that explores the psychological depths of the self. The *Confessions* is an extended address to God in which Augustine lays bare his dark secrets and weaknesses and calls upon the mercy of God. In a famous passage he tells how as a

---

51. *NPNF* 4:205 (*Contra Faustum* 13.16).
52. Kelly, *Early Christian Doctrines,* 416.

teenage boy he, along with friends, denuded a pear tree of its fruit simply for the thrill of destroying something. Teenage boys out of control: hardly an uncommon event. But to Augustine it was revelatory of an evil will to undo that grips the self and leads it to desire destruction. He caught a glimpse of the human condition in its waste and void. He confesses to God: "It was filthy and I loved it. I loved my own destruction. I loved my own fault; not the object to which I directed my faulty action, but my fault itself, was what I loved, my vile soul leaping down from thy support into extinction. . . ."[53] In this terrible discovery, Augustine goes even further into the dark night of the soul than St. Paul does in his honest agony about not understanding "my own actions. For I do not do what I want, but I do the very thing I hate" (Romans 7:15). Augustine learned something much worse: that he hated good and loved to hate. A human being is *non posse non peccare* — "not able not to sin." What is confession and forgiveness in this context? And how can the church be holy?

53. Augustine, *Confessions*, 41 (2.4).

CHAPTER III

Luther and the Binding Key

Penance as Blessed Repetition

In March 1525, Nicholas Hausmann (c. 1478-1538), Lutheran reformer in the city of Zwickau, pastor at St. Mary's church, sent Martin Luther a number of masses in the German language for review. This was part of Hausmann's effort, supported by the city council at the time, to bring orderly evangelical reform to a city that had seen a good deal of conflict. Luther replied in a letter dated March 26, in which he proposed one textual revision: the replacement of the preface with its versicles in the inherited Roman mass with "An Exhortation to Communicants." The precedent for this goes back to the year before, to the first evangelical German mass celebrated in Nuremberg (April 1524), in which an exhortation prepared by Andreas Osiander (1498-1552) was read aloud immediately before communion.[1] Luther's exhortation reads as follows:

> Dearest Friends in Christ: You know that our Lord Jesus Christ, out of unspeakable love, instituted at the last this his Supper as a memorial and proclamation of his death suffered for our sins. This commemoration requires a firm faith to make the heart and conscience of everyone who wants to use and partake of this Supper sure and certain that Christ has suffered death for all his sins. But

---

1. Ronald K. Rittgers, *The Reformation of the Keys* (Cambridge: Harvard University Press, 2004) 83-85. For the text of the Nuremberg exhortation, see *EKO* 11/1:48.

whoever doubts and does not in some manner feel such faith should know that the Supper is of no avail to him, but will rather be to his hurt, and he should stay away from it. And since we cannot see such faith, and it is known only to God, we leave it to the conscience of him who comes and admit him who requests and desires it. But those who cling to open sins, such as greed, hatred, envy, profiteering, unchastity, and the like and are not minded to renounce them, shall herewith be barred and be warned faithfully not to come lest they incur judgment and damnation for their souls as St. Paul says [1 Cor. 11:29]. If however someone has fallen because of weakness and proves by his acts that he earnestly desires to better himself, this grace and communion of the body and blood of Christ shall not be denied to him. In this fashion each must judge himself and look out for himself. For God is not mocked [Gal. 6:7], nor will he give that which is holy unto the dogs or cast pearls before swine [Matt. 7:6].[2]

The exhortation, dramatic and blunt, spoken not in remote Latin but in the vernacular, is evidence of how deeply concerned early Lutheranism was to witness to the holiness of the Lord's Supper over against the unrepentant, the unbelieving, and the casual worshiper. St. Paul's command to examine oneself is given paramount importance within the liturgy itself. The aspect of judgment is placed before the worshiper in such a way that he or she is forced to pay attention. Luther draws upon the traditional catalogue of sins going back to the early church, "greed, hatred, anger," etc., and warns that if these sinful acts are intentional and no effort is made to amend one's behavior, then the sacrament is of no avail. This is the traditional Catholic teaching, whether it is explicitly acknowledged or not, concerning mortal sin. This calls to mind the eschatological consciousness and concern for holiness in behavior so common in the liturgy of the early church that we examined in the last chapter. The exhortation to communicants became a standard feature of Lutheran liturgy in the sixteenth century.[3] Exceptions to its use are rare.

2. *LW* 51:104. On Hausmann, see Helmar Junghans, "Hausmann, Nicholas," in Hans J. Hillerbrand, ed., *The Oxford Encyclopedia of the Reformation* (New York, Oxford: Oxford University Press, 1996): 2:214-15.

3. Here are examples of two orders of public worship from the sixteenth century that have come down to us in which the exhortation holds a prominent place:

The similarity in intention between Luther's exhortation and the rigorous liturgical warnings of the early church is not explained by the argument that worship practices are being preserved by tradition. One thousand years separated Luther from the early church. In that vast expanse of time the fundamentals of Christian worship regarding repentance in preparation for communion had changed in the West. The common practice in the Roman Church, persistent to the sixth century, was to allow the fallen sinner but one chance to repent in a lifetime, most often in a ritualized public act. Divine grace was limited, holiness a fearful and unbending mandate on all believers. Over the course of the seventh and eighth centuries repentance was reconceived as a repeatable act. The sinner could confess to a priest in private again and again and be assured of the forgiveness of the church. Sins were catalogued, lesser to greater, and gradations of penalties applied. This change came about through Celtic influence. Why this happened among the Irish is unclear. What is known is that in Ireland Christianity came late (mid-fourth century) and developed a vigorous and intellectually inquisitive morphology in relative isolation from inherited Roman tradition. The Irish, it appears, were more forgiving to fallen sinners. Perhaps the reason for this is that St. Patrick, great missionary to the Irish tribes, came to Ireland with a record of scandal in his past. Empathy for the sinner comes from one who knows sin himself; Patrick knew sin. The empathy of the founder shaped Celtic faith and theology. St. Columba or Colmcille, Irish missionary to the continent in the dark age of barbarian conquest, stated that a chief principle of the

---

Bugenhagen Type	Brandenburg-Nuremberg Type
Congregational hymn	Exhortation to the Supper
Exhortation to the Supper	Words of Institution
Lord's Prayer	Sanctus, Lord's Prayer, Peace
Words of Institution	Distribution
Distribution	Post-Communion Collect
Agnus Dei	Benedicamus Domino
Post Communion Collect	Blessing
Blessing	

In the so-called "Bugenhagen type" the exhortation "in certain orders or at certain times could be preceded, replaced, or followed by the Preface and Sanctus." Hans-Christoph Schmidt-Lauber, "The Lutheran Tradition in German Lands," in Geoffrey Wainwright and Karen B. Westerfield Tucker, eds., *The Oxford History of Christian Worship* (New York: Oxford, 2006) 403.

gospel is *"Amor non tenet ordinem"* — "Love has nothing to do with order." Discipline must give way to charity.[4] As Celtic influence spread in Western Europe, repeated repentance and forgiveness became part of the rhythm of Christian life.

In this new context, certain aspects of Scripture, especially Jesus' teaching in the Gospels regarding the radical nature of divine forgiveness, emerged with new clarity and relevance.

> Then Peter came and said to him, "Lord, if another member of the church sins against me, how often should I forgive? As many as seven times?" Jesus said to him, "Not seven times, but, I tell you, seventy-seven times." (Matthew 18:21-22)

> He also told this parable to some who trusted in themselves that they were righteous and regarded others with contempt: "Two men went up to the temple to pray, one a Pharisee and the other a tax collector. The Pharisee, standing by himself, was praying thus, 'God, I thank you that I am not like other people: thieves, rogues, adulterers, or even like this tax collector. I fast twice a week; I give a tenth of all my income.' But the tax collector, standing far off, would not even look up to heaven, but was beating his breast and saying, 'God, be merciful to me, a sinner!' I tell you, this man went down to his home justified rather than the other; for all who exalt themselves will be humbled, but all who humble themselves will be exalted." (Luke 18:9-14)

> Then Jesus said, "Father, forgive them; for they do not know what they are doing." (Luke 23:34)

> All have sinned and fall short of the glory of God. (Romans 3:23)

> For I received from the Lord what I also handed on to you, that the Lord Jesus on the night when he was betrayed took a loaf of bread. . . . (1 Corinthians 11:23)

> If we say that we have no sin, we deceive ourselves, and the truth is not in us. (1 John 1:8)

Scripture affirms that the church is a "mixed body," a *corpus permixtum;* it is wheat and tares, clean and unclean, saint and sinner. This mixture

---

4. Thomas Cahill, *How the Irish Saved Civilization* (New York: Anchor Books, 1995) 176.

can be found in each individual Christian. While the Christian aspires to holiness, he or she cannot claim holiness without falling into sin, like the Pharisee thumping his breast in pride. To be a Christian is to know that one has betrayed Christ and that Christ, though knowing this, still extends an invitation to the Lord's Table.

This awareness of grace did not make penance easy in the Celtic tradition. Sin is a serious affair; penance must be made fitting for the offense. "If any layman commits theft," states *The Penitential of Columban* (c. 600):

> that is, steals his neighbor's ox or horse or sheep or any animal, if he does it once or twice he shall first make restitution to his neighbor for the damage which he has done, and he shall do penance for the three forty-day periods on bread and water. But if he has been accustomed to commit theft often and is not able to make restitution, he shall do penance for a year and the three forty-day periods and shall promise in no circumstances to do it henceforth; and so he shall take communion in the Easter of the following year, that is, after two years having moreover previously given alms to the poor . . . and thus shall he be absolved from the guilt of his evil course.[5]

These are stern penalties. What is new is not only that the one-time thief can secure absolution, but that the chronic thief, the repeat offender, is not barred from the grace of God and a place at the Lord's Table.

As the medieval church developed, penance, as a repeated sacramental act, became routinized in the liturgical calendar and subject to theological rationale. According to canon law, every Christian of the age of reason (seven years) was required to confess sins and receive communion at least once a year, most commonly during Lent. The fundamental question facing the penitent was the same as that of the young rich man who came to Jesus: "Teacher, what good deed must I do to have eternal life?" (Matthew 19:16). For priest, monk, and nun, Jesus' challenge to the young man to go beyond obedience was taken as the rule: "If you want to be perfect, go, sell your possessions and give to the poor, and you will have treasure in heaven" (v. 21). This word had guided great ecclesiastical figures of the church: St. Anthony of Egypt

5. John T. McNeill and Helena M. Gamer, *Medieval Handbooks of Penance* (New York: Columbia University Press, 1938) 255.

(251-356), St. Augustine, St. Francis of Assisi (c. 1181-1226). For the laity, obedience to the commandments was sufficient, the summary of which Jesus gives as follows: "'You shall love the Lord your God with all your heart, and with all your soul, and with all your mind.' This is the greatest and first commandment. And a second is like it: 'You shall love your neighbor as yourself.' On these two commandments hang all the law and the prophets." (Matthew 22:37-40).

Certainly, neither cleric nor layperson fulfills these demands to perfection. This fact the church now fully realized and was willing to express. "What is the debt we owe to God?" asks St. Anselm (1033-1109). The answer is that "every inclination of the rational creature ought to be subject to the will of God. . . . None who pays it sins, everyone who does not pay it sins."[6] Humanity is incapable of paying the debt. But God requires it and this requirement cannot be rescinded. What is to be done? Anselm answers with his theory of atonement. The solution to the predicament of sinful humanity is Jesus Christ the God-Man. As God Christ carries out the divine will and is perfectly obedient. As human he suffers the penalty that human beings deserve. His atoning death pays the original debt. Human beings, if they believe in Christ, receive pardon.

Reconciled to God through Christ, Christians are still obligated to the divine law to love God and neighbor. Love is the test and fruit of faith. But human beings still sin. How then can they love? This question was hotly debated in medieval scholastic theology as the theology of penance developed. On one side stood Peter Lombard (1100-1160), called "the Master," who authored the most influential theological textbook at the beginning of the Middle Ages, the *Sentences*. He asks: "Is that love by which we are saved a created habit of our soul or is it the very person of the Holy Spirit dwelling within us?"[7] He answers that it is the Holy Spirit. The Holy Spirit allows us to say "Jesus is Lord" (1 Corinthians 12:3). The Holy Spirit does works of love through us. Without the Spirit, we can do nothing. On the other side stood Thomas Aquinas (1225-1274), writing a century later, who disagreed with "the Master." Acts of love to be authentic must be voluntary acts of will. While it

6. Anselm, *Why God Became Man* 1.9. Eugene Fairweather, ed. and tr., *A Scholastic Miscellany: Anselm to Ockham* (New York: Macmillan, 1970) 119.

7. Peter Lombard, *Sentences* 1.17, a. 2. Quoted in Steven Ozment, *The Age of Reform: 1250-1550* (New Haven and London: Yale University Press, 1980) 31.

is not to be doubted that God provides an infusion of grace for humanity to respond to the divine will, it is still the case that the human being is obligated to cooperate.[8]

The theology of penance "was notorious for producing differences of opinion."[9] The dominant position was that of Thomas. "Moral cooperation" became the accepted view in the Roman church and undergirded the practice of confession and absolution in the Middle Ages.[10]

On the basis of this theology, confession and absolution were understood as follows. The penitent went through a four-step process with the priest in privacy: confession of the heart *(contritio cordis)*, oral confession to the priest *(confessio oris)* which involved the penitent reciting all sins and the circumstances surrounding the sins, and also responding to the examining questions of the confessor, questions that could be formally organized according to, for instance, the Ten Commandments;[11] satisfaction for sin in the form of good works *(satisfactio operis);*

---

8. A. M. Fairweather, *Aquinas on Nature and Grace* (Philadelphia: Westminster, 1954) 344-45 (*Summa Theologia* IIa IIae q. 23 a. 2).

9. Jaroslav Pelikan, *The Christian Tradition: A History of the Development of Doctrine* 4: *Reformation of Church and Dogma (1300-1700)* (Chicago: University of Chicago Press, 1984) 11.

10. "Following Aquinas, most late medieval theologians thought that God planted divinely created habits of virtue in believers via the sacraments, which helped them realize and develop their natural love for the good, God himself. In this way salvation was always a gift, but it still took place within an individual and required human agency...." Rittgers, *The Reformation of the Keys,* 57.

11. These leading questions asked by the priest could be highly invasive of a person's private life. Steven Ozment quotes and translates examples from *The Mirror of the Sinner* (c. 1470), a popular confessional in the vernacular. Questions concerning sins against the First Commandment: "Have you honored temporal rulers and lords more than God, Mary, and the sacraments? Are your prayers, alms, and religious activities done more to hide your sins and impress others than to please God? Have you loved relatives, friends, or other creatures more than God? Have you had doubts about Scripture, the sacraments, hell, the afterlife, the Last Judgment, or that God is the creator of all things? Have you befriended the excommunicated? Have you practiced or believed in magic?" The Second Commandment: "Have you questioned God's power and goodness when you lost a game? Have you muttered against God because of bad weather, illness, poverty, the death of a child or a friend? Have you murmured against God because the wicked prosper and the righteous perish? Have you committed perjury in a court of law? Have you sworn in the name of God that you would do something you had no intention of doing?" The Third Commandment: "Have you skipped mass on Sundays and holidays without a good excuse? Have you conducted business on Sundays rather than reflecting on your sins, seeking indulgence, counting your blessings, meditating on

absolution by the priest *(ego te absolvo a peccatis tuis in nomine Patris, et Filii, et Spiritus Sancti. Amen)*. In the practice of the church, satisfaction and absolution were reversed so that the penitent need not return to the priest. The good works of "satisfaction" were understood to be enabled by the mercy of God. God infuses the believer with grace. The believer cooperates willingly by "doing the best one can" *(facere quod in se est)*. In this way Christian faith is formed by acts of charity *(fides caritate formata)* and shapes the worthy Christian life. This life receives as its merited reward the gift of eternal life. As to the works required in satisfaction, the church provided clear guidance. There were the seven acts of corporal mercy derived from Scripture that are meant for the neighbor's physical well-being[12] and seven acts of spiritual comfort to minister to the neighbor's soul, also derived from Scripture.[13] The number seven was thought of as the sacred number of completeness. There was a good deal of variation as to how much satisfaction was required, depending

death, hell and its penalties, and heaven and its joys? Have you dressed proudly [a question especially for women], sung and danced lustily, committed adultery [a doubly deadly mortal sin on Sundays], girl-watched, or exchanged adulterous glances in church or while walking on Sundays?" Translated and quoted in Steven Ozment, *The Reformation in the Cities* (New Haven and London: Yale University Press, 1975) 24.

12. To feed the hungry: "For I was hungry and you gave me to eat." Mt. 25:35
   To give drink to the thirsty: ". . . I was thirsty and you gave me to drink. . . ." Mt. 25:35
   To clothe the naked: "I was . . . naked and you clothed me. . . ." Mt. 25:36
   To visit the imprisoned: "I was in prison and you came to me." Mt. 25:36
   To shelter the homeless: ". . . I was a stranger and you took me in. . . ." Mt. 25:35
   To visit the sick: ". . . I was sick and you cared for me. . . ." Mt. 25:36
   To bury the dead: "Amen, I say to you, insofar as you did it for one of these least of my brothers, you did it for me." Mt. 25:40

13. To admonish the sinner: ". . . there will be more joy in Heaven at the repentance of one sinner than at ninety-nine of the righteous who had no need of repentance." Lk. 15:7
   To instruct the ignorant: "Go into the whole world and proclaim the good news to all creation." Mk. 16:15
   To counsel the doubtful: "Peace I leave with you, my peace I give to you. . . . Let not your hearts be troubled. . . ." Jn. 14:27
   To comfort the sorrowful: "Come to me, all you grown weary and burdened, and I will refresh you." Mt. 11:28
   To bear wrongs patiently: ". . . Love your enemies, do good to those who hate you, bless those who curse you." Lk. 6:27-28
   To forgive all injuries: "And forgive us our debts, as we forgive our debtors." Mt. 6:12
   To pray for the living and the dead: "Father, I desire that they, too, may be with me where I am. . . ." Jn. 17:24

on the circumstances and the seriousness of the offense. Over time, however, there developed a tendency to impose lighter penalties.[14] The rigor of the early church was self-consciously left behind while continuing to be admired as an example of uncompromising discipline. The "primitive church" was a harsh master, said Alain de Lille (ca. 1128-1202): its people more able to endure punishment. Early Christians lived in a heroic age closer to God. Now the church is larger, but weaker in character. Its weaknesses must be accommodated: "For then human nature was stronger than it is now for bearing the burdens of penance; and that is why penance must be moderated."[15]

This moderation meant that fewer demands were placed on the faithful. The penitent sinner could confess his or her sins by "attrition" or imperfect contrition and still receive absolution. In the thirteenth century the notion of *opus operatum* was introduced (first used by Peter of Poitiers [ca. 1130-1215]), asserting that the beneficial effects of the sacraments depended neither on the merits of the minister nor the recipient, but on the objective character of the sacrament which itself produces grace by the virtue inherent in it (*opus operatum* — "the work wrought"). This meant that the sacrament could be worthily received with only a virtual intention: a person received the grace of God just by participating, as long as one did not place an obstacle in the way such as conscious resistance or outright rejection. At the Council of Trent the teaching of *opus operatum* would be elevated to official doctrine. The objective character of the Sacrament of the Altar was enhanced by the doctrine of transubstantiation, ratified at the Fourth Lateran Council (1215). This doctrine taught that bread and wine of the Lord's Supper were "changed in substance," or "transubstantiated" at consecration by the priest, becoming the body and blood of the Lord. Christ's real presence in the Mass is a presence of things divine in and through things material.

Fundamental to medieval theology was the distinction of *fides implicata* — "implicit faith" — and *fides explicata* — "explicit faith." The duty of the laity or the "simpler minded" is implicit faith: obedience to the instructions of the "wiser," who are the clergy, those who have ex-

14. Thomas N. Tentler, *Sin and Confession on the Eve of the Reformation* (Princeton: Princeton University Press, 1977) 16-27.

15. Alain de Lille, *Liber poenitentialis*, in Jacques Paul Migne, ed., *Patrologiae cursus completus, Series latina* (Paris, 1844-1890) 210:293. Translated and quoted in Tentler, *Sin and Confession on the Eve of the Reformation*, 17.

plicit knowledge of the content of revelation and faith. Divine truth is made known by a hierarchy. "Now divine revelation," says Thomas,

> reaches lower creatures through higher creatures, in a certain order. It is given to men through the angels, and to the lower angels through higher angels, as Dionysius explains (*Coel. Hier.*, caps. 4, 7). In the same way, it is through wiser men that the faith must be made explicit for the simpler. Hence just as higher angels have a fuller knowledge of divine things than the lower angels whom they enlighten, so also are wiser men, to whom it pertains to instruct others, required to have a fuller knowledge of what ought to be believed, and to believe it more explicitly.[16]

That hierarchy mirrors the order of heaven means that it is the inevitable and natural order of earthly things.

The medieval theology of penance and the church practices derived from it should not be thought of as miring the church in legalism and works righteousness. If anything, they represented a certain laxity of demand as the church tried to carry out the biblical imperative of self-examination and to do so by creating an inclusive system of discipline for penance that was private and repeated and was geared to reach all members of society at least once a year. According to the Protestant historian of doctrine Reinhold Seeberg (1859-1935), this had "beneficial results" for society in that age: "The sinner was compelled to scrutinize his whole life in search of his sins; he was induced to look for and to recognize and mourn as sins, not only gross outward offenses, but also the inward evil desire itself."[17] This challenge to examine the self was softened insofar as the church made allowance for the weakness of faith on the part of the majority of believers. The ultimate effect of teachings such as *opus operatum,* confession by attrition, and *fides implicata* was to relax the demand for subjective holiness on the part of the individual believer that had determined the liturgical practice and discipline of the early church. In the medieval church, the stringent demands of holiness could be set aside or at least neutralized. Penance became a matter of fixed liturgical custom and guaranteed effect, em-

---

16. A. M. Fairweather, *Aquinas on Nature and Grace* (Philadelphia: Westminster, 1954) 250 (*Summa Theologia* IIa IIae, q. 2, a. 6).

17. Reinhold Seeberg, *Textbook of the History of Doctrines,* tr. Charles E. Hay (Grand Rapids: Baker Book House, 1952) 2:42-43.

bracing the masses with the assurance of grace. This placed baptism and the Lord's Supper in a more congenial context of "sacramentality": that is, the general and largely comforting medieval idea that things divine are disclosed in and through things material to represent the intimate presence and protection of God; to use the phrase of Martin Buber, "the having of God in space and time."[18]

Sacramentality emphasized the visibility of the church as a public institution at the center of society; its central paradigm was the Incarnation, the Word becoming flesh and dwelling among us (John 1:14), an idea that Catholic authorities would readily exploit over against Protestant rebels at the beginning of the Reformation. According to Catholic teaching, Christian truth is that which is taught "always, everywhere, and by all" *(semper, ubique, omnibus)*.[19] "Our doctrine of the church," claimed Robert Cardinal Bellarmine (1542-1621),

> is distinguished from the others in this, that while all others require inward qualities *(internas virtutes)* in everyone who is to be admitted to the church, we believe that all the virtues, faith, hope, charity and the others, are to be found in the Church. We do not think that any inward disposition *(ullam internam virtutem)* is requisite from anyone in order that he may be said to be part of the true Church whereof the Scriptures speak: all that is necessary is an outward confession of faith and participation in the sacraments *(sed tantum externam professsionem fidei et sacramentorum communionem)*. The Church, in fact, is a company of men *(coetus hominum)* as visible and palpable as the assembly of the Roman people, or the Kingdom of France, or the Republic of Venice.[20]

18. Martin Buber, *I and Thou*, tr. Walter Kaufmann (New York: Charles Scribner's Sons, 1970) 161-62.

19. This is the famous definition of Vincent of Lérins (d. c. 445), an obscure semi-Pelagian theologian of the fourth century whose essay *The Commonitory* (434) was rediscovered in 1528 and used for polemical purposes against the relatively small band of upstart reformers at the time, who represented small numbers and few cities and territories. "We hold," says Vincent, "to that which has been believed everywhere, always, and by all men" *(teneamus quod ubique, quod semper, quod ab omnibus creditum est)*. George E. McCracken, ed., *Early Medieval Theology*, Library of Christian Classics 9 (Philadelphia: Westminster, 1957) 38.

20. *De ecclesia militate*, chapter 2. Quoted and tr. J. S. Whale, *The Protestant Tradition* (Cambridge: University Press, 1955) 185.

This is the morphology of the church type in full display: Christian faith as conventional Christendom.

In the Middle Ages sacramentality involved a wide range of "ritual structures" and "symbolic gestures" that helped to order daily life and give it meaning.[21] Priests could be employed to consecrate a wide range of secular activities through blessings of salt and water that worked as a kind of exorcism: "to bless houses, cattle, crops, ships, tools, armour, wells and kilns. There were formulae for blessing men who were preparing to set off on a journey, to fight a duel, to engage in battle or move into a new house . . . [for] driving away thunder, for making the marriage bed fruitful."[22]

Liturgy marked the rhythms of the yearly agricultural cycle as God's time and nature commingled. The canonical hours, eight daily prayers that measured the day, and the ringing of church bells along with three (or four) prayers at night were a primary way by which time was kept day in, day out. Seasons also had their liturgical markers. At Candlemas (February 2), which celebrates the Lord as the Light of the world, the medieval peasant farmer would bring his oxen, horses, and plows to the church to be blessed for the breaking of the soil in anticipation of the end of the winter freeze. The spring crop was planted to be harvested in late summer or early fall. On St. John's Day, the summer solstice, farmers harvested the winter crop that had been planted back in October and lay dormant under the winter snow. St. Michael's Day (September 29) marked the end of the harvest season: the crop was taken in and taxes paid (usually in kind) to the lord of the manor. On St. Martin's Day (November 11) the stubble in the fields was burned, the ashes used to fertilize the ground for the year to come. Farm animals that could not be kept over the winter were slaughtered to make sausage and salted meat. In winter people mostly slept and did their best to keep warm and survive for the return of the light and activity at Candlemas. The liturgical calendar brought the visible and invisible, the profane and the holy, together for rural life. The proclamation of the gospel that "God became flesh

21. See Keith Thomas, *Religion and the Decline of Magic* (New York: Charles Scribner's Sons, 1971) 3-50; Eamon Duffy, *The Stripping of the Altars: Traditional Religion in England 1400-1580* (New Haven and London: Yale University Press, 1992) 11ff.; Jacques Le Goff, *Time, Work, and Culture in the Middle Ages,* tr. Arthur Goldhammer (Chicago: University of Chicago Press, 1980).

22. Thomas, *Religion and the Decline of Magic,* 29.

and dwelt among us" (John 1:14) was made part of common life in the everyday.

This mingling of divine and human in the common things of life could lead to outright superstition, especially among the unlettered laity. A friar's cloak, a church key, even dirt from the churchyard could all be used as amulets to ward off various ills. Above all there was the sanctified bread of the Lord's Supper. The doctrine of transubstantiation had the effect of making the consecration of the elements by the priest the center of the mass, instead of the communing of believers. Consecrated bread and wine became objects of devotion believed to hold magical powers above all other things, working, according to a common phrase of the time in England, "like a charm upon an adder."[23] If a communicant did not swallow the bread (the cup was withheld from the laity) but saved it, it could be used as a talisman to protect against misfortune, employed as a cure for fever or blindness, even crumbled in the garden to keep insects away.[24]

The mingling of the divine and the human could also involve great sums of money as the practice of penance (that most intimate of the sacraments) became entangled in the doctrines of Purgatory and indulgences. This was not a positive development. The first mention of Purgatory dates to the eleventh century, although early fathers as diverse as Tertullian, Origen (185-254), Clement of Alexandria (c. 150-c. 215), and Ambrose (c. 337-397) spoke in various ways about the purifying of the dead.[25] The scriptural basis for the doctrine is found in 2 Maccabees,[26] which speaks of "atonement" being made for the dead

23. Thomas, *Religion and the Decline of Magic*, 33.

24. Thomas, *Religion and the Decline of Magic*, 34.

25. Angelo di Berardino, ed., *Encyclopedia of the Early Church*, tr. Adrian Walford (New York: Oxford University Press, 1992) 2:725.

26. 2 Maccabees 12:39–13:1: 39On the next day, as had now become necessary, Judas and his men went to take up the bodies of the fallen and to bring them back to lie with their kindred in the sepulchres of their ancestors. 40Then under the tunic of each one of the dead they found sacred tokens of the idols of Jamnia, which the law forbids the Jews to wear. And it became clear to all that this was the reason these men had fallen. 41So they all blessed the ways of the Lord, the righteous judge, who reveals the things that are hidden; 42and they turned to supplication, praying that the sin that had been committed might be wholly blotted out. The noble Judas exhorted the people to keep themselves free from sin, for they had seen with their own eyes what had happened as the result of the sin of those who had fallen. 43He also took up a collection, man by man, to the amount of two thousand drachmas of silver, and sent it to Jerusalem to provide for a sin

that "they might be delivered from their sin" — the atonement in the form of a money gift to be given to the Temple. Purgatory is a state intermediate between life and heaven where sinners undergo purifying punishment as satisfaction for sins. For those who confess their sins by attrition, Purgatory is required for full satisfaction. It is significant that the official scriptural basis for the teaching should mention atonement by money gift. That the payment of money can be a means of satisfaction is an idea that goes far back in the church. In the thirteenth century it was tied to a supposed "treasury of merit" built up by the works and witness of saints and martyrs, the key to which belongs to the pope. By paying the church to access this treasury, one could draw on this merit for oneself, a relative, or a friend and so reduce the time required in the purging fire. The church used this teaching to raise money. To draw a connection among money, grace, and merit may have been profitable for the church, but it was also vulgar and prone to abuse. Penance as blessed repetition was a great achievement of the medieval church: it deepened religious life by making the sacraments more clearly vehicles of grace. By giving repeated penance a price tag in monetary indulgence, however, the church courted the danger that "a lamentable superficiality" would take over ecclesiastical discipline.[27] It is exactly this danger that an upstart monk and Bible teacher from Wittenberg would lift up for attention and decry.

The Necessity of Explicit Faith

The way the story of the Reformation is usually told, Luther rebelled against the Roman church because of the oppressive burden of what he thought of as "works righteousness" placed on the shoulders of believers. One needs only to think of the generic Lutheran illustration showing Luther, resolved, hammer in hand, ready to awaken the common people to the abuses of a tyrannical institution, the "Ninety-Five The-

---

offering. In doing this he acted very well and honorably, taking account of the resurrection. 44For if he were not expecting that those who had fallen would rise again, it would have been superfluous and foolish to pray for the dead. 45But if he was looking to the splendid reward that is laid up for those who fall asleep in godliness, it was a holy and pious thought. Therefore he made atonement for the dead, so that they might be delivered from their sin.

27. Reinhold Seeberg, *Textbook*, 2:43.

ses," nailed to the church door, looking something like the Declaration of Independence. The Reformation, as the conventional narrative goes, was about freedom. "The rise of Protestantism," asserts Ferdinand Christian Baur (1792-1860) "can be thought of as an act of free self-determination that required the highest spiritual and moral energy."[28] But the exhortation to communicants quoted at the beginning of this chapter does not read like a call to freedom. Instead it makes clear in plainspoken language that the mandate of self-examination is a burden on the individual conscience. Luther demands that Christians coming to the Lord's Table "feel" genuine faith. If fallen in sin, the believer must prove by action the earnest desire to "better himself." Those who cling to sin are "warned faithfully not to come lest they incur judgment and damnation for their souls as St. Paul says [1 Cor. 11:29]. . . . In this fashion each must judge himself and look out for himself. For God is not mocked [Gal. 6:7], nor will he give that which is holy unto the dogs or cast pearls before swine [Matt. 7:6]."[29]

The exhortation demonstrates the seriousness with which the Lutheran tradition at its beginning understood sincere faith as the validation of liturgical worship. This is in continuity with the disciplined severity of the early church and its eschatological consciousness. It is also a mark of the sectarian tradition as it would later develop. The purpose of public worship, according to Luther, is to change people and make them Christians. This is clear from the beginning of Luther's public career. In the "Ninety-Five Theses," Luther's primary attack is on the laxity of Christian discipline in repentance. In the first thesis he asserts: "When our Lord and Master Jesus Christ said, 'Repent' [Matt. 4:7], he willed the entire life of believers to be one of repentance." Repentance means "that the sinner has a change of heart and hates his sin." There is no place for attrition or routine custom. Repentance demands contrition in the deepest sense: ". . . hatred of oneself should involve one's whole life, according to the passage, 'He who hates his soul in this life, preserves it for eternal life' [Matt. 10:39]. And again: 'He who does not take his cross and follow me, is not worthy of me' [Matt. 10:38]."[30] Sacramental penance cannot begin to fulfill this demand, first, because it

---

28. Ferdinand Christian Baur, *Lehrbuch der christlichen Dogmengeschichte* (3rd. ed., 1867, reprint Darmstadt: Wissenschaftliche Buchgesellschaft, 1974) 273.

29. *LW* 51:104.

30. *LW* 31:83-84.

is "temporal and cannot be done all the time," and second, because it is "external" and can thus be a "sham."[31] Insofar as it is "legally instituted by popes and the church" and is subject to a false theology, it can serve to lessen the demands that God actually makes on those who would be his followers, thus placing believers under an illusion as to their true condition. Thus "the bounty of indulgences" that the church peddles and "the need for true contrition" are in opposition. A Christian who is "truly contrite" does not want to escape punishment but "seeks and loves to pay penalties":[32] "Christians should be exhorted to be diligent in following Christ, their Head, through penalties, deaths, and hell. . . . And thus be confident of entering into heaven rather through many tribulations, than through the false security of peace."[33]

Martin Brecht argues that the "Ninety-Five Theses" "can be understood as an expression of a strict theology of humility," reflecting a stage in Luther's emerging consciousness that predates his mature theology.[34] There is evidence to back this claim. Two years after the posting of the Theses, Luther appears to move away from adherence to the strict demands of contrition to an emphasis on forgiveness and faith. In a teaching sermon, *The Sacrament of Penance* (1519), he declares: "the forgiveness of guilt, the heavenly indulgence, is granted to no one on account of the worthiness of his contrition over his sins, nor on account of his works of satisfaction, but only on account of his faith in the promise of God, 'Whatever you loose . . . shall be loosed,' etc." This is the work of Christ, not a priest; and it can be conveyed to you by "any Christian," even "a woman or child."[35]

This argument encouraged a number of Luther's followers to abandon auricular confession as a requirement for communion. This happened, for example, during Christmas 1521 under the leadership of Andreas Bodenstein von Karlstadt (1486-1541), professor of theology at Wittenberg. In addition to abandoning private confession, Karlstadt also celebrated mass in the vernacular, discarded traditional vestments, and distributed communion in both kinds. Less than a month later he married. This all took place while Luther was hidden away at the Wartburg. In all this revolutionary activity, Karlstadt sought nothing

31. *LW* 31:85.
32. *LW* 31:196-97.
33. *LW* 31:251.
34. Martin Brecht, "Luther," in *The Oxford Encyclopedia of the Reformation*, 2:462.
35. *LW* 35:12.

less than to carry out what he thought were the clear implications of Luther's radical teaching. But Luther was not always ready to embrace the fullest implications of his own teaching, especially if he thought that that teaching could confuse laypeople or if it was taken up by someone Luther thought suspicious. The fact is that Luther lost trust in his old colleague. What concerned Luther was the spirit in which Karlstadt acted. Here, he thought, was a man impatient with all externals of the faith, a man all too willing to move quickly to overturn the delicate frame of the inherited social order on the basis of abstract principle. In acting so boldly, Karlstadt relied on the resources of his personal faith; indeed, he was convinced that he himself was a vehicle of divine truth. "The Spirit of God," he said, "to which all things ought to be subjected, cannot be subject even to Scripture."[36] In Karlstadt, the individual conscience, bolstered by the Spirit, became the sole criterion of faith.

Luther recoiled. He saw Karlstadt as the first in a frightening line of radical reformers, a general in a dangerous new army of religious subjectivists. If this attitude spread to the population as a whole, it would be a disaster. No one can live out of the resources of private conscience alone. In 1525 he wrote: "That which God has made a matter of inward faith and spirit they convert into a human work. But what God has ordained as an outward word and sign and work they convert into an inner spirit."[37] Karlstadt, said Luther, was a child of the devil.

For a time after Karlstadt had done his work, Luther allowed communicants to receive the sacrament without confessing their sins before a priest. But he also warned them that "evil abuses" needed to be ended. "The prospect of laypeople participating in the Eucharist without sufficient preparation frightened Luther and his colleagues."[38] After 1524, examination of faith and conduct was mandated for the people of Wittenberg by civil decree.

Why was formal confession so important? Certainly Luther did not want to discourage believers from receiving the sacrament. He writes in the *Large Catechism* (1529) that "true Christians who cherish and honor the sacrament will of their own accord urge and impel themselves to come."[39] He interprets Christ's words of institution to be an offer to re-

---

36. Quoted in Whale, *The Protestant Tradition,* 200.
37. *LW* 40:148-49.
38. Rittgers, *The Reformation of the Keys,* 82.
39. *BC,* 451.

ceive the sacrament "frequently, whenever and wherever you will, according to everyone's opportunity and need."[40] He cites the rule of "St. Hilary" (actually St. Augustine, *Epistle* 54) approvingly: "Unless a man has committed such a sin that he has forfeited the name of Christian and has to be expelled from the congregation, he should not exclude himself from the sacrament."[41] He assures Christians "that it is the highest wisdom to realize that this sacrament does not depend upon our worthiness."[42] He even goes so far as to say in a section on confession added to the *Large Catechism* in the revised edition, also from 1529, that mandated confession is "the pope's tyranny" and that "we have been set free from his coercion and from the intolerable burden he imposed upon the Christian church."[43] But Luther also understood human weakness and sin and knew that to honor the sacrament "we must make a distinction among men. Those who are shameless and unruly must be told to stay away, for they are not fit to receive the forgiveness of sins since they do not desire it and do not want to be good."[44] The sad fact is that people may have the gift of freedom in confession but this freedom is abused:

> Unfortunately, men have learned it only too well; they do whatever they please and take advantage of their freedom, acting as if they will never need or desire to go to confession any more. We quickly understand whatever benefits us, and we grasp with uncommon ease whatever in the Gospel is mild and gentle. But such pigs, as I have said, are unworthy to appear in the presence of the Gospel or to have any part in it.[45]

Luther's observation that people "do not want to be good" calls to mind St. Augustine's doctrine of *non posse non peccare* ("not able not to sin") and the dramatic example of the pear tree in the *Confessions* when Augustine confesses to sinning with no other cause than the love of the will to undo.

Luther appears to say contradictory things about confession: it

40. *BC,* 452.
41. *BC,* 453.
42. *BC,* 453.
43. *BC,* 457.
44. *BC,* 453.
45. *BC,* 457.

must be free, and it must be mandated. How are these claims to be reconciled? Can they be? The *Treatise on Good Works* (1520) may provide a helpful perspective. In this important early essay, Luther writes in detail about distinctions among people, contending that there are "four kinds" of persons. The first is the person of faith who needs "no law." This is the ideal Christian: "Such men do willingly what they know and can, because they alone are distinguished for their firm confidence that God's favor and grace rests upon them in all things."[46] Such people do not need the externals of ritual, ceremony, and formal confession of sins to do the will of God. They go to confession freely. The second type is the schemer, ever willing to abuse the freedom of faith as, in the words of St. Peter, "a cover for sin" (I Peter 2:16). They only see in the gospel what makes them comfortable. The third type is the "wicked," who love sin and seek its perverted pleasures. "They must be restrained like wild horses and dogs by spiritual and temporal laws, and where this does not help, they must be put to death by the temporal sword."[47] The fourth are the immature, "lusty and childish in their understanding." For such people, prey to human weakness, is the discipline of the liturgy with its blessed repetition, its customs and practices, including auricular confession, which is necessary and beneficial: "they must be coaxed . . . enticed with external, definite, concomitant adornment, with reading, praying, fasting, singing, churches, decorations, organs, and all those things commanded and observed in monasteries and churches, until such time as they too learn to know the teaching of faith."[48]

There is no more eloquent defense of the church type in its best sense than Luther gives in this last sentence. He does not glorify the institutional church as the organ of redemption, thus risking the danger of making the church an idol. Instead, Luther sees the church as an accommodation to a fallen world. If Christians consider the four types of human beings that Luther describes, and do so honestly, they will see themselves in all four. This is what it means to be *simul iustus et peccator* — at the same time saint and sinner. That people are both saints and sinners is why Karlstadt's revolutionary subjectivism was rejected as a grave danger and the mandate for auricular confession reinstituted.

46. *LW* 44:35.
47. *LW* 44:35.
48. *LW* 44:35.

But Luther also defends auricular confession in dramatic, existential terms, calling on Christians to make the decision of faith to engage in spiritual warfare: "I will allow no one to take private confession from me and would not give it in exchange for all the wealth of the world . . . no one knows what [confession] can give unless he has struggled much and frequently with the devil. I would have been strangled by the devil long ago if confession had not sustained me."[49] The path to salvation is through tribulations: "through penalties, deaths, and hell." This is *Anfechtung* or personal affliction: spiritual and physical assault on the Christian that is meant to destroy faith, a theme that characterized Luther's theology throughout his career as reformer. Luther identified personal affliction as the mark of the genuine Christian. A human being lives "between God and the devil,"[50] between judgment and grace. This is the heavenly drama of individual human life. It is the explicit faith *(fides explicata)* that is incumbent on all Christians. Luther never abandoned this idea or watered it down, before or after the encounter with Karlstadt.

To the end of his life, Luther argued that leaders in the church do not serve the people when they "preach much about the grace of Christ, yet they strengthen and comfort only those who remain in their sins, telling them not to fear and be terrified by sins, since they are all removed by Christ." Caring only about preaching the assurance of grace (which is the hallmark of the church type), priests and false pastors "let the people go on in their public sins, without any renewal or reformation of their lives. Thus it becomes quite evident that they truly fail to understand the faith and Christ, and thereby abrogate both when they preach about it."[51] The true path to Christ is through personal affliction. It is the "primal experience" *(Urerlebnis)* of explicit faith. In his exposition of Psalm 90 (1534), his great "Christian thanatopsis"[52] or meditation on death, Luther describes this affliction. To stand before the judgment of God is "the climax of the drama which God enacts with us." The divine intention is that "we play our part," and be "in full awareness of our sins and of death"; indeed "to conclude that there is nothing within us but damnation." In this full contrition

49. *WA* 10/3:62. Quoted and tr. in Rittgers, *The Reformation of the Keys,* 82.

50. Heiko Oberman, *Luther: Man between God and the Devil,* tr. Eileen Walliser-Schwarzbart (New Haven: Yale University Press, 1989).

51. *LW* 41:147.

52. *LW* 13:xii.

or humiliation of the self, "it will happen that one becomes aware of salvation."[53]

Luther's theology of worship can only be fully understood in this existential context of explicit faith: changing people through contrition that leads them to embrace the faith. This will also become the hallmark of the sect type. In *The German Mass and the Order of Service* (1526), Luther says that the public worship service of the church, open to all people, "should be arranged for the sake of the unlearned lay folk . . . for all people, among whom are many who do not believe and are not yet Christians. Most of them stand around and gape, hoping to see something new, just as if we were holding a service among the Turks or the heathen in a public square or out in a field. . . . [T]he gospel must be publicly preached [to such people] to move them to believe and become Christian."[54] This public worship, he believed, would lead to "truly evangelical" private worship among those "who want to be Christians in earnest." If liturgy has any purpose whatsoever, it is not to leave Old Adam as a lump of coal in the bin, but to move him to believe and become a Christian.

To move such people, Luther entered into the full vitality of Christian speech regarding worship, not only its promises and assurances, but also its judgments, challenges, and imperatives; a vitality that calls to mind the rigors of the early church when "human nature was stronger than it is now," as Alain de Lille had argued in the twelfth century.[55] This rigor is evident in Luther's teaching regarding baptism, the office of the keys, the discipline of confession and absolution, and the Lord's Supper.

Baptism

For Luther, baptism is the beginning of the perilous journey of life. It makes the person a child of God, but also places him or her between God and the devil. So, for example, in *The Holy and Blessed Sacrament of Baptism* (1519), Luther speaks in familiar terms of "a blessed dying unto sin and a resurrection in the grace of God, so that the old man . . . is there drowned, and a new man . . . comes forth."[56] But he also says that

---

53. *LW* 13:116.
54. *LW* 53:63.
55. Quoted and tr. in Tentler, *Sin and Confession on the Eve of the Reformation*, 17.
56. *LW* 35:30.

baptism "establishes a covenant between us and God to that effect that we will fight against sin and slay it, even to our dying breath, while he for his part will be merciful to us, deal graciously with us and — because we are not sinless in this life until purified by death — not judge us with severity."[57] Luther warns against "a false security" that says "If baptism is so gracious and great a thing that God will not count our sins against us. . . . I will live and do my own will."[58] This is an illusion: we cannot "wickedly and wantonly sin [and go on presuming] God's grace."[59]

In his early baptismal orders of 1523 and 1526, Luther places the idea of baptism as covenant in the context of the ancient tradition of spiritual warfare. The battle against Satan begins as soon as we enter the world. In baptism we flee from the Prince of Darkness. Baptism is an exorcism. This is ancient church teaching and is preserved in the Roman rite. In obedience to ancient liturgical tradition, Luther emphasizes exorcism, an emphasis made especially dramatic because it is done in the vernacular. Recognizing that the devil is *princeps mundi* who owns us at our birth, the order begins by calling on the devil to vacate his property: "Depart thou unclean spirit and give room to the Holy Spirit."[60] The minister prays in "the name of the eternal God and of our Savior Jesus Christ" to adjure the devil and cause him to "depart trembling and groaning, conquered together with [his] hatred, so that [he shall] have nothing to do with the servant of God who now seeks that which is heavenly and renounces [the devil] and [his] world." After prayer, the exorcism follows directly: "I adjure thee, thou unclean spirit, by the name of the Father and of the Son and of the Holy Ghost that thou come out of and depart from this servant of God, for he commands thee, thou miserable one, he who walked upon the sea and stretched forth his hand to the sinking Peter."[61]

Baptism is indeed the beginning of a perilous journey. The devil is ever ready to ensnare the believer. Luther considered the lordship of Satan over the world "an article of faith."[62] Satan is the greatest enemy

57. *LW* 35:35.
58. *LW* 35:42-43.
59. *LW* 35:42.
60. *LW* 53:96, 107.
61. *LW,* 53:98, 108.
62. "Aber der Teuffel ist herr jnn der welt, und ich have es selbs nie können gleuben, das der Teuffel solt Herr und Gott der welt sein, bis ichs nu mals zimlich erfahren, das es

that Christians face: "Satan is his name, that is, adversary. He must obstruct and cause misfortune; he cannot do otherwise. Moreover, he is the prince and god of this world, so that he has sufficient power to do so."[63] Satan teaches us to acquiesce to his terrible divinity by attacking our health and well being,[64] disturbing marriage,[65] upsetting the rhythms of daily life, including religious practice,[66] inciting murder,[67] mixing politics and religion,[68] and confusing the interpretation of Scripture.[69] This is *Anfechtung*. As Luther put it in the first stanza of "A Mighty Fortress" (Hedge translation):

> For still our ancient foe
> Doth seek to work us woe;
> His craft and power are great,
> And armed with cruel hate,
> On earth is not his equal.

---

auch ein artickel des glaubens sey [is an article of faith]: Princeps mundi [prince of the world], Deus huius seculi." *WA* 50:473, quoted in Heiko Oberman, *The Reformation: Roots and Ramifications* (Grand Rapids: Eerdmans, 1994) 67.

63. *LW* 37:17. I am indebted to Mark L. Nelson, *Luther's Conception of the Devil* (St. Paul: Luther Theological Seminary M.Th. thesis, 1979), for gathering quotations from Luther on the devil.

64. "In all grave illnesses the devil is present as the author and cause . . . [and] he is the author of death." *LW* 54:33.

65. "At first everything goes all right, so that, as the saying goes, they are ready to eat each other up for love. The devil comes along to create boredom in you, to rob you of your desire in this direction, and to excite it unduly in another direction." *LW* 21:89.

66. "The devil comes at unsuitable places and times, as in the choir during songs of praise to God, or at night when one ought to sleep, in order to ruin the head. Or elsewhere, when other things are being done in common, so that he hinders these things or sees that they are done with less dedication." *LW* 10:348-49.

67. "[The devil] incites the Cainites against their brother, just as Christ declares in John 8.44 that the devil was a murderer from the beginning." *LW* 1:322.

68. "The devil never stops cooking and brewing these two kingdoms into each other. In the devil's name the secular leaders always want to be Christ's masters and teach Him how He should run His church and His spiritual government. Similarly, the false clerics and schismatic spirits want to be the masters, though not in God's name, and to teach people how to organize the secular government. Thus the devil is very busy on both sides, and he has much to do." *LW* 13:194.

69. "When we wish to deal with Scripture, [Satan] stirs up so much dissension and quarreling over it that we lose our interest in it and become reluctant to trust it." *LW* 37:17. "It is the supreme art of the devil that he can make the law out of the gospel." *LW* 54:106.

Many in the modern church consider these lines a colorful trope. Luther meant them literally.

This is why at baptism the minister intercedes on behalf of the baptized as their journey of life begins. Spiritual warfare is a dangerous enterprise, and many lose their way. Thus the minister prays, "that [the one being baptized] may be sundered from the number of the unbelieving, preserved dry and secure in the holy ark of Christendom, serve thy name at all times, fervent in spirit and joyful in hope, so that with all believers he may be made worthy to attain eternal life according to thy promise; through Jesus Christ our Lord. Amen."[70] In his instructions to the Christian reader at the end of his baptismal order, Luther warns that "it is no joke to take sides against the devil." Baptism means that the child will be burdened with "a mighty and lifelong enemy." The child needs the "heart and strong faith" of fellow Christians along with their earnest intercession through prayer. Corporate faith demonstrated in intercessory prayer is the key to the sacrament, not the traditional customs of a rite. "Signing with the cross . . . anointing the breast and shoulders with oil, signing the crown of the head with chrism, putting on the christening robe, placing a burning candle in the hand . . . are not the sort of devices and practices from which the devil shrinks or flees. He sneers at greater things than these! Here is the place for real earnestness." Luther laments that for most people baptism makes no difference. They lose their way on the perilous journey on earth. This is the fault of the church: "I suspect that people turn out so badly after baptism because our concern for them has been so cold and careless; we, at their baptism, interceded for them without zeal."[71] "Real earnestness" in corporate faith and "zeal" in intercessory prayer are both necessary to the effectiveness of the sacrament.

When baptism is not attended to in the church by prayer and faith, Satan rears his ugly head. Over time, his effect is destructive: "though [Satan] could not quench the power of baptism in little children, nevertheless [he succeeds] in quenching it in all adults so that now there are scarcely any who call to mind their own baptism, and still fewer who glory in it. . . ."[72] What is the glory of baptism? Baptism is and remains throughout a person's life the means "for remitting sins and getting to

70. *LW* 53:97.
71. *LW* 53:102.
72. *LW* 36:57-58.

heaven." There should be no confusion about the relation of baptism and penance. Baptism is the basis of penance because it is the source of forgiveness. Rejecting St. Jerome's famous metaphor that penance is "the plank" for the "shipwrecked,"[73] Luther asserts that for the faithful there is no shipwreck. Baptism is the "ship" that does not sink or founder; it is "the first plank" which the believer may safely ride through all storms of life.[74] "The ship remains one, seaworthy and invincible; it will never be broken up into separate 'planks.' In it are carried all those who are brought to the harbor of salvation, for it is the truth of God giving us its promise in the sacraments."[75] Penance does not succeed baptism in order to counter the curse of post-baptismal sins, as if baptism were powerless to forgive such sins. Rather, penance serves baptism by driving the repentant sinner to the promise of God, which is given to the believer unwaveringly, despite the fact that he or she falls into sin again and again through life:

> Now, the *first* thing to be considered about baptism is the divine promise, which says: "He who believes and is baptized will be saved" [Mark 16:16]. This promise must be set far above all the glitter of works, vows, religious orders, and whatever else man has introduced, for on it all our salvation depends.[76]

Baptism is, however, subject to faith. It is only effective when "we exercise our faith in it." Absent faith, "baptism will profit us nothing."[77] As Luther memorably puts the matter in his church postil or expository sermon for Ascension Day 1523 on Mark 16:16 ("The one who believes and is baptized will be saved; but the one who does not believe will be condemned"):

> A man can believe even though he be not baptized; for baptism is nothing more than an outward sign that is to remind us of the divine promise. If we can have it, it is well; let us receive it, for no one should despise it. If, however, we can not receive it, or it is denied us, we will not be condemned if we only believe the Gospel. For

73. *NPNF* 6:266 (*Epistle* 130.9).
74. *LW* 36:58.
75. *LW* 36:61.
76. *LW* 36:58-59.
77. *LW* 36:59.

where the Gospel is, there is also baptism and all that a Christian needs. Condemnation follows no sin except the sin of unbelief. Therefore, the Lord says "He that disbelieveth shall be condemned"; he says not: He that is not baptized. He is silent concerning baptism; for baptism is worth nothing without faith, but is like seals affixed to a letter in which nothing is written. He that has the signs that we call sacraments and has no faith has only seals upon a letter of blank paper.[78]

Through faith, which is the assurance of the gospel, we can rightly say "once we have been baptized, we are saved."[79] Without faith, we are in peril. Returning to the metaphor of baptism as a ship, Luther warns: "Of course, it often happens that many rashly leap overboard into the sea and perish; these are those who abandon faith in the promise and plunge into sin." Nevertheless: "the ship remains intact and holds its course unimpaired."[80]

The Office of the Keys

The office of the keys is vitally important to the purpose of worship as a means of challenging worshipers through repentance and renewal. The binding and loosing of sins keeps Christians in a living relationship with the Lord, protecting them from the illusion of a false security that takes God for granted. In *On the Councils and the Church* (1538), one of his most important essays from his later life, Luther puts it this way:

> Christ bequeathed [the keys] as a public sign and a holy possession, whereby the Holy Spirit again sanctifies the fallen sinner redeemed by Christ's death, and whereby the Christians confess that they are a holy people in this world under Christ. And those who refuse to be converted or sanctified again shall be cast out from this holy people, that is, bound and excluded by means of the keys, as happened to the unrepentant Antinomians.[81]

78. John Nicholas Lenker, ed., *Luther's Works* (Minneapolis: Lutherans in all Lands, 1903-1910) 3:204.
79. *LW* 36:59.
80. *LW* 36:61.
81. *LW* 41:153.

To have the two keys of binding and loosing sins together is, as Luther famously argues in *The Keys* (1530), a sure means that Christ uses to get the sinner's attention so that he can free the sinner:

> . . . the purpose of Christ's binding is to free the sinner from his sins. With his "binding" Christ attempts nothing else but to free and rid the sinner's conscience of sins. It is for this reason that he "binds" and punishes the sinner so that he might let go of his sin, repent of it, and avoid it. One may call such "binding" a saving.[82]

Binding sin is the means to break the iron grip of pride, and it prepares the sinner for the grace of God. Receiving grace by the loosing of sins requires no merit on the part of the believer. Luther asserts that it is wrong to "want to become holy by our own righteousness, beyond and outside of divine grace."[83] But the keys "demand faith in our hearts, and without faith you cannot use them with profit."[84] Faith begins with the binding key. Faith allows us to heed the threat of divine judgment and "thereby come to fear God." Faith comes to rest in the loosing key. Faith allows us to believe the "consolation" of divine mercy and accept the promise of eternal life and "so learn to love God and receive a joyful, confident, and peaceful heart." The keys place us before the existential situation of faith, the primal emotions of fear and consolation, emotions that are never satisfied by the performing of works. Even repentance itself is subservient to these primal emotions. As the consolation of the loosing key grips our hearts we become ready for the life of faith and its responsibilities. Thus: "He who has faith in the [loosing] key, has satisfied it by means of such faith, before and without performing any works. The key demands no other works. Afterward such faith will indeed perform works."[85]

When Luther talks about "Christians," it must be remembered that a proviso stands over all of his theology: namely, his firm belief that the "Christian" is a *rara avis* — a "rare bird." In Luther's view, there is no such thing as "Christendom" traditionally defined. Luther attacks the very idea of a "Christian" society or a "Christian" government. He makes this attack on sacramental grounds:

82. *LW* 40:328.
83. *LW* 40:330.
84. *LW* 40:330.
85. *LW* 40:375-76.

... the world and the masses are and always will be un-Christian, even if they are all baptized and Christian in name. Christians are few and far between (as the saying is). Therefore it is out of the question that there should be a common Christian government over the whole world or indeed over a single country or any considerable body of people, for the wicked always outnumber the good.[86]

The world is unconverted; the mass of the baptized are unconverted. Most people love darkness and hate the light. The Roman polemic that Christian truth is taught "always, everywhere, and by all" is false. Christian truth is not subject to the law of majority but the law of minority. This is the reason, as Philip Melanchthon (1497-1560) puts it, that "there is an infinite number of ungodly within the church who oppress it."[87] The true church is "scattered throughout the world"; "wolves and ungodly teachers" are "rampant" within it; it is beset by "weak people" who build "perishing structures of stubble, that is, unprofitable opinions."[88] "Human doctrine, ceremonies, tonsures, long robes, miters, and all the pomp of popery only lead far away from it into hell."[89]

Among the most pernicious of Catholic teachings is the doctrine of *opus operatum*. Melanchthon asks rhetorically: "Why will faith be necessary if sacraments justify *ex opere operato*, without a good attitude in the one using them?"[90] The fact is that outward participation in the sacrament is not enough to receive its benefits. The sacrament requires faith. Faith is "the proper attitude in the recipient."[91] If people are to be Christian, they must become Christian. They must be evangelized: "the gospel must be publicly preached [to such people] to move them to believe and become Christian."[92] This includes even the "earnest Christians" for whom Luther proposes a private service; what he calls

... a truly evangelical order [that] should not be held in a public place for all sorts of people. But those who want to be Christians in earnest and who profess the gospel with hand and mouth should sign their

86. *LW* 45:91.
87. *BC* 169.
88. *BC* 171-72.
89. *LW* 41:211.
90. *BC* 172.
91. *BC* 115.
92. *LW* 53:63.

names and meet alone in a house somewhere to pray, to read, to baptize, *to receive the sacrament, and to do other Christian works. According to this order, those who do not lead Christian lives could be known, reproved, corrected, cast out, or excommunicated, according to the rule of Christ, Matthew 18[:15-17].* Here one could also solicit benevolent gifts to be willingly given. . . . Here would be no need of much and elaborate singing. Here one could set up a neat and brief order for baptism and the sacrament and center everything on Word, prayer, and love.[93]

Notice the passage in italics. Even among the "dearest Christians," the "earnest Christians," there is the exercise of the binding key.

Luther does not blink from the conditional expression of divine grace when he believes Christ leads him so to speak. In *Sermons on the Gospel of John* (1537), Luther comments on Christ's words in John 15:10: "If you keep my commandments, you will abide in my love":

. . . it behooves everyone to search his heart and examine himself. Let no one bank on thoughts like these: "I am baptized and am called a Christian. I hear God's Word and go to the Sacrament." For here Christ Himself separates the false Christians from those who are genuine, as if He were saying: "If you are true believers in Me and are in possession of My treasure, it will surely become evident that you are My disciples. If not, do not imagine that I will acknowledge and accept you as My disciples. You will never cheat and deceive any but yourselves — to your eternal shame and harm. Christ and the Gospel will surely not be cheated and defrauded."

Christ found this admonition necessary, and it must constantly be repeated in Christendom, because we see that there are always many Christians of this sort among us. Christ is determined not to have or to acknowledge any false Christians. In Matt. 7.23 He passes a terrible sentence on them, when He says that on the Day of Judgment He will address them with the words: "I never knew you; depart from Me you evildoers." Such false Christians would fare far better if they were heathen and non-Christians. Then they would at least not do harm to Christianity with their offensive example and would not disgrace and blaspheme the holy name of Christ and of His Word.[94]

93. *LW* 53:63-64, italics added.
94. *LW* 24:250.

This is Luther exercising the office of the keys in preaching, placing believers before the privilege and duty of explicit faith. The word of God calls a person out of custom, lethargy, obedience to a hierarchy, and outward participation in sacramental life *(opus operatum)* into the fullness of an individual relation to Jesus as Lord and Master.

Why does Luther say these things — things which make many a church-type Christian from a later age cringe? Trusting that the Holy Spirit calls and sanctifies, Luther felt free to speak plain language in the church, language not only of comfort, but also of admonition and command, language that is contingent and conditional in that it demands a response on the part of the hearer — above all fear of the judgment of God and faith in the divine promise of salvation. To be Christian is to know the forgiveness of sins, the glory of Christ's mercy. Christ alone makes the Old Adam alive. But, as Luther says, in *Bondage of the Will* (1525): "[God] does it by killing."[95] In the drama of human life *coram Deo,* God breaks us down, brings us to fear, which is "the beginning of wisdom" (Proverbs 9:10), which then leads us to the promise of salvation.

Private Confession

Luther's original understanding of private confession, as seen in his *Short Order of Confession before the Priest for the Common Man* (1529) and in his instructions on *How One Should Teach Common Folk to Shrive Themselves* (1531), offers a worthy ideal for the church. Luther conceives confession primarily as an intimate act within the fellowship of believers in which Christians, burdened by their sins and repentant, make oral confession to a fellow Christian, usually a minister, and receive this assurance: "As thou believest, so be it done unto thee [Matt. 8:13]. And I by the command of Jesus Christ our Lord, forgive thee all thy sin. . . ."[96] Absolution is from God, not the church: "the forgiveness of guilt is not within the province of any human office or authority, be it pope, bishop, priest, or any other."[97] But this word of forgiveness is to be spoken within the fellowship of believers from one Christian to another so that it is made concrete and personal: "For any Christian can say to

---

95. *LW* 33:62.
96. *LW* 53:121.
97. *LW* 35:12.

you, 'God forgives you your sins, in the name,' etc., and if you can accept that word with a confident faith, as though God were saying it to you, then in that same faith you are surely absolved."[98]

In medieval Europe, the office of the keys was placed exclusively in the hands of the clergy. It was a chief means by which clerics exercised political power. The papacy had used the binding key in its ultimate form of excommunication to claim the jurisdiction of *sacerdotium* over *regnum* — church over state. Political reformers such as Marsilius of Padua (ca. 1245-ca. 1342) and John Wycliffe (ca. 1324-1384) rejected the claim that the church can exercise coercive power in the secular realm and further declared that the clergy derive their privileges from the congregation of the faithful, the priesthood of all believers. This was a revolutionary idea at the time. Luther takes it up, especially in his early writings, as he declares the right of lay people to absolve the sins of fellow Christians.

But as wonderful as the ideal form of private confession is, with its genuineness, spontaneity, and equality, it is very hard to regularize in liturgy and church order. What ended up being regularized was a practice of private confession that, like the Roman doctrine of penance, became mandated in Lutheran churches as a preparation for Holy Communion; indeed, it became an article of faith: "Confession has not been abolished in our churches, for it is not customary to administer the body of Christ except to those who have previously been examined and absolved."[99] The clergy received exacting instructions as to how to examine individuals regarding their sins and shortcomings. The emphasis was not, as in Roman Catholic penance, on the recounting of specific sins through detailed and invasive questioning by the priest. "No one," asserts the Augsburg Confession, "should be compelled to recount sins in detail, for this is impossible. As the psalmist says [Psalm 19:12], 'Who can discern his errors?'"[100] But this did not mean that confession was to be lax. Parishioners were expected to recount serious sins that burdened the conscience. Pastors were expected to examine an individual's understanding of both the content of faith and the meaning and consequence of sin. This was in effect an assessment of a layperson's responsibility for explicit faith.

98. *LW* 35:12.
99. *BC* 61.
100. *BC* 62.

This regularized clerical examination of laypeople in private confession came to be called the *Verhör* or "interrogation," as in a court of law. As we have already seen, it was instituted by Luther himself in Wittenberg in 1524 to counter Karlstadt and "to insure the devout reception of the sacrament."[101] From Wittenberg the practice grew: "Fifty Lutheran church ordinances between 1525 and 1591 decreed individual confession with the *Verhör* as a precondition to admission to the Lord's Supper: no Lutheran polities failed to adopt it, and many forbade general absolution of the congregation."[102]

The instructions for the *Verhör* itself could be elaborate and detailed. A good example is the church order for Courland (Latvia) from 1570. This calls for "each Christian to be assiduously instructed in proper confession."[103] The penitent is called "to examine himself" at least four times a year and to go before the "priest" who stands "in the stead of God." He or she is to engage in heartfelt confession. It is expected that such confession will involve the disclosing of specific sins. If any are particularly grievous or involve important matters, the priest is to refer the individual to "deputy inspectors" or "superintendents" for disposition.[104] The confessional process of examination in preparation for communion involves twelve steps from turning to God in contrition and confession, through trusting divine forgiveness in Christ, to seeking harmony and fellowship with other believers in the church.[105] The

---

101. Thomas Tentler, "Confession," in *The Oxford Encyclopedia of the Reformation*, 1:403.

102. Tentler, "Confession."

103. *EKO* 5:84.

104. *EKO* 5:86.

105. The steps are as follows: (1) turning to God with one's heart; recognizing one's sins and confessing them; (2) hearing that God is true and righteous and forgives sins; (3) knowing that absolution, the loosing of sins on earth and in heaven as proclaimed in Matthew 16 and John 20, is "the goal and benefit of confession"; (4) realizing that the promise of the gospel is spoken "particularly and privately" to the penitent and (5) that what is given to the individual penitent is "justification through faith" as St. Paul teaches in Romans 4; (6) taking comfort in the fact that divine forgiveness consoles the conscience and relieves the penitent of "anger, personal affliction [*affecting*], and secret sorrows"; (7) knowing that Jesus promises that whoever acknowledges him before men will be acknowledged by him before his heavenly Father (Matthew 10); (8) rejoicing that God will send many blessings and mercy to the penitent; (9) knowing that the forgiven penitent is under obligation to the church and that "that which is sacred is not given to dogs nor pearls cast before swine" (Matthew 7); (10) in this regard, having fear in the knowledge that any baptized and believing Christian who evades God's offer of grace in forgiveness will be subject to God's wrath and fearful judgment on the Last Day;

"inexperienced and unknowing" who undergo examination — that is, those who lack "understanding" in whole or part — are to be admonished for their ignorance and then examined in the catechism as to the nature of true confession. They must be able to define sin and recognize the law, know how to confess properly and how to repent, and pledge themselves to new obedience and Christian life.[106]

The church order demands that all Christians who come to the Table must be able to answer five questions:

1. What is the sacrament of the altar? Answer: It is the true body and blood of Christ.
2. What are the words of institution? Answer: "On the night in which he was betrayed. . . ."
3. What moves one to receive the sacrament? Answer: The command of God "to take and eat," the gracious promise of Christ that it is done "for the forgiveness of sins," and the need of the sinner to be unburdened of sins.
4. What makes the sacrament efficacious? Answer: Not merely the eating and drinking, but "the firm faith that Christ died for my sins."
5. What are the benefits of the sacrament? Answer: The forgiveness of sins, the strengthening of faith, reconciliation with God, and union with Christ.[107]

Finally the Courland church order takes up the problem of the "Easter Christian" who "seldom or never comes to confession and sacrament." Such a person should be upbraided, punished, and, if need be, banned from the church.[108]

After such examination the private absolution was applied. In Courland, this meant a brief, unconditional declaration of forgiveness and assurance:

---

(11) knowing that God in Christ is the penitent's example, directing one's way in divine righteousness (Psalm 32, etc.); and finally, (12) the forgiven sinner seeking harmony in the church and the increase of brotherly love. *EKO* 5:84-85.

106. *EKO* 5:85. In some territories, the *Verhör* called for occasionally *(zu zeiten)* testing a person's knowledge of the catechism by recitation; if they failed, they were to be admonished to go home and learn the parts they missed. See *EKO* 6/1:560.

107. *EKO* 5:85-86.

108. *EKO* 5:86.

The almighty, truthful, merciful God and Father of our Lord Jesus Christ who through the will of his Son has forgiven thy [second person familiar] sins, wants further to have mercy on you and continue what has been begun to the praise of his holy name and your salvation. Amen.[109]

It is common, but by no means a set rule, for the *Verhör* to be accompanied by an unconditional declaration of absolution for sins. A particularly elaborate, even extravagant example of such an unconditional absolution may be found in the church order from Lüneburg, 1564. Its instructions for the *Verhör* are much less detailed and rigorous than those from Courland. They amount to two brief paragraphs stating that receiving the sacrament must be preceded by confession of sins to the priest and that priests are expected to examine "simple folk" *(einfeltige leut)* in recitation of the catechism, admonishing them to learn any passages they miss. The absolution reads as follows:

The Almighty God and Father of our Lord Jesus Christ wills to be gracious and merciful to you [second person singular familiar] and will forgive you all your sins for this sake, that his dear Son Jesus Christ has suffered and has died for this; and in the name of the same, our Lord Jesus Christ, at his command and in the power of his word when he says, John 20.23 "To whomever you remit sin, to him they are remitted," I declare you free from all your sins; I declare you free, quit, and rid of all your sins that they should be forgiven you always as richly and perfectly as Jesus Christ has effected the same through his suffering and dying and has commanded the same to be preached through the gospel in all the world, and this trustworthy promise which I now make to you in the name of the Lord Christ that you will peacefully accept, joyfully fix your conscience on this, and firmly believe your sins are certainly forgiven you.[110]

This is indeed a sublime word of forgiveness, an unqualified expression of the loosing key that has as its purpose to release the sinner and offer the assurance of salvation. But the instructions make it clear

109. *EKO* 5:87.
110. *EKO* 6/1:560.

that any absolution must be earned by fulfilling the requirements of the *Verhör*.[111]

A second, optional form of absolution attached to the Lüneburg order makes the essential connection between contrition and absolution clear:

> Since you [familiar plural] confess that you are afflicted with sin and with your sins have angered God and desire comfort against the devil's assault [*Anfechtung*], and since I am ordained to comfort poor sinners, male and female, a servant of God, after Christ has spoken to me [Joh. 20,23]: "which sins you forgive, they are forgiven"; also [Mt. 18,18]: "what you loose on earth is loosed in heaven," on such a promise of God and speaking according to his command, I declare you in God's stead free from all of your sins in the name of the Father, Son, and Holy Spirit. Amen.
>
> Go in peace and sin no more.[112]

Public Confession

Martin Luther never prepared a public order for confession and absolution. But he did get involved in bitter controversy over a rite of public confession and absolution in the imperial city of Nuremberg that pitted the city council against the polarizing figure of Andreas Osiander (1498-1552).

The circumstances were as follows. The majority of the citizenry of Nuremberg had stopped practicing sacramental penance by 1524.[113] In May of that year private penance had been replaced by an order for public confession and absolution in a mass in the German language at which Wolfgang Volprecht (d. 1528), prior of the Augustinian order in Nuremberg, presided. As part of that mass, the confession of sins read as follows:

> I, a poor, miserable, and sinful human being, acknowledge to God my heavenly Father, to the Lord Jesus Christ my Savior, to you my

---

111. ". . . *darumb sol keener sum sacrament des altars gehen, er hab sich den bey dem priester angeben und sich vor einem sunder bekand in die privatam absolutionemn erlanget.*" *EKO* 6/1:560.

112. *EKO* 6/1:560.

113. Rittgers, *The Reformation of the Keys,* 80; see also 84-85.

brothers and sisters, and to the whole Christian community, that I, unfortunately, have sinned frequently and seriously against God my Lord, by disbelief and lack of trust, [and by] not loving him above all things and my neighbor as myself. This is readily apparent to me and causes me great sorrow in the depths of myself. O Lord God, almighty Father, I, a poor sinner, remind you of your most gracious pledge and promise, where you promise forgiveness of sin through the blood of your Son Jesus Christ, who died for us and poured out his blood for our forgiveness. The same Jesus Christ, my Lord, also spoke through his holy mouth that where two or three are gathered in his name he will be in their midst [Matthew 18:20], and, that what they ask from you in his name will be granted them [Matt. 18:19]. Therefore, we ask for forgiveness of our sins in his name.

After this the pastor proclaimed the divine response to confession, which included not only the declaration of forgiveness but also divine imperatives to the penitent: "The Lord God says to us, 'according to your [second person familiar] faith it will happen to you! Go forth in peace! Sin no more! Thy sin is forgiven, removed, and left behind." There then follows a brief formula of absolution: "My dear brothers and sisters, God has mercy on us, pardoned our sin, and will give us eternal life. Amen."[114]

This public order was well crafted for its purpose. Its text is concentrated in expression. The confession emphasizes, in good evangelical fashion, sins against faith — disbelief and lack of trust and dependence upon Christ. The absolution is subtly conditional. Forgiveness is declared to be by God's own word and dependent upon the faith one holds along with the conviction to amend one's life. The absolution itself is not from priest to parishioner, but from God to "us."[115] To insure proper reception of the sacrament, the mass also included an exhortation to communicants, which was in fact prepared by Osiander, pastor at St. Lorenz Church, that reminded worshipers of St. Paul's demand to examine oneself (1 Corinthians 11:28). Holy Communion, declared the exhortation, requires a hungry soul that confesses sin, fears God's wrath and death, and thirsts for righteousness. To such a soul, the exhortation declares: "As we however examine ourselves, we find

114. *EKO* 11:39. Quoted and tr. in Rittgers, *The Reformation of the Keys*, 84.
115. *EKO* 11:39.

nothing in us but sin and death; we cannot in any way help ourselves out of them. Therefore has our dear Lord Jesus Christ had mercy on us and for the sake of us become flesh, fulfilled the law for us, and suffered. . . ." To receive his blessing requires "firm faith."[116]

The following year Wenzeslaus Linck (1483-1547) of New Hospital Church prepared a public confession to follow Osiander's exhortation in the service that became widely popular in the churches of the city:

> And because we have all sinned and need God's grace, humble your hearts before God the Lord, confess your sins and transgressions with heartfelt love and desire for his divine grace and help, with firm belief and trust in his gracious promise, and forgive from your hearts your neighbors so that your heavenly Father will also forgive you your sins and transgressions. If you do this, I will then release you from all of your sins on behalf of the holy Christian Church and by the command and promise of our Lord Jesus Christ when he said, "He whose sins you forgive, to him they are forgiven," in the name of the Father, the Son, and the Holy Spirit. Amen.[117]

In this confession, the Christian is challenged with imperatives: to confess "with heartfelt love and desire," to believe firmly in the divine promise of forgiveness, and to forgive the neighbor so that God forgives "you your sins and transgressions." The absolution is then promised on a conditional basis: "If you do this," says the text, the minister representing "the holy Christian Church," by the command of Christ will forgive sins.

Despite his involvement in the preparation of the new Protestant liturgy, Osiander was uneasy with the liturgical practice of public confession followed by conditional absolution. He argued that to give a public absolution to a "mixed assembly" made up of unbelievers, impenitent, adulterers, drunkards, and the like, people who neither deserve nor want to confess sins and receive absolution, is without warrant in Scripture and follows no practice condoned by the ancient church. His concern for discipline was not in any way unusual. The early reformers were, without exception, opposed to indiscriminate mass communion. But he was also concerned about the nature of absolution. If the absolution is given conditionally in the form, "if you have faith, I absolve you," it is

---

116. *EKO* 11:48. See Rittgers, *The Reformation of the Keys*, 85.
117. Quoted and tr. in Rittgers, *The Reformation of the Keys*, 92.

"no real absolution" said Osiander.[118] Thus he demanded the resumption of private confession and absolution "to the exclusion of general, public confession and absolution . . . advocated by the majority of Nuremberg clergy."[119] The theological question at stake in this controversy was this: Can there be such a thing as a general or public absolution, especially when the argument is clearly made that any conditions placed upon an absolution means that it is no true absolution?

The clergy in the city did not agree with Osiander, nor did the city council. The council's interest in defending a public order for confession was at least partly political. They knew from their long experience governing an imperial city and protecting its independence that the Roman clergy often exploited the office of the keys in the sacrament of private penance to exercise influence and authority over the fate of individual lives in a way that rivaled the power of secular rulers. Public confession and absolution in official liturgical wording made the office of the keys a matter of church order regulated by government. If this regulated liturgical wording states that God alone forgives and clergy along with laity are recipients of grace, as is the case in the liturgical text for absolution in the German mass used by Volprecht, then the interests of secular government are all the more protected from clerical abuse. In this regard, Osiander was not unmindful of the political implications of his protest.

In 1533, after several years of debate, the city council asked Luther and Melanchthon for advice on the matter. In a letter sent April 18, 1533, Luther and Melanchthon argued that both forms of confession and absolution, private and public, should be retained. "The preaching of the holy gospel itself is principally and actually an absolution." Through preaching "forgiveness of sins is proclaimed . . . in public to many persons, or publicly or privately to one person alone. Therefore absolution may be used in public and in general, and in special cases also in private. . . ."[120] They then go on to describe absolution itself:

> . . . for each absolution, whether administered publicly or privately, has to be understood as demanding faith and as being an aid to those that believe in it, just as the gospel itself also proclaims for-

118. H. E. Jacobs, "Confession of Sins," *The Lutheran Cyclopedia* (New York: Scribner's, 1899) 128-29.

119. *LW* 50:75.

120. *LW* 50:76.

giveness to all men in the whole world and exempts no one from this universal context. Nevertheless the gospel certainly demands our faith and does not aid those who do not believe it; and yet the universal context of the gospel has to remain [valid].[121]

One can presume that this letter was written with special care since two people had to agree on its wording and since it was a public utterance meant for a public controversy. In Wittenberg, both Luther and Melanchthon gave preference to the practice of private confession and absolution. But this preference did not prevent them from affirming the validity of public confession in Nuremberg and also, in effect, defending the practice of conditional absolution. A liturgical absolution, they argue, must conform to two characteristics: (1) it demands faith, and (2) it is an aid or comfort to those who believe in it. To make the demand of faith is to subject absolution to a condition.

Osiander refused to accept this judgment, although he did not wish to argue against Luther directly. In September 1533 he presented an expert report on the matter of absolution, *Opinion Concerning the Use of Absolution (Gutachten über den Gebrauch der Absolution)*, in which he reasserted that a public order for confession and absolution was illegitimate and that a proper absolution can never be conditional.[122] He complained directly about the conditional absolution formulated by Wenzeslaus Linck:

> It requires humility, sorrow, heartfelt desire for God's grace and help, [and] a firm faith and trust in his promises. These are the highest and most difficult works and virtues one can wish or require from a human being. . . . Who can believe that he has been absolved [according to this teaching]? Truly, no one, unless he believes and knows beforehand that he possesses all the above-mentioned virtues.[123]

Authentic absolution, declared Osiander, is conveyed by the pastor's word, speaking in God's stead, unconditionally. It requires no faith or

---

121. *LW* 50:77.

122. Gerhard Müller and Gottfried Seebaß, *Andreas Osiander D. Ä. Gesamtausgabe* 5 (Gütersloh: Gütersloher Verlagshaus Gerd Mohn, 1983) 413-90. See Rittgers, *Reformation of the Keys*, 150-58.

123. *Gesamtausgabe* 5:465. Quoted and tr. Rittgers, *Reformation of the Keys*, 153.

moral obedience on the part of the recipient. "In the absolution with the laying on of hands is not a sign of loosing but is the loosing [of sins] itself," just as Christ himself is present in the bread and wine and just as the act of baptism is itself a dying to sin and a rebirth.[124] Throughout this argument, Osiander refers for authority to Luther's essay *The Keys* (1530).[125] According to Osiander, Luther teaches that the loosing of sins and the promise of eternal life is the judgment of Christ alone.[126] Everything has to do with Christ, nothing with us. This unconditional absolution is what the pastor conveys. It must be done directly, privately, one-on-one, not indiscriminately in a public service where the graciousness of God is lost on those attending who are uncaring.

In his *Gutachten,* Osiander ignores what Luther and Melanchthon said in their letter to the city council concerning the demand of faith. That faith is essential is also Luther's argument in *The Keys,* an argument that Osiander distorts. To be sure, as we have already argued above, Luther asserts in *The Keys* that to have sins forgiven does not require moral obedience: it is wrong to "want to become holy by our own righteousness, beyond and outside of divine grace."[127] On this Osiander and Luther agree. Luther goes even further by declaring that the loosing key does not depend on repentance,[128] an assertion that contradicts the demand of his own exhortation to communicants and the instruction in the various conditional absolutions that we have considered in this chapter. It is not atypical for Luther to engage in overstatement, and this seems to be an example of it. But let the statement stand. Here again Osiander and Luther seem to be in agreement. But, according to Luther, the keys "demand faith in our hearts, and without faith you cannot use them with profit."[129] Faith begins with the binding key and comes to rest in the loosing key. Thus: "He who has faith in the key, has satisfied it by means of such faith, before and without performing any works."[130] Here Luther and Osiander do not agree. That Osiander ignored Luther on the demand of faith makes his position appear eccentric and willful. It is as if, ironically, he is yearning

124. *Gesamtausgabe* 5:489.
125. *Gesamtausgabe* 5:450ff. *passim.*
126. *Gesamtausgabe* 5:451.
127. *LW* 40:330.
128. *LW* 40:375.
129. *LW* 40:375.
130. *LW* 40:375-76.

for the laxity of Roman practice. His argument evokes in a curious way the Roman doctrine of *opus operatum* — the teaching that one receives the grace of God by mere participation — a position that would come to haunt the Lutheranism of a later age as it conformed more and more to the morphology of the church type.

It is no wonder that Osiander found himself outside the consensus of church leaders in Nuremberg. Rittgers describes Osiander's stance as "extreme absolutionism," a theological position which to his detractors recalled the "remnants of the sacerdotal religion they had rejected."[131]

The Lord's Supper

For Luther the validity of the Lord's Supper depends on the word of Christ alone. The so-called canon of the mass, "also called Eucharistic prayer, mass canon, Prayer of Thanksgiving, Great Thanksgiving,"[132] in other words, the central rule according to which the Lord's Supper is to be received, is unnecessary and misleading, even dangerous to the faith. The Words of Institution are all that is needed. To add to them the elements of the mass "is like imbedding the holy words in a heathen temple."[133] As Luther puts it in *An Order of Mass and Communion for the Church at Wittenberg* (1523), complaining about that portion of the mass called the "offertory" and what follows after it,

> From here on almost everything smacks and savors of sacrifice. And the words of life and salvation [the Words of Institution] are imbedded in the midst of it all, just as the ark of the Lord once stood in the idol's temple next to Dagon. . . . Let us therefore repudiate everything that smacks of sacrifice, together with the entire canon and retain only that which is pure and holy, and order our mass.[134]

When Luther says to "repudiate everything that smacks of sacrifice," he means it. It was for him a matter of firm theological principle, enun-

131. Rittgers, *Reformation of the Keys,* 158.
132. Oliver K. Olson, *Reclaiming the Lutheran Liturgical Heritage* (Minneapolis: Reclaim Resources, 2007) 88.
133. Olson, *Reclaiming,* 33.
134. *LW* 53:26. See Olson, *Reclaiming,* 33.

ciated forcefully in *The Babylonian Captivity of the Church* (1520), and adhered to throughout his life:

> . . . we must be particularly careful to put aside whatever has been added to [the sacrament's] original simple institution by the zeal and devotion of men: such things as vestments, ornaments, chants, prayers, organs, candles, and the whole pageantry of outward things. We must turn our eyes and hearts simply to the institution of Christ and this alone. . . . For in that word, and in that word alone, reside the power, the nature, and the whole substance of the mass.[135]

The idea that "the mass is a good work and sacrifice" is "the most wicked abuse of all" with regard to the Sacrament of the Altar.[136] It makes the sacrament captive to the ecclesiastical hierarchy, which seeks to control the grace of Christ for the sake of power. The sacrament is Christ and belongs to Christ.

> Let this stand, therefore, as our first and infallible proposition — the mass or Sacrament of the Altar is Christ's testament, which he left behind him at his death to be distributed among his believers. . . . Let this truth stand, I say, as the immovable foundation on which we shall base all we have to say. For, as you will see, we are going to overthrow all the godless opinions of men which have been imported into this most precious sacrament.[137]

"Mass and prayer, sacrament and work, testament and sacrifice" must never be "confused." The former is from God, the latter the false human effort to be in command of the means of grace: "The former descends, the latter ascends."[138] Prayer does have its legitimate place in sacramental administration. As we have seen, the congregation's zealousness in prayer makes baptism effective in the life of the believer as he or she begins the journey of life.[139] And in the mature life of the individual believer, "baptism is worth nothing without faith, but is like seals affixed to a letter in which nothing is written."[140] This faith is

135. *LW* 36:36.
136. *LW* 36:35.
137. *LW* 36:37.
138. *LW* 36:56.
139. *LW* 53:97, 102.
140. Lenker, *Luther's Works* 3:204.

nurtured by the confession of sins in preparation for receiving the Lord's Supper. But in the liturgy of the Lord's Supper, the context in which this reception takes place, there is no necessary human action, no ritual of enactment, no ascending to divine being that takes place. God comes to us, even "on the night in which he was betrayed."

An Arduous Liturgical Tradition

In the practice of worship both Catholics and reformers took seriously the fundamental duty to call Christians to self-examination. They accepted the teaching that repentance could be repeated. They realized that this teaching represented a moderation of the severity of the early church, in which forgiveness for serious sins could be given only once in a lifetime. The Roman Church sought to lessen the burden of penance for sinners in the secure environment of sacramentality, teaching that divine grace is an intimate and assured presence in the blessed repetition of ritual action and participation — forgiveness guaranteed by formula. Whatever moralism and legalism attended the interrogation of the penitent by the priest in private confession, the fact is that the church in the Middle Ages relaxed the demand for subjective holiness on the part of the laity. This is the effect of the teachings of *opus operatum,* confession by attrition, and *fides implicata.* Penance became a matter of fixed liturgical custom. Cardinal Bellarmine was right to describe the morphology of the Roman church as not requiring "inward qualities." The believer can rest assured that the theological virtues of faith, hope, and love inhere within the visible, institutional church itself. Thus: "all that is necessary is an outward confession of faith and participation in the sacraments."[141] Repentance as a blessed repetition in liturgical worship led Catholicism to embrace a church-type morphology, Christian faith as Christendom.

The reformers sought to call Christians to self-examination in a much different way. They eschewed sacramentality with its rituals and formulas as the superficial trappings of "human traditions" and false religion. There is no Christendom: "the world and the masses are and always will be un-Christian."[142] "Human doctrine, ceremonies, tonsures,

---

141. *De ecclesia militate* 2. Quoted and tr. Whale, *The Protestant Tradition,* 185.
142. *LW* 45:91.

long robes, miters, and all the pomp of popery only lead far away from it into hell. . . ."[143] When Luther speaks of hell, he means it. The world belongs to the devil, who engages Christians in spiritual warfare, seeking to make them his own through assault on body and soul *(Anfechtung)*. The reformers sought to ground the church in inward qualities, the very thing that Cardinal Bellarmine decries. Outward participation in the sacrament is not enough to receive its benefits. There must be faith. Faith is a gift of the Holy Spirit. It is "the drama which God enacts with us."[144] Faith must be nurtured and tended so that people are not left as "heathen in a public square or out in a field" but actually "become Christian."[145] In this regard, private confession is a mandate, a formal exhortation to communicants is a common feature of the worship service, and absolution, especially when delivered in a public order for confession and absolution, is usually given in a conditional form. Private confession is not a sacrament mediated by a priest. It is not a moralistic or legalistic exercise in recounting the particulars of one's sins. But it is an examination of oneself, standing before God's judgment and undergoing "Christ's binding."[146] To fulfill the responsibility of *fides explicata,* the confessing sinner must know the fundamental content of faith: what sin is, what the sacrament of the altar is, what makes it efficacious, what its benefits are, etc. In all this the church sought to speak plain language: language of admonition, command, and comfort, language that demands a response on the part of the hearer — above all, fear of the judgment of God and faith in the divine promise of salvation, a promise that comes to the struggling Christian again and again in blessed repetition. "God will not let the sinner go," proclaims the church; "receive Him in simple faith." This style of worship bespeaks a church that, at least in the early decades of its formation, demonstrated a tendency toward a sect-type morphology, a morphology that shaped itself less moralistically or legalistically than existentially.

In 1746, Henry Melchior Muhlenberg (1711-1787), a pastor serving in America, reported to his superiors back in Halle in Saxony-Anhalt on his method of administering Holy Communion. His letter, dated October 30, 1746, was but one of many he would write throughout his life,

143. *LW* 41:211.
144. *LW* 13:116.
145. *LW* 53:63.
146. *LW* 40:328.

the so-called *Hallesche Nachtrichten,* in which he described the conditions and spiritual state of Lutheran churches in the new land.
Muhlenberg had been sent to the colonies just four years before to provide leadership among Lutherans who had settled in Pennsylvania and
surrounding colonies and were desperate for a spiritual guide and
steady hand. Muhlenberg was the right man for the job. He would
spend the rest of his life in America, organizing the Pennsylvania
Ministerium in 1748 and helping to educate two generations of pastors.
The sacrament, writes Muhlenberg, is given twice yearly in each congregation.[147] Those wishing communion are expected to speak with the
pastor the week preceding. "One talks with them about the inner feel-
ings of the heart and looks for growth and also gives the necessary ad-
monitions, encouragement and consolation as the situation requires."[148] Through this private encounter, Muhlenberg as pastor
learned about the congregation: "one gains an understanding of inner
and outer conditions and one also gets an insight into relationships in
the estate of marriage, between neighbors, parents, children and
friends." On Saturday evening a preparatory service of confession was
held, the sermon being directed to repentance and the concerns and
tribulations of parishioners: "Without reference to specific persons
one arranges the preached word according to the concerns and circumstances one has noted in the particular conversation." After the sermon
the parishioners "form a half moon around the altar." Those guilty of
"public offense" are singled out. They are once more examined by the
pastor in front of the gathered congregation and urged to "true repentance" and "improvement of life." Thus private confession as interrogation or *Verhör* and public confession are joined together. The congregation is urged to reconciliation with the offenders. Muhlenberg reports
that most often parishioners readily forgive their brothers and sisters
of public sins. "Then when everything has been settled members of the
group bow their knees before God, and the pastor, kneeling in their
midst, prays the confession." Catechetical questions about faith and
the meaning of the sacrament are directed to the entire gathering.
These are followed by a conditional absolution: forgiveness is declared

---

147. "Letter 58" (October 30, 1746), *The Correspondence of Heinrich Melchior Mühlenberg* 1:
1740-1747, ed. and tr. John W. Kleiner and Helmut T. Lehmann (Camden, ME: Picton
Press, 1993) 293-307.
148. *Correspondence of Heinrich Melchior Mühlenberg* 1:296.

to the penitent and the warning is given "that the sins of the impenitent shall be retained until they do an about-face." After this the pastor is still not done. "Those who perhaps still have something against one another go to the parsonage with the pastor, are reconciled with one another and forgive each other their faults." On Sunday the sermon focuses on Holy Communion. The elements are consecrated and distributed. "Afterwards the school teacher has to read the history of the Passion from the four Evangelists so that one may proclaim the Lord's death and consider the price he paid to redeem us."[149]

In late spring, 1867, Herman Amberg Preus (1825-1894) reported to his home church in Norway on the conditions and spiritual state of Norwegian Lutheran churches in America. He did so in person, traveling back to Norway for a visit after sixteen years of service as pastor, fourteen of them in the Norwegian Evangelical Lutheran Church in America, later known as the Norwegian Synod or Old Synod, which had been established in 1853. Preus gave a series of lectures, "Seven Lectures on the Religious Situation among Norwegians in America," in part to entice ministers to serve in the far-off and rugged land of Midwest America, but also to describe and, if need be, defend the new church.[150] The Church of Norway was wary of its offspring, and with good reason. The religious leaders of the Norwegian immigrants disapproved of the latitude of the territorial church in Norway. They saw America "as an opportunity to restore what they thought of as proper Lutheran practice." Thus they embraced older Lutheran rites instead of nineteenth-century revisions, congregational freedom, which befitted the American religious environment, and stricter penitential practice. The most important reform involved membership: "Where baptism alone had been sufficient for membership in the Church of Norway, the pioneer pastors provided for a rigorous examination of the faith and life of applicants for membership in their congregations and required the congregations or congregational councils to vote on the admission of prospective members."[151]

In Lecture II, on "Congregational Polity," Preus summarized communion discipline. "Private confession," he said, "is to be considered the goal toward which we must strive," though he admitted that it was not

---

149. *Correspondence of Heinrich Melchior Mühlenberg* 1:296.

150. Herman Amberg Preus, *Vivacious Daughter: Seven Lectures on the Religious Situation in America,* ed. and tr. with intro. Todd W. Nichol (Northfield: The Norwegian-American Historical Association, 1990) 10.

151. Preus, *Vivacious Daughter,* 15-16.

practiced everywhere and was frequently hard to do given the isolation of many churches and rural conditions. Nevertheless, he asserted: "In spite of the difficulties with respect to time and place standing in the way of private confession, in spite of the great trouble and time it costs the pastor, in spite of the ignorance and misunderstanding and ill will the common people show toward this ordinance, it has made its way into many of the congregations."[152] Examination of communicants is necessary to fulfill Christ's admonition, "Give not that which is holy unto the dogs, neither cast ye your pearls before swine" (Matthew 7:6).[153] Christ expects the congregation and pastor "to take care and stand guard so that the plainly unfit and unrepentant do not go to the altar and profane what is holy while bringing judgment upon themselves."[154] At the preparatory or "confessional service," held usually on Saturday, people gather in "as many as ten to twelve at once" or "in special cases [as] individuals," and the pastor gives instruction on "the conditions for a worthy reception," "the truths of faith," and "the knowledge of Christianity."[155] The service begins with "prayers and hymns, after which followed catechization. The five parts of Luther's Small Catechism are gone through along with "the section on absolution."[156]

> When the catechization is over, each individual comes to the pastor in the sacristy or in a room set apart. Confession takes place either as the penitent himself makes confession or as he answers certain questions directed to him by the pastor. The pastor pronounces absolution [in unconditional form along with the laying on of hands] when the confession is finished, if there is no evidence of impenitence. While private confessions are in progress, the rest of the congregation sings hymns or someone reads to them from the Bible or a book of communion devotions.[157]

On Sunday, those who have been prepared receive the Lord's Supper preceded by "a communal address." Preus was well aware that this com-

152. Preus, *Vivacious Daughter*, 69.
153. Preus, *Vivacious Daughter*, 68.
154. Preus, *Vivacious Daughter*, 68.
155. Preus, *Vivacious Daughter*, 69.
156. Preus, *Vivacious Daughter*, 70. The five chief parts of the Catechism are: the Ten Commandments, the Apostles' Creed, the Lord's Prayer, Holy Baptism, and the Sacrament of the Altar.
157. Preus, *Vivacious Daughter*, 70.

munion discipline could easily be subject to abuse "by an arrogant, domineering pastor or in an unevangelical manner." But, he declared, "we believe that the blessings attending upon a proper evangelical administration of private confession are so great that we ought not to preclude or abolish its usage."[158]

Muhlenberg wrote his letter exactly two centuries after Luther's death; Preus delivered his lectures one hundred and twenty-one years after that. Both men represent the austere Lutheran liturgical tradition in faithful transmission. Muhlenberg is recognized as the patriarch of American Lutheranism. His influence and inspiration extended through the Pennsylvania Ministerium to the Joint Synod of Ohio, the General Synod, the General Council, the United Lutheran Church in America, and the Lutheran Church in America. Herman Amberg Preus is the patriarch of a distinguished church family that created deep ties among the Norwegian Synod, the Missouri Synod, the Evangelical Lutheran Church, and the American Lutheran Church. To be sure, the rituals and customs that Muhlenberg and Preus describe are particular to their times and places. Lutheran worship has always had variations. But everything that Muhlenberg did from the week preceding communion through Saturday and Sunday and Preus did on Saturday and Sunday is grounded in practices established in the Reformation. The penitential disciplines of Muhlenberg and Preus thus conform to the morphology of Lutheran identity, emphasizing, above all, its sect-type elements, centered in the vigorous exercise of the binding key that recalls the eschatological consciousness and moral rigor of the early church. These disciplines were especially well-suited to the rugged religious environment of eighteenth- and nineteenth-century America where the evangelicalism of sectarian denominations held sway. Above all, Muhlenberg and Preus, in their administration of Holy Communion, sought to obey the divine imperative that undergirds Christian devotion to the Sacrament of the Altar: examination of oneself. These pioneers in the American wilderness give eloquent and poignant witness, from their time and place to ours, to the fundamental purpose of worship: *to call Christians to repentance, to warn them to be under no illusion as to who they are and how far they fall short when they stand before God and holy things, to teach them to worship God in humility, to feed them the Bread of Life, and to make them ready to give testimony to Christ in word and deed.*

158. Preus, *Vivacious Daughter,* 70.

CHAPTER IV

The Attack on Private Confession

Schmucker's Challenge

In 1855 a pamphlet called the *Definite Platform* was published under the auspices of the General Synod, the largest Lutheran denominational organization in America at the time.[1] Although no author was identified in the document itself, it was soon learned that the pamphlet was written by the guiding spirit of the General Synod, Samuel Simon Schmucker (1799-1873), Professor of Didactic Theology and chairman of the faculty at Gettysburg Theological Seminary. In the *Platform* Schmucker proposed that Lutherans revise their historic confessions to bring the church more in line with the evangelical environment of American Christianity, an environment that emphasized the priority of individual religious conversion and distrusted ecclesiastical hierarchy and ritual observance. This process of revision for the purpose of Americanization could only be accomplished, in Schmucker's view, if the Synod rejected the binding authority of any formal confession except the Augsburg Confession. Subscribing to Augsburg was not a matter of obedience to every word. In Schmucker's view, the Confession is to be accepted "insofar as" *(quatenus)* it conforms with the teaching of Scripture not "because" *(quia)* it conforms with the teaching of Scripture. Finally, certain inherited teachings and practices of European

---

1. *Definite Platform, Doctrinal and Disciplinarian, for Evangelical Lutheran District Synods; Constructed in Accordance with the Principles of the General Synod* (Philadelphia: Miller & Burlock, 1855).

Christianity not determined to be biblical or relevant to the new society in America needed to be eliminated. These included exorcism, the doctrine of original sin and guilt, baptismal regeneration, the real presence in the Sacrament of the Altar, and confession and absolution.

In making these proposals, Schmucker took great care to assess the needs of the Christian faithful in America. He believed that American Christians, including Lutheran Christians, could only accept what made sense to them in their own cultural environment. In his own way, Schmucker also took the Lutheran tradition seriously. He understood that Lutheran history was a story of contention and change. Most of the confessions collected in the Book of Concord had been rejected by the majority of Lutheran kingdoms in Europe.[2] Dutch Lutherans, who pioneered Lutheranism in America, were accustomed by the beginning of the seventeenth century to administer the sacrament of baptism without exorcism and eschewed private confession.[3] The doctrine of the bodily presence in the Lord's Supper had been hotly disputed by rival faculties in Lutheran territories in the sixteenth and seventeenth centuries. In America during the colonial period, Lutherans had not demanded formal subscription to the Augsburg Confession. On the contrary, they debated openly the doctrinal content of the Lutheran tradition. In 1837 rebellious Lutherans from the Harwick Synod formed the Franckean Synod, named after the Pietist leader August Herman Francke (1663-1727), and purposely deemphasized the sacraments in favor of a theology of revival and conversion. They declared openly that they "did not believe everything" in the Augsburg Confession.[4] The Bible, not doctrine, is the key to authentic faith. Schmucker and other leaders in the General Synod thought themselves to be in this long and distinguished line of critical thought. They believed that engaging in the process of revision, using the *Platform* as a statement of principles, the General Synod would participate in the legitimate historical evolution of its own Lutheran identity.

With regard to the matter of confession and absolution, Schmucker was specifically opposed to the practice of private confession that takes place between pastor and parishioner and that is affirmed in Article XI

2. *Definite Platform*, 2.

3. Henry Eyster Jacobs, *A History of the Evangelical Lutheran Church in the United States* (New York: Charles Scribner's Sons, 1893) 40.

4. E. Clifford Nelson, ed., *The Lutherans in North America* (Philadelphia: Fortress Press, 1975) 144.

of the Augsburg Confession, where it is declared that "private absolution should be retained in the church." Schmucker labeled this claim a doctrinal "error." He also dismissed Article XXV of the Confession. It states: "the custom is retained among us, not to administer the Sacrament unto those who have not been previously examined and absolved." The article goes on to commend "the comfort afforded by the words of absolution, and the high and great estimation in which it is held. . . . [I]t is the word of God who here forgives sins . . . for it is spoken in God's stead, and by his command. Concerning this command and the power of the keys, it is taught with the greatest assiduity how comfortable, how useful they are to alarmed consciences, and besides how God requires confidence in this absolution." Schmucker objected to all these confessional assertions in the article. Finally, he argued that a portion of Article XXVIII is to be cast aside, that portion which reads: "the power of the keys or of the bishops, according to the Gospel, is a power and commission from God to preach the Gospel, *to remit and retain sins.*"[5]

Schmucker declares that "the entire doctrine of absolution and sinforgiving [sic] power of the ministry" is "dangerous" to the "doctrine of justification by grace alone through faith." "Pardon and justification" are obtained through "the merits of Christ." These merits "must be apprehended by a living faith" which is found "only in the regenerate or converted." For a person who has such faith, attendance at confession is superfluous; if he or she has no such faith, confession and "the priest's absolution" accomplish nothing. Schmucker's reference to "the priest's absolution" was a deliberate insult meant to identify the practice of confession and absolution as a holdover from Roman Catholicism that, in his view, the reformers had neglected to abolish and should have done so. People need to distinguish true faith from false faith. The line he draws in the sand is between "converted and unconverted . . . mere formalists and true Christians." "No rite can replace the command that *'a man be born again.'* (see I Pet. 1.23)."[6]

That Schmucker placed so much emphasis on conversion is no surprise. His focus on born-again theology as the measure of faith reflected his belief, and the belief of many of his colleagues in the General Synod, that evangelical Christianity was the future of the church in America,

5. *Definite Platform,* 25-26.
6. *Definite Platform,* 24-26.

not denominations who trace their heritage to the territorial churches of old Europe. Evangelicalism, the classic form of the sect type in modernity, teaches that the normal beginning of genuine Christian life is spiritual transformation. It emphasizes "crisis conversion" as "an arduous and often extended rebirth experience" followed by a commitment to a devout life and morality that ratifies the conversion as authentic.[7] The template for evangelicalism is the Reformed tradition, exemplified by the Puritans, Scottish and Irish Presbyterians, Baptists, and Methodists but also influential in Lutheran Pietism. Evangelicalism as a transdenominational force triumphed in America in two nationwide revivals, the First and Second Great Awakenings. The first took place during the 1730s and 1740s in the American colonies and was led by the great revival preacher George Whitefield (1714-1770). Inspired by the example of John Wesley (1703-1791), Whitefield traveled throughout all thirteen colonies, inviting people to receive the gospel of Christ in their hearts under the power of the Holy Spirit. The Second Great Awakening began in the 1790s when the United States was just a fledgling nation. Revival preachers brought the gospel to the expanding frontier and helped to civilize the west. The Second Awakening continued well into the 1830s. The result of these two momentous events was the triumph and dominance of sect-type morphology in American Protestantism.

The most important of the revival preachers in the Second Awakening was Charles Grandison Finney (1792-1875). Finney preached that a relationship to Christ requires human response in emotion, reason, and will and that sanctification defines authentic faith and brings salvation. Under Finney's influence, revival became a technique, the so-called "new measures," in which people at meetings that would extend over days had their spirits aroused by dramatic appeals to make a decision for Christ. The meetings were deliberately staged and choreographed with preaching, sustained prayer, and hymn singing to pressure people to commit themselves, this in the belief that excited emotions were the channel through which the Holy Spirit worked to bring an individual to the judgment of God and the grace of Christ. The imperative to examine oneself, the fundamental purpose of Christian worship, was not a matter of blessed repetition, but rather a concentrated single event. Those who were moved to respond would go

---

7. Paul K. Conkin, *Cane Ridge: America's Pentecost* (Madison: University of Wisconsin Press, 1990) 11.

one-by-one to the front of the group, sit on the seat called the "anxious" or "mourner's bench," and receive the intercessory prayers of the evangelist and the group, culminating in conversion. Conversion was the goal of worship. This practice was considered by many to be manipulative, but it was very successful.

It also had a history. Its origins trace back to the unique worship practice of communion among Scottish Presbyterians beginning in the early seventeenth century.[8] The Presbyterian ideal for receiving the Lord's Supper was to obey as closely as possible New Testament practice, the earliest account of which is to be found in 1 Corinthians 11. This ideal was grounded in the desire to rid worship of all traces of high-church ritual, whether of the Roman variety espoused by Mary Queen of Scots (1542-1587) or the high Anglican version adopted by her son and grandson, James I (1566-1625) and Charles I (1600-1649). Presbyterian practice was to serve communion at a long table (one table per parish), ministers, elders, and lay people seated together, passing bread and wine in healthy portions, as at an actual meal. The members of a parish properly could take an entire day for communion since only so many could be seated at one time.

To obey the Pauline imperative to examine oneself, there were long preparatory sermons that included explicit warnings, called "fencing the Table": no one could take communion unprepared. Over time, the process of preparation became more and more elaborate as it included fasting and prayer, sermons on Friday and Saturday preceding, the use of leaden tokens to admit communicants to the meal, and a thanksgiving service celebrated on the Monday following,[9] all this to be done in an expectant atmosphere of emotional intensity and sincerity.

There were also joint communion services in which several churches participated together at one location. This meant setting up a number of tables, each led by a different minister. Such gatherings could involve churches from miles around and include thousands of people. They became:

> . . . a festival or fair, the most exciting time of the year, with thousands of noncommunicants attending. The joint services were a proper time for courtship, for the formation of new friendships,

8. On the following, see Conkin, *Cane Ridge*, 16ff.
9. Conkin, *Cane Ridge*, 18.

and for various reasons a time of joy and celebration. Presbyterian communion was usually the peak experience of the year; at some communions it could be the peak experience of a lifetime.[10]

This was in effect the Presbyterian version of sacramentality: a dramatic demonstration of the visibility of the divine in the mundane world. Communion services became extended revival services serving a theology of conversion. But they also in their own way sought to fulfill the fundamental purpose of worship that has been argued throughout this book: to call Christians to self-examination and repentance.

Presbyterian immigrants from Scotland and Ulster in Ireland brought this practice of communion to America. The word "communion" came to mean this Presbyterian type of extended service. "Communions" were employed as a tool of evangelism in a country where the vast majority did not attend church. In 1798, James McGready (1763-1817) was called from his Presbyterian congregation in Orange County, North Carolina, to be pastor to three small congregations in Logan County, Kentucky, named Red River, Gasper River, and Muddy River.[11] Kentucky and its neighbor Tennessee were then considered the wild frontier of America. Many of the people who inhabited these lands were thought to have lost their souls. After a visit to Tennessee in 1794, Francis Asbury (1745-1816), Methodist bishop and famous circuit rider, observed despairingly: "When I reflect that not one in a hundred came here to get religion, but rather to get plenty of good land, I think it will be well if some or many do not eventually lose their souls."[12] The same year that McGready was sent to his new call, the Presbyterian General Assembly resolved to set aside a day for fasting and prayer to lament the "Egyptian darkness" that imperiled the frontier. In June 1800, McGready held a communion at the Red River church that got a decent response. For the next communion at Gasper River in August he sent out advance notice. Scores of settlers showed up, some from as far as one hundred miles. This is often considered the first "camp meeting" in America, although the term was not in currency until two years later. In August 1801 a communion was held at Cane Ridge Meeting House in Bourbon County, Kentucky, twenty miles northeast of Lexington. Pre-

10. Conkin, *Cane Ridge*, 18.
11. On the following see, Mark Galli, "Revival at Cane Ridge," *Christian History* 45 (1995): 9-14 = http://www.christianitytoday.com/ch/1995/issue45/4509.html.
12. Quoted in Galli, "Revival at Cane Ridge," 10.

vious communions that summer had attracted 4,000 (Concord), 6,000 (Lexington), and 10,000 (Indian Creek). The Cane Ridge assembly was an explosive event; one estimate put the number at 12,000. "Sinners [were] lying powerless in every part of the house, praying and crying for mercy," wrote McGready of those who were able to attend the sermons of preparation on Friday and Saturday, squeezing into the small, primitive building. Emotion and ecstasy gripped the huge crowd outside; even soaking rain could not dampen their spirits.

This was the event that gave momentum to the Second Great Awakening as a broad national phenomenon. Gradually over time, sacramental communions morphed into revival meetings, participation in the Lord's Supper being replaced by an effort to induce conversion by preaching. Sacramental communion was a repeated event in which worshipers sought the spiritual presence of Christ in the sacred meal. Revivals had a different goal: a one-time permanent change of heart on the part of those attending; if such change was not permanent, the person was in a "backslidden" condition. It was Finney's "new measures" that turned the revival into a method calculated to produce results. Finney's working assumption, shared among evangelicals of the time, was that "the common man, listening to the preaching of the church, was capable by the use of reason of assessing the full scope of his moral predicament as a lost creature under the judgment of God who has nowhere to turn but the love of Christ."[13] Faith in Christ was an act of free will not unlike the ballot cast by an enfranchised voter in an election or the member of a jury at a trial. This was a theology fit for a republic founded on Enlightenment ideals and especially suitable for the age of Jacksonian democracy. The greatest itinerant evangelist of his time, Finney claimed to have reached 500,000 people in America and Great Britain. His influence, like that of Whitefield and Wesley before him and Billy Graham more than a century later, transcended denominational allegiance.

Finney's success got the attention of Lutherans. Benjamin Kurtz (1795-1865), an ally of Schmucker, grandson of the first Lutheran pastor ordained by a Lutheran synod in America and editor of the *Lutheran Observer* (1833-1861), called the anxious bench "the archimedean lever which with the help of God can raise our German church [by which he

13. Roy A. Harrisville and Walter Sundberg, *The Bible in Modern Culture*, 2nd ed. (Grand Rapids: William B. Eerdmans Publishing Co., 2002) 200.

meant the Lutheran church in America] to that position of authority in the religious world which is its rightful due."[14] At the annual meeting of the Synod of Maryland in 1845, the effort was made to incorporate a revivalist theology of free choice into the church in a document entitled "Abstract of Doctrines and Practice of the Evangelical Lutheran Synod of Maryland," which defined "the power of choice" as a person's "natural gift" by which at all times he or she "possesses the ability to choose the opposite of that which was the object of his choice." God "places before man the evil and the good," urging him to choose the good. If he does so, it is by the persuasion of "the truth" — that is to say, by an act of reason. Thus "the sinner is persuaded to abandon his sins and submit to God, on terms made known in the gospel." The sacraments are symbolical representations of gospel truth. They are ancillary to the change of heart that follows voluntary submission to God: "This change, we are taught, is radical, and is essential to present peace and eternal happiness. Consequently, it is possible, and is the privilege of the regenerated person to know and rejoice in the change produced in him."[15] The synod neither accepted nor rejected the proposed "Abstract," but tabled it for the following year. It was not taken up again.

This setback did not discourage the evangelical party in the General Synod, but spurred them on to a more ambitious effort a decade later in the *Definite Platform*. The *Platform* was given widespread distribution. Arrangements were made to send it to a prepared list of leaders all over the church who had not otherwise obtained it, with the request that "25 cents in silver or post-paid stamps" be sent to the publisher, Miller and Burlock in Philadelphia, or, "should any not desire to retain it, they will please to enclose it carefully in paper, and send it, post-paid, to the same address."[16] The purposeful effort to get the document in the hands of church leaders demonstrated how serious the *Platform* was to the strategic plan of the General Synod.

The effort to distribute the document widely was also a sign of fear. Schmucker worried that the attempt to bring the Lutheran church into line with the dominant force of evangelical Christianity might fail be-

14. *Lutheran Observer*, November 17, 1843, quoted in Arie J. Griffioen, "Charles Porterfield Krauth and the Synod of Maryland," *Lutheran Quarterly* 8 (1993): 279.

15. Quoted in Griffioen, "Charles Porterfield Krauth," 283.

16. *Definite Platform*, insert.

cause the General Synod was under siege by immigrant Germans who began arriving in large numbers in the 1840s. The *Platform* argued that, "being surrounded by German churches, which profess the entire mass of former symbols," that is, not just the unaltered Augsburg Confession, but the Book of Concord as a whole, the doctrine, liturgical practices, and ecclesiastical ordinances of the Lutheran territorial churches, American Lutheranism could be overwhelmed by foreign members who believed superfluous doctrines. The church would then be turned into a European artifact and become irrelevant to American culture.[17] "We are not in Europe anymore," said the *Platform* in effect, "we need to make our new home in this great land that Christ may be proclaimed. We need to practice revival before we are left behind. We cannot let immigrants who do not understand America and who retain outmoded religious practices of the past, to hold us back."

William Julius Mann's Response

In the following year, 1856, William (Wilhelm) Julius Mann (1819-1892) replied to Schmucker's argument in the *Platform*, defending a Lutheran confessional position in his essay *A Plea for the Augsburg Confession*. Mann served as pastor of St. Michael and Zion churches in Philadelphia at the time and was one of the new German immigrants Schmucker feared, having arrived in America in 1844 with his good friend from student days at the University of Tübingen, Philip Schaff (1819-1893), who came to America to teach at the Reformed Seminary in Mercersburg, Pennsylvania. Schaff eventually became the most prominent church historian in America in the nineteenth century. Mann also had a distinguished career. He would become Professor of Symbolics at Lutheran Theological Seminary in Philadelphia, beginning at its inception in 1864.

Mann's position over against Schmucker and the *Definite Platform* has been aptly described by the scholar D. G. Hart as a "confessionalist piety [that] was essentially churchly; participation in the forms and rites of the church, as opposed to the convert's solitary quest to lead an earnest moral life, was the way to be Christian."[18] With regard to the

---

17. *Definite Platform*, 3.

18. D. G. Hart, *The Lost Soul of American Protestantism* (Lanham, MD: Rowman & Littlefield, 2002) 47.

matter of confession and absolution, Mann concedes in his *Plea* that private confession and absolution in the American context may appear too Roman Catholic, especially if it is mandated to be administered by a pastor in conjunction with receiving the Lord's Supper. This makes the pastor look like a Catholic priest, which is not what the church needs. But having no rite of confession and absolution is un-Lutheran; it means falling to "revival excitement" of Finney and his ilk, in which Christian faith is reduced to individualistic subjective emotion.[19] Instead, there is a "a middle way [between private confession and no confession], one where the Lutheran pastor actually declares pardon to those who confess their sin, but does so in the context of public worship and in response to a corporate confession of sin."[20] Public confession and absolution, done in public worship, is exactly what is required to counter the distortions of evangelical decision theology in the religious environment of America. Mann declares: "Our Lutheran Church knows of no priesthood in the sense of the word in the Roman Church." Rather, ministry is grounded in "the universal priesthood of all believers in Christ." Mann adhered to a functional view of ministry which meant that the pastor can never be understood by Lutherans as "the embodiment of the power of heaven or hell"; nor is he "the "representative of a caste" put in place "to decide on the fate of poor miserable sinners."[21] The church instituted confession and absolution not to serve the clergy but to serve the mandate of the Scriptures.

What is this mandate? "We all know how urgently," writes Mann, "the Gospel enjoins us to beware of an unworthy participation of the body and blood of Christ." In light of this mandate, "the Church could not do better than institute a particular service, preparatory to the celebration of the Lord's Supper." This is "an occasion to move the hearts of men, to preach to them repentance, and to warn them of a portentous responsibility." To those who "are lingering after the comfort of forgiveness of sins," there is heard "the blessed word of pardon."[22]

It is proper for a minister as representative of the universal priesthood to lead Christians in self-examination, not at the one-time event of a revival meeting, but at regular occasions of liturgical worship, in

19. W. J. Mann, *A Plea for the Augsburg Confession* (Philadelphia: Lindsay & Blakiston, 1856) 25.

20. Hart, *Lost Soul*, 48.

21. Mann, *A Plea for the Augsburg Confession*, 22.

22. Mann, *A Plea for the Augsburg Confession*, 23.

particular by conducting on set and accustomed occasions a service of confession and absolution. This is the office of the keys commanded in Scripture: "Whatsoever ye shall bind on earth, shall be bound in heaven; and whatsoever ye loose on earth, shall be loosed in heaven" (Matthew 18:18). In Mann's view, following the Lutheran tradition going back to Luther himself, this verse gives the office of the keys to the church — the church understood exclusively as the universal priesthood. The keys are not given to the pastor standing over against the congregation: "It is the view of the Lutheran theologians from the beginning, that these words apply to the ecclesiastical rights of the whole congregation." Mann continues:

> Of course, in the congregation as such, the minister is the duly appointed officer, who, in the name of Christ, will proclaim the good tidings of forgiveness to the penitent, and the awful wrath of God to the impenitent and to the hypocrite. But this does not forbid that under certain circumstances a member of the church may confess his sins to another member, and be comforted by the cheering exhortation of his brother, who is no minister.[23]

This last sentence, about brother hearing the sins of brother, raises the matter of private confession. The *Definite Platform* argued that private confession and absolution is an error. Mann replied: "We may well ask now, whether the Augsburg Confession commits an *error* in maintaining private confession. . . . We allow a minister to hear a confession from his whole flock. Why in the name of common sense should we regard it as wrong in him to hear the confession of individual members thereof?" Private confession is no error. Private confession heard by a pastor is no error.

But private confession did have a problem in the American environment of the mid-nineteenth century. The problem is that "under the influence of a revival excitement" there is an expectation that the converted will give evangelical testimony about being lost and then found, testimony that borders "very near upon, not private, but auricular confession."[24] The converted individual feels constrained, like an unlettered medieval peasant before a priest, to catalogue his or her sins before an itinerant preacher on the sawdust trail. In Mann's view modern-day

23. Mann, *A Plea for the Augsburg Confession*, 24.
24. Mann, *A Plea for the Augsburg Confession*, 24.

evangelicalism and old Romanism are foxes tied by the tail. Lutheranism must battle on two fronts to protect the integrity and fundamental intent of its liturgical tradition. With this understanding, Mann is willing to concede that private confession may have outlived its usefulness to the church, especially in the distorted environment of American revivalism. Even if this is the case in this particular context, it is not true in all contexts. Private confession is no error.

To demonstrate to his reader that his theological argument for public confession and absolution is grounded in authentic Lutheran liturgical practice, Mann quotes in full an absolution from a public order for confession and absolution that he claims was used in Wittenberg — "the cradle of the Reformation" as he calls it — as early as 1559. This absolution bears a strong family resemblance to ones we considered in the previous chapter. After the admonition to repentance and faith in Christ the minister shall say:

> Therefore to all such as are here present with a penitent and believing spirit, who turn themselves to God and fear his anger at their sins, who believe that their sins are forgiven for the sake of Jesus Christ, and who earnestly resolve to die unto sin, to all such I proclaim the forgiveness of their sins according to the word of the Lord: Whosoever sins you remit, they are remitted unto them. Therefore, according to the command of Christ, I pronounce to you this forgiveness, that your sins are pardoned for the sake of Jesus Christ. And of this voice of the Gospel you ought to accept, and enjoy true comfort in Christ, and walk faithfully and obediently before God, having a good conscience.[25]

This liturgical formulation of the absolution fits exactly Mann's description of the purpose of preparation through confession to receive the Lord's Supper: "to move the hearts of men, to preach to them repentance, and to warn them of a portentous responsibility," so that those who "are lingering after the comfort of forgiveness of sins" can hear "the blessed word of pardon."[26] For Mann, the wording of this absolution validates the practice of public confession and absolution as it has been carried on by Lutherans from the sixteenth century to the nineteenth. It contains the promise of forgiveness and a sobering list of

25. Mann, *A Plea for the Augsburg Confession*, 22-23.
26. Mann, *A Plea for the Augsburg Confession*, 23.

the conditions of faith which serve to encourage the communicant to examine oneself. Mann concludes his defense of the liturgical practice with these words: "This is nothing but what the Bible authorizes, and has been the practice of the Lutheran Church from the beginning until the present time, even in this country."[27]

Mann and the Lutheran Liturgical Tradition

Mann's arguments that the pastor hearing confession and declaring absolution is no priest, that the office of the keys resides in the congregation, and that private confession, while no error, may have limitations as a matter of church practice were all familiar in the history of Lutheran theology and liturgical practice. While these claims are all important for understanding confession and absolution in Lutheran morphology, there is no doubt that the most important of the issues in the debate between Schmucker and Mann was the priestly status of the pastor.

The priestly authority of the pastor to impart absolution was a much-debated issue going back to the very beginning of the Reformation. As we saw in the last chapter, the city council of Nuremberg, supported by the majority of clergy interested in evangelical reform, introduced a public order of confession and absolution in 1524 in which the liturgical declaration of forgiveness is not from priest to parishioner, but from God to the people, clergy and laity receiving divine mercy together — this to emphasize that absolution is from God alone and requires no priestly mediation to have effect. The city council also discouraged the practice of private sacramental penance, thus seeking to deny to the clergy their most intimate sacramental connection to the laity. These radical reforms were a direct assault on the religious authority of ministers to exercise the power of the keys. It also affected adversely the political power of the clergy to influence and control individual lives. In reaction, Andreas Osiander defended private confession and made the self-consciously "priestly" argument that absolution is conveyed by the pastor's word, speaking in God's stead, delivering forgiveness unconditionally to the laity, who are to receive it in passive obedience: ". . . absolution with the laying on of hands is not

27. Mann, *A Plea for the Augsburg Confession*, 23.

a sign of loosing but is the loosing itself."[28] Forgiveness requires no faith or works. Unconditional absolution, conveyed by the pastor, must be done directly and privately, minister to individual parishioner. This position of "extreme absolutionism" appeared to the evangelical party in Nuremberg to be the "remnants of the sacerdotal religion they had rejected."[29]

Osiander did not get his way in Nuremberg; even Luther and Melanchthon sided with the city council against him. But they did so by endorsing both private and public confession as valid; so the argument carried on. Luther had mandated private confession in Wittenberg in 1524 against the reforms of Karlstadt, introducing the practice of the *Verhör* or interrogation. Mandated private confession to the exclusion of a public order of confession was taken up by a number of Lutheran territories,[30] this against the practice in Nuremberg. Also, the pastor's authority to exercise the keys and declare absolution to the people remained a commonly accepted practice among Lutherans. There was no consistent effort to ban pastors from speaking in the first person singular in exercising the keys, nor from interpreting this as a priestly or mediating function, a privilege of the pastoral office. Often there was a mix of elements, what Thomas Tentler calls "a paradoxical combination." As he explains: "A typical early formula [of absolution] might mention the fact of the sinner's repentance; then make an announcement of God's general forgiveness of the sinner; and then continue with a formula signifying that the pastor himself by divine authority absolved the penitent."[31] An example of this combination (if not exactly in the same order) can be found in the liturgical wording of a public or general absolution adopted in Wolfenbüttel in 1569 and Oldenberg in 1573:

> Almighty God hath had mercy on thee [second person plural familiar] and through the merits of the most holy suffering, death, and resurrection of our Lord Jesus Christ, his beloved Son, forgiveth

28. Gerhard Müller and Gottfried Seebaß, *Andreas Osiander D. Ä. Gesamtausgabe* 5 (Gütersloh: Gütersloher Verlagshaus Gerd Mohn, 1983) 489.

29. Ronald K. Rittgers, *The Reformation of the Keys* (Cambridge: Harvard University Press, 2004) 158.

30. Thomas Tentler, "Confession," in *The Oxford Encyclopedia of the Reformation* (New York, Oxford: Oxford University Press, 1996) 1:403.

31. Tentler, "Confession," 403.

thee all thy sins, and I as an ordained servant of the Christian Churches declare to all those [third person plural] who do truly repent and through faith place all of their trust in the sole merit of Jesus Christ, and who intend to order their life under the command and will of God, such forgiveness of all their sins in the name of the Father and of the Son and of the Holy Spirit. Amen. On the other hand, however, I say to the unrepentant and unbelieving, on the basis of the Word of God and in the name of Jesus Christ, that God has retained their sins and certainly will punish them.[32]

In the first clause of this rather elaborate absolution, it is God who is the subject and who does the forgiving directly, the people being addressed in the intimate form of second person familiar. The ordained pastor is the subject of the next clause, speaking in the first person singular; his responsibility is to clarify the demand of faith for believers and to warn the unbelieving and unrepentant. He addresses the people indirectly in the third person. This formulation reverses the customary Lutheran order of law and gospel: gospel or forgiveness is spoken first, the law or the conditions of faith is spoken second: the "binding" thus comes after the "loosing."[33]

In the seventeenth century, however, the diverse and sometimes paradoxical combination of elements in the Lutheran practice of confession and absolution began to fall apart, the pieces sorting themselves out along the battle lines that had first appeared in Nuremberg: on one side those asserting the adequacy of public confession and absolution according to a set liturgy, on the other those demanding private confession before an ordained pastor who speaks absolution in God's stead.

Mandatory private confession and absolution before a minister in preparation for Holy Communion, a widespread legal requirement in Lutheran territories in the sixteenth century, began to be questioned in the seventeenth century by educated laity and pastors who were influenced either by the emerging Enlightenment, by the new movement of Pietism, or in some cases by a combination of the two. The Enlightenment fostered a secular mentality and revived the ancient Epicurean suspicion that the priestly class in society exercises power in an illegiti-

---

32. *EKO* 6/1:144-45; 7/2/1:1146.

33. This echoes a most important verse in the biblical tradition: from the old ending of Mark, 16:16: "He who believes and is baptized will be saved; but he who does not believe will be condemned," where the warning follows the promise.

mate manner by manipulating the fear of God. Private confession, in this view, is a form of political and social control.

Pietist leaders had the same suspicion, but they came to it by theological conviction. Pietists did not like the ecclesiastical development that led to the identification of confession with the *Verhör*, which thus subjected the divine imperative to examine oneself to the regulations of the territorial governments. Legally mandated confession, they believed, did not encourage sincere, heart-felt repentance, but made for conventional, superficial Christians. They saw mandatory private confession as a ritual exercise, "a mechanical going through of a set of memorized responses to pastoral questions."[34] In the social and political climate of the territorial church, it also led to abuses as clergy exercised "a potentially effective hold on the lives and emotions of parishioners."[35] They further objected to the way ministers had come to be defined in relation to the rituals of the church. In the teaching of some Lutheran scholastic theologians such as Johann Gerhard (1582-1637) and his nephew Johann Andreas Quenstedt (1617-1688), ministers were theologically defined in a similar way to Catholic priests. They were thought to possess "a sacral status as persons deriving from ordination." This blatant assertion of clerical authority was combined with a doctrine of "the objective efficacy inhering in the supernaturally effective word of God," a variation of the doctrine of verbal inspiration extended to formal ritual declarations of the clergy: "The servants of the church have the power of forgiving sins in such a way that they forgive sins, not merely historically by way of declaration [declarative] and announcement [annunciative], but also effectively [effective], yet instrumentally *(werkzeuglich)* they forgive sins."[36] This doctrine had the bizarre effect of turning the pastor's personal speech in liturgical settings, including what he says in the private confessional, into the equivalent of the infallible word of God.

Pietists could not abide such blatant clericalism. They wished to encourage instead the long-neglected Lutheran doctrine of the "priesthood of all believers" through Bible study and the establishment of conventicles where laypeople, men and women together, could meet indepen-

34. John Stroup, *The Struggle for Identity in the Clerical Estate: Northwest German Protestant Opposition to Absolutist Policy in the Eighteenth Century* (Leiden: E. J. Brill, 1984) 29-30.

35. Stroup, *Struggle for Identity*, 30.

36. J. A. Quenstedt, *Theologia didactico-polemica* (1691) 4:402, quoted in Emanuel Hirsch, *Hilfsbuch zum Studium der Dogmatik* (Berlin and Leipzig: Walter de Gruyter, 1951) 369. Cited in Stroup, *Struggle for Identity*, 31.

dently, examine their faith, and upbuild each other. In Brandenburg-Prussia, a territory where they were welcomed by the government and developed a strong base, Pietist leaders led the attack against mandated private confession in the so-called *Berliner Beichtstuhlstreit* (1696-1698), or conflict over the confessional. They persuaded Friedrich III (1657-1713) — later Friedrich I of Prussia — to end mandatory private confession as a legal requirement, replacing it with a public order of "General Confession and General Absolution."

The attack on mandatory private confession by Pietists may be seen as following both an historical precedent and a certain inevitable Protestant logic. The precedent is Nuremberg, where already in 1524 the city fathers and the majority of clergy had discouraged private confession as a "Roman" practice in the interest of reform. As for the logic, Thomas Tentler observes:

> ... when Luther proclaimed "Christian liberty," denied that ordination conferred on priests an inherent power to absolve, affirmed that all believers had the right to pronounce forgiveness, discouraged detailed inquiry into sins (especially secret sins), and rejected the possibility of a complete confession, he prepared the way for the decline and eventual demise of [mandatory private] confession, even though the religious and secular authorities in Lutheran Germany tried to maintain it.[37]

Prince Friedrich's action was received favorably and became broadly influential. During the course of the eighteenth century, the general order of confession and absolution, uncommon in the sixteenth century, became more common in Lutheran liturgies. The general confession and absolution was the means by which public worship became the focus to fulfill the biblical command for self-examination and to protect the laity from clerical abuse of the *Verhör*. A Lutheran church order from Berlin in 1778 exemplifies the order of service that followed from these seventeenth-century reforms:

Morning Hymn
Greeting and a prayer for the beginning of the day
Epistle of the day
Gospel of the day

37. Tentler, "Confession," 403.

Sermon
General confession with absolution
Luther's sanctus hymn
Prayer to Jesus, the Lord's prayer, and the institution narrative
  sung by minister
Hymn verse
Peace of the Lord
Communion
Hymn[38]

Extreme Absolutionism

The position of extreme absolutionism — that is, the teaching that absolution is conveyed solely by the pastor's word, speaking in God's stead and imparted unconditionally — did not fare well up through the eighteenth century. Osiander found himself outside the consensus of church leaders in Nuremberg. The scholastic position lost out in Berlin: "[The] heightening of the Orthodox claims with regard to clerical powers was in fact the immediate preparation for an Orthodox defeat."[39] The consensus position that emerged from the conflict over the confessional in Berlin was that absolution was not "effective" simply by being spoken. What made it effective was the faith of the recipient.[40] This recalls Luther himself. The keys, he said, "demand faith in our hearts, and without faith you cannot use them with profit."[41]

This did not mean that the position of extreme absolutionism disappeared. Especially insofar as it emphasizes the exclusive priestly au-

---

38. Hans-Christoph Schmidt-Lauber, "The Lutheran Tradition in German Lands," *The Oxford History of Christian Worship* (New York: Oxford, 2006) 403, 409. Notice that the general confession and absolution follows the sermon. This echoes the sixteenth-century practice as found in Nuremberg. Professor Karlfried Froehlich of Princeton Seminary, who came from six generations of Lutheran pastors in Saxony, grew up on a service of this general outline and maintained to generations of students that having confession and absolution follow the sermon was the best form because it enhanced the seriousness of the preaching of God's Word.

39. Stroup, *Struggle for Identity*, 32.

40. Paul Graff, *Geschichte der Auflösung der alten gottesdienstlichen Formen in der evangelischen Kirche Deutschlands* I: *Bis zum Eintritt der Aufklärung und des Rationalismus* (Göttingen: Vandenhoeck & Ruprecht, 1937) 377.

41. *LW* 40:375.

thority of the pastor to impart absolution, it is an argument that periodically raises its head within Lutheranism; usually it is associated with a conservative, "high-church" position that conceives society in hierarchical terms. In the nineteenth century, at the time of the debate between Schmucker and Mann, it had been taken up by so-called "Neolutherans" in Germany in the aftermath of the Napoleonic Wars.

The immediate catalyst for the Neolutheran protest was the formation of the Prussian Church of the Evangelical Union by royal decree of the Prussian King, Friedrich Wilhelm III (1770-1840) in 1817. The king was a pious Christian, Reformed in faith, who found it intolerable that he could not share the Lord's Supper with his Lutheran wife. He believed that a united church would advance the Christian cause. Emboldened by Napoleonic precedent of the reorganization of German territories[42] and exercising his legal rights as *summus episcopus,* the King created a "union" church. He prepared his own liturgy and regulations and imposed them on the churches of the territories he controlled. The reaction was fierce, especially among Lutherans. 1817 was, after all, the tercentenary of Luther's revolt. Echoing the first thesis of Luther's "Ninety-Five Theses," Claus Harms (1778-1855), a Lutheran pastor from Kiel in Schleswig-Holstein, laid down the gauntlet: "When our Lord and Master Jesus Christ says, 'Repent,' He wants men to conform themselves to His teaching; He does not conform His teaching to men, as is now the custom in accord with the changed spirit of the time."[43] Any compromise with new political arrangements, or with a theology that might support such arrangements, was thought to be anti-confessional, nothing less than a political form of synergism.

By the mid-nineteenth century conservative Lutherans believed they faced a further threat. The revolutions of 1848 brought down governments from Paris to Prague and had reached as far north as Denmark and as far south as Italy. Progressive forces called for an end to monar-

---

42. After the defeat of German forces at the Battle of Jena-Auerstedt in October, 1806, Napoleon (1769-1821), by a stroke of his pen, ended the formal organization of German states as the Holy Roman Empire and reorganized German territories into confessionally mixed states, Catholic, Lutheran, and Reformed. This reorganization made irrelevant the Peace of Westphalia (1648), which had made peace among the warring Christian parties by defining the religion of particular territories according to the faith of the prince, *eius regio, cuius religio.*

43. Translated and quoted in Carl S. Meyer, *Moving Frontiers* (St. Louis: Concordia, 1964) 66.

chy and the beginning of representative government. Unreconciled to confessionally mixed states and churches, conservative authorities now feared the return of the chaos of the French Revolution with its secular, anti-Christian spirit.

In this political context, the Neolutherans attempted to practice "confessional theology," and they did so in a self-conscious, ideological manner. They honored Luther not only for his doctrine, but as the patriarch of German culture and nationalism. They revived confessional studies, employing an idealistic, historical hermeneutic in which the teachings of the confessions, including the ancient symbols of the Apostles', Nicene, and Athanasian Creeds, were conceived as a development of dogma through which the church experienced both continuity and change in the understanding of revelation across time. This allowed conservative ecclesiastics to claim that the Lutheran church retains its core identity even in the face of the relativism of political change. As a hymn from the 1840s put it:

> Secure Church, our Church
> Her wall, her safety and defense
> Is Augsburg's conquering creed
> A mighty rampart round her.[44]

Despite their declared commitment to Luther and the Confessions, Neolutherans found it difficult to embrace the more radical elements of Reformation theology regarding the church. Luther's early commitment, for example, to the priesthood of all believers, his rejection of ordination as "an invention of the church of the pope" that creates a "detestable tyranny of the clergy over laity by which clergy and laymen should be separated from each other farther than heaven from earth, to the incredible injury of the grace of baptism and to the confusion of our fellowship in the gospel,"[45] his declaration that Scripture gives "overwhelming power to the Christian congregation to preach, to permit preaching, and to call,"[46] were impossible to accept for fear that they would open the floodgates to revolution. According to August Friedrich Christian Vilmar (1800-1868), professor of theology at Mar-

44. Quoted in Karl Barth, *Theology and Church,* tr. Louise Pettibone Smith (London: SCM, 1962) 115.

45. *LW* 36:112.

46. *LW* 39:311.

burg and leader of the Hessian Lutheran Church, the congregation is "a violent sea of all kinds of opinions, contradictory ideas, worldly cares, doubts and contradictions to God's Word."[47] In his view, confessional identity and the popular will were incompatible and this meant that only the ordained ministry can protect the integrity of church teaching. The ordained minister must rule over the congregation. The ministerial office proceeds "directly" from the Lord Christ as "his express mandate, his command." Christ "is behind the exercise [of the office], is active in it, and himself goes in advance of it."[48] This is the source of pastoral authority: "Only from this certainty flows our total fearlessness and absence of regard for person . . . our power through Word and Sacrament to gather the community from out of the new heathenism . . . the power to descend into a soul in which the arch foe has set up his dwelling. . . . The congregation cannot do all this."[49]

Wilhelm Loehe (1808-1872) of Neuendettelsau in Bavaria, one of the most influential and representative of Neolutherans who developed close connections with Lutherans in America, especially the Missouri Synod, took a similar position. The office of ministry stands over against the congregation and is nothing less than the authentic source of the congregation: "Not the office originates from the congregation, but it is more accurate to say, the congregation originates from the office."[50] Without the ministry, the congregation is in danger of being separated from the Lord. Any collegial church order that gives congregations the right to vote on ecclesiastical affairs is "not only unapostolic, but highly dangerous."[51] The idea that congregations can choose their own ministers is out of the question. The clergy must be seen as the "strong princes of the church":[52] like princes they cannot be elected by the people; rather, the ministry arises by succession to the ministerial office, "from person to person, by reason of God."[53]

47. August Friedrich Christian Vilmar, *The Theology of Facts versus the Theology of Rhetoric,* tr. with notes by Roy Harrisville, introduction by Walter Sundberg (Fort Wayne: Lutheran Legacy, 2008; first published 1856) 99.

48. Vilmar, *Theology of Facts,* 101.

49. Vilmar, *Theology of Facts,* 101-2.

50. Wilhelm Loehe, *Gesammelte Werke,* ed. Klaus Ganzert, 7 vols. (Neuendettelsau: Freimund Verlag, 1951-1986) 5/1:262.

51. Loehe, *Gesammelte Werke* 5/1:287-88.

52. Loehe, *Gesammelte Werke* 5/1:274.

53. Loehe, *Gesammelte Werke* 5/1:294.

Loehe was highly suspicious of the interference of the government in church affairs. The prince should not be *summus episcopus*. But this viewpoint did not mean that Loehe embraced the Reformation principle of the freedom of individual Christians and congregations. Rather, it is the clergy, representing their people in synods, who are responsible for the life of the church. If exclusive clerical control cannot be permitted — that is, if there must be leadership in the church directly from the laity — then it is better that the prince rule and not the members of the church: "a tyrant is easier to endure, if indeed one there must be, than the many."[54] Loehe conceived the office of ministry not only as the center of authority in church order, but also as itself a means of grace. Ordination, by the laying on of hands, is nothing less than a consecration. Ordination provides "capability," "privilege," and "charism" for ministry; it is entirely other than "a naked ceremony."[55]

Just how far Loehe was willing to take this notion is apparent in his "New Aphorisms" of 1851, where he declares that there is an essential difference between the word of forgiveness spoken by one Christian to another and the word of forgiveness spoken by the office of the minister: only the latter provides the gift of absolution.[56] He deplored the fact that in his church in Bavaria private confession had devolved into a general preparatory confessional service in which the pastor absolves people by the group. "The preacher absolves people with whom he is not acquainted; he also absolves those addicted to vice and unbelievers."[57] "Without private confession and private absolution, one cannot effectively carry out the pastoral care of awakened souls."[58] Although he preferred private confession, he allowed "both general confession and private confession to remain in use."[59]

When in his *A Plea for the Augsburg Confession* William Julius Mann grounds ministry in "the universal priesthood of all believers," when he claims that the pastor can never be for Lutherans "the embodiment of

54. Loehe, *Gesammelte Werke* 5/1:325.
55. Loehe, *Gesammelte Werke* 5/1:296.
56. Loehe, *Gesammelte Werke* 5/1:549.
57. Wilhelm Loehe, "Einfältiger Beichtunterricht für Christen evangelisch-lutherischen Bekenntnisses" (1836), *Gesammelte Werke*, 3/1:181; see Fred L. Precht, "Confession and Absolution: Sin and Forgiveness," *Lutheran Worship: History and Practice,* ed. Fred L. Precht (St. Louis: Concordia Publishing House, 1993) 347.
58. Loehe, "Einfältiger Beichtunterricht," 182; Precht, "Confession and Absolution," 348.
59. Loehe, "Einfältiger Beichtunterricht," 182.

the power of heaven or hell" or "the representative of a caste," when he makes clear that the church practices confession and absolution not to enhance the power of the clergy but to follow the mandate of Scripture, and when he concedes that private absolution may be too easily misused in a religious environment of revivalism, he is not only defending the Lutheran liturgical tradition against the evangelical Schmucker, who fears a European invasion of the American church by waves of German immigrants. He is also seeking to preserve its fundamental tenets against a conservative confessional party in Europe that claims Lutheran identity exclusively for itself.

And Mann was not without support in German Lutheranism, especially on the matter of pastoral authority. The authoritarian understanding of ordained ministry that Vilmar endorsed was vigorously opposed by prominent Lutherans at the time, especially Johann Wilhelm Friedrich Höfling (1802-1853) and Gottlieb Christoph Adolph von Harless (1806-1879). Höfling insisted that the ministry belongs *iure divino* to the entire Christian community. Ordained ministry is a function of "the universal priesthood."[60] Harless asserted that while the office of ministry has "fullness of power" (that is, while it represents the Lord Jesus Christ independently of congregational control), this independence is nevertheless the result of the call of the church. The authority of the clergy is not grounded in a particular, individualized power and grace that resides within the office itself. Power and grace belongs to the Word, rooted in the living Christ. Christ alone is the foundation of the Word. He alone establishes the office of ministry.[61] The promise of Christ is bestowed on the entire congregation. It does not require the mediation of a priest. In this understanding, democracy and confessional identity are compatible. Mann is on solid ground when he rejects the claim of Schmucker and his companions that the Americanization of Lutheranism mandates revision of the confessions.

---

60. Johann Wilhelm Friedrich Höfling, *Grundsätze evangelisch-lutherischer Kirchenverfassung* (Erlangen: T. Bläsing, 1853) 62, 225. See Holsten Fagerberg, *A New Look at the Lutheran Confessions, 1529-1537*, tr. Gene J. Lund (St. Louis: Concordia Publishing House, 1972), 226.

61. Gottlieb Christoph Adolf Harless, *Kirche und Amt nach lutherischer Lehre* (Stuttgart: Samuel Gottlieb Liesching, 1853), 25.

Forgiveness as Unconditional

The other aspect of extreme absolutionism, originating with Osiander, is the teaching that absolution imparts forgiveness unconditionally: even faith is not required. Faith as a requirement was not an issue in the debate between Schmucker and Mann. Both understood that faith is essential to confession and forgiveness. Their argument concerned different understandings of faith. Schmucker understood faith in evangelical fashion as an act of the will to accept Christ; Mann viewed faith as a gift of God, the sign of which is repentance. But neither doubted that faith was essential to absolution. The issue of faith as a requirement for absolution does come up, however, at least tangentially, in a theological debate among Norwegian Lutherans that began in 1861 and continued for over forty years.

Between June 26 and July 2, 1861, the Norwegian Synod met in Rock Prairie, Wisconsin. Two months earlier the Civil War had begun. Lutherans, like other denominations, were divided over slavery. Among the leaders attending was Peter Laurentius Larsen (1833-1915), at the time serving as the Norwegian professor of theology at Concordia Seminary in St. Louis, the school of the Missouri Synod, where the Norwegian Synod had decided to send its ministerial candidates for theological education. Missouri was a border state. The Missouri Synod held to the position that slavery was not a sin, thus in effect justifying its existence. Larsen wanted to avoid the subject at all costs since the majority of Norwegians as well as many Germans and other Scandinavians were fiercely opposed.[62] He had been asked to give a theological paper on absolution. This he was glad and relieved to do. He brought with him a report from the Missouri Synod on the theology of absolution that had been given the previous October, prepared by Theodore Julius Brohm (1808-1881), a prominent pastoral leader in Missouri who also lectured on Old Testament at Concordia Seminary. Brohm formulated the church's position in eight articles or theses:

1. Absolution, or the forgiveness of sins, is, according to Luther's teachings, the Gospel, whether proclaimed to many or few.
2. Private Absolution is consequently not a power outside, or by the side of, the Gospel to forgive sins; it is nothing else than the preaching of the Gospel to the individual sinner.

---

62. Nelson, ed., *Lutherans in North America*, 239-40.

3. The guardians and givers of Absolution in the public ministry are the preachers of the Gospel. Otherwise it is the function of all Christians, as the whole Church originally was the keeper of the keys; but the one who by the services of these forgives sins is the Triune God.

4. Absolution consists: (a) not in this that the confessor (the pastor) sits as a judge, and returns a verdict concerning the inner condition of the confessant; (b) nor in an empty pronouncement or wish that the sinner be forgiven; but (c) in a powerful impartation of the forgiveness of sins.

5. The effect of Absolution (a) is not contingent upon man's repentance, confession, and atonement, (b) but Absolution demands faith, creates and strengthens faith; (c) without faith it does not profit a man in the least, (d) although it is not therefore a *clavis errans* (a failing key).

6. In private Absolution, no essentially different, or better, forgiveness is given than in the preaching of the Gospel. Further, it need not necessarily be thus administered in order to get the forgiveness of sins, as though no forgiveness of sins takes place without Absolution. Still it has its own peculiar worth and usefulness, because by it the individual is made more certain that he also has the forgiveness of sins.

7. In close connection with private Absolution stands private confession, which latter is nothing else than a request for Absolution. It has moreover also this advantage, that it gives the confessor (the pastor) opportunity to examine people, to apply the Word of God and the *Catechism*, to guard against the unworthy use of the sacraments, and to give all sorts of advice in difficult questions of conscience. Finally, it is a training in self-humiliation. Summa: it is an application of the Law and the Gospel.

8. Confession is not commanded by God, but is, nevertheless, of the greatest usefulness. Consequently this should not be forced upon anyone as a necessary act, but where it exists, it ought to be maintained; where it has fallen into disuse, it ought to be revived by recommending it and praising its usefulness.[63]

63. Translated and quoted in J. Magnus Rohne, *Norwegian American Lutheranism up to 1872* (New York: Macmillan, 1926) 227-28. The theses and a summary of the debate at the meeting of the Norwegian Synod were published in the monthly periodical of the Synod, *Kirkelig Maanedstidende,* in 1861.

This document expresses much that is common to traditional Lutheran understanding. Against a post-Reformation trend, it affirms private confession and absolution, a practice commended by Neolutherans in Germany, above all Wilhelm Loehe, and defended by the Missouri Synod, largely in practical, pastoral terms as an aid to examination of oneself and opportunity for pastors to give advice on "difficult questions of conscience." It does not argue, as Osiander had, that private absolution is the only form to obtain forgiveness. Also against Osiander, the document states that absolution requires faith: "without faith it does not profit a man in the least." Against Loehe, the document declares pointedly that absolution "is the function of all Christians," not just the clergy. What else would one expect given the tumultuous early history of the Synod in which its first leader, Martin Stephan (1777-1846), who brought the original group from Saxony to America, ended up being dismissed in disgrace for reasons of financial mismanagement and sexual misconduct? This made the small band of immigrants distrustful of pastors. But the document also speaks of the objectivity of the ritual act of absolution, asserting that it is "a powerful impartation of the gospel"; that it "creates" faith; that in no circumstances can it be understood as "a failing key," meaning, presumably, that it does what it says. In such claims there is some of the spirit, if not the letter, of Osiander's old argument.

In supporting the theses, Larsen emphasized these objectivist elements in the theses. John Magnus Rohne (1891-1958) summarizes Larsen's argument as follows:[64] "the impartation of the forgiveness of sins on God's part [is] not contingent upon anything human, which always is uncertain and faltering, but wholly upon God's work and word." The Gospel is "nothing but a declaration of the forgiveness of sins," such forgiveness having been accomplished for "the whole world" by the merit of Christ and the affirmation of Christ by God in raising him from the dead. "Absolution is powerful in the case of the unconverted as well as in the case of the converted." Faith "is a mere empty hand which lets itself be filled by God." The sole condition for absolution "is Christ's perfect satisfaction." Thus the pastor is called to preach repentance, "but must not demand it in such a way that people base their hope of forgiveness on it."

Bernt Julius Muus (1832-1900), pastor of Holden Church in Kenyon,

---

64. See Rohne, *Norwegian American Lutheranism*, 228-29.

Minnesota, was given responsibility to lead the discussion that followed. Muus questioned the notion of "impartation," suspicious that it made forgiveness unconditional, extended even to unbelievers. In reply it was argued that "the forgiveness of sins were actually given to both believers and unbelievers, penitent and impenitent . . . in short, unconditionally to all who hear it." That which is "holy" remains holy, even if it is given to "dogs" (Matthew 7:6). The sinner receives forgiveness, although he may despise it or "refuse to believe." The general sympathy in the meeting was for an objectivist position that recalled, if it did not directly follow, Osiander. "Extreme absolutionism" was back on the table. If any group of Norwegian Lutherans in America represented the church type which "is able to receive the masses, and to adjust itself to the world, because, to a certain extent, it can afford to ignore the need for subjective holiness for the sake of the objective treasures of grace and of redemption,"[65] it was the Norwegian Synod. God gives his grace to all who hear it. "For this reason," said Ulrik Vilhelm Koren (1826-1910), prominent pastor and church leader of the Norwegian Synod, writing in 1867, "we use the expression 'The Gospel gives the forgiveness of sins to all who hear it, both believers and unbelievers.'"[66] This is unconditional absolution.

Other Norwegians in the Midwest took up the issue. The Scandinavian Augustana Synod, pietist and evangelical in its morphology, objected to the idea of impartation in a synod meeting in 1864. The gospel bestows forgiveness on believers, not unbelievers. With this position other evangelical Lutheran groups such as the Eielsen's Synod agreed. The pietist strain representing the sect-type morphology within the Lutheran fold ran deep among Norwegian Lutheran immigrants to the Midwest.

The Norwegian Synod decided to let go of the phrase "powerful impartation" in 1872.[67] The argument among Lutherans in the Midwest between "objectivism" and "subjectivism" in the understanding of salvation was transformed at the end of the decade into a full-scale debate over election. This time the Missouri Synod became fully involved in the debate. Conflict over absolution continued as a subset of the larger

65. Ernst Troeltsch, *The Social Teachings of the Christian Churches,* tr. Olive Wyon (New York: Harper Torchbooks, 1960) 2:481.

66. S. C. Ylvisaker, ed., *Grace for Grace: Brief History of the Norwegian Synod* (Mankato: Lutheran Synod Book Co., 1943) 158.

67. Rohne, *Norwegian American Lutheranism,* 233.

issue. In March 1906, meeting at United Church Seminary (Luther Seminary after 1917), the United Norwegian Lutheran Church, the Hauge Synod (both groups evangelical in temperament), and the Norwegian Synod came to a compromise agreement on absolution, expressed in five theses:

1. Absolution, which according to God's command and in His name is given those who desire the consolation of the Gospel, is God's own absolving act through the office of the Word.

2. In Absolution God declares to the sinner the forgiveness of all his sins as a gracious and promised good, which is established and procured by the merit of Christ's blood, and stored up for reception in the Gospel's gracious promises.

3. The means whereby the sinner receives, appropriates, and becomes partaker of the gift of forgiveness, and, in Absolution as if by God Himself, must be tendered, declared, and presented, is faith.

4. Absolution is always a genuine and valid Absolution of God, although it does not benefit without faith, and although an impenitent and unbelieving hypocrite does not become a partaker of the gift of the forgiveness of sins which is declared unto him.

5. When, according to customary church language, it is rightly said that only the penitent should be absolved, it is not thereby said that the administrators of the office of the keys are able to try the hearts and pass judgment on the condition of the confessant's heart, but only that it is their duty conscientiously to exercise care in regard to the confessant's confession in word and life in order not to give that which is holy to the dogs or throw the pearls to the swine (Matt. vii.6).[68]

This agreement moved the Norwegians into the direction of mainstream American Lutheranism as it had developed by the end of the nineteenth century. There is no mention of private confession and absolution. The default position appears to be a public order. As is fitting for such an order, absolution is declared to be conditional. It is conditional in that "it is given to those who desire the consolation of the Gospel." Faith is the "means" by which forgiveness is "tendered, declared, presented" and "received." In declaring absolution, the "administrators of the office of the keys" are duty bound "conscientiously to

68. Rohne, *Norwegian American Lutheranism,* 232.

exercise care in regard to the confessant's confession in word and life in order not to give that which is holy to the dogs or throw the pearls to the swine (Matt. vii.6)." In these assertions, there is not even a hint of extreme absolutism. The spirit of Osiander, at least for the time being, is nowhere to be found.

A Public Order of Confession

To return to the primary debate in American Lutheranism over confession and absolution — that between Schmucker and Mann — there is no doubt that Schmucker lost. His program for Americanization failed. His attempt to revise the wording of the hallowed Augsburg Confession was the wrong strategy. The *Definite Platform* was in fact so controversial that it led to the formation of a rival ecclesiastical organization, the General Council, in 1864. Mann, the confessional theologian, won the day, carried on the shoulders of scores of German immigrants who flooded America after 1840, a number so huge that two and a quarter million claimed membership in the Lutheran Church by 1910, making Lutherans the third largest Protestant denomination in America.[69] As long as the debate over the *Platform* lasted, however, it was a powerful and significant influence on pastors and teachers in the Lutheran church. Many theological debates are not worth the paper they are printed on, but this one was.

The debate was important because it raised the fundamental theological issue of Lutheran identity. How essential is, to use Mann's words, "the practice of the Lutheran Church from the beginning"? Can such practice evolve? What about Schmucker's argument concerning historical change and the claims of culture? In the nineteenth century, Lutherans decided that Schmucker's proposal of Americanization went too far. "We cannot conceal our sorrow," said Charles Porterfield Krauth (1823-1883), comrade in arms with William Julius Mann, "that the term, 'America' should be made so emphatic, dear and hallowed though it be to our heart." "Why," he asked, "should we break or weaken the golden chain which unites us to the high and holy association of our history as a church by thrusting into a false position a word

---

69. Abdel Ross Wentz, *A Basic History of Lutheranism in America*, rev. ed. (Philadelphia: Fortress, 1964) 177.

which makes a national appeal?"[70] The Lutheran liturgical tradition cannot give way to the "new measures" of revivalism. The divine imperative to examine oneself is rightly conceived and executed in a churchly order of confession and absolution in which both the binding and the loosing keys are exercised clearly and specifically. Private confession may be used, but it may not work in the American environment. A public order of confession and absolution, however, is necessary and salutary to fulfill the biblical command to examine oneself.

Already in the sixteenth century, Lutherans in Holland, who appeared to have had a good handle on how to examine oneself, employed a public order exclusively. The particulars of this order are quoted admiringly by Henry Eyster Jacobs (1844-1932) in his *History of the Evangelical Lutheran Church in the United States* (1893), the first great classic account of the story of Lutheranism in America. Jacobs was professor of systematic theology at Lutheran Seminary at Philadelphia (Mount Airy) and later president. He was a long-time colleague of William Julius Mann. In his *History,* Jacobs identifies with Dutch Lutherans of the Reformation. They were "the pioneers of Lutheranism in America"[71] and thus the forebears of all Lutherans who are Americans. As Lutherans in colonial America lived in a religious culture dominated by the Reformed Protestantism, so did the Dutch Lutherans before them. And they prospered. Jacobs quotes a Jesuit from the sixteenth century named Strada who observed religious competition in the city of Antwerp: "The Lutherans . . . excelled the Calvinists or Reformed, and the Anabaptists, with respect to the quality of their adherents and followers, who consisted of the principal inhabitants."[72] Whether the judgment of this Jesuit was true or not may be debated. What is clear is that Jacobs identifies with the claim. It is a way for him to praise the ancestors. As part of this praise he quotes in full the public order for confes-

---

70. Charles Porterfield Krauth, *The Conservative Reformation and Its Theology* (1872), quoted in Theodore G. Tappert, ed., *Lutheran Confessional Theology in America, 1840-1880* (New York: Oxford, 1972) 47. Krauth was a graduate of Gettysburg Seminary, a prominent pastor, and a rival of Schmucker eventually denied the opportunity to be Schmucker's successor at Gettysburg and then becoming Professor of Dogmatics at the new Lutheran Theological Seminary in Philadelphia, the competing school to Gettysburg established by the General Council, then finally Professor and Provost at the University of Pennsylvania.

71. Jacobs, *History of the Evangelical Lutheran Church,* 22.

72. Jacobs, *History of the Evangelical Lutheran Church,* 28.

sion and absolution that the Dutch Lutherans formulated in the late sixteenth century.

Confession was not private, but public: "a preparatory service with public absolution . . . held the preceding Friday" to Sunday Communion. In this public order, the pastor leads the congregation in rigorous, existential self-examination of their sins and directs them to promise amendment of life:

1. I ask you, in God's stead, whether you experience in yourselves, and with humble hearts, confess that you are poor, lost sinners, who have often and grievously offended the Lord your God, secretly and openly, knowingly and ignorantly, in thoughts, words, and deeds, and besides have in various ways also injured your neighbors, and have thus deserved all temporal and eternal punishments? And do you pray God to forgive you? *Answer*, Yes.

2. I ask you whether you firmly believe that God, according to his infinite mercy, for the sake of the precious merits of Jesus Christ, his Son, not only forgives you all your sins, but also, as a seal thereof, in the Lord's Supper gives us his Body and Blood, under the bread and wine to eat and drink? Is this your sincere belief? *Answer*, Yes.

3. I ask you whether it be also by God's grace, your purpose to amend your sinful lives, to bring forth the true fruits of repentance and faith, to show yourselves to be new creatures in Christ, to walk in the Spirit, after the new man, and not only to forgive from the heart your neighbor who has offended you, but also to prove your love to him, and henceforth to remain faithful to God's everlasting Word, and our true Christian religion even unto death? *Answer*, Yes.

The minister then assures the congregation that by grace God will enable Christian obedience:

The Faithful and Merciful God, who has given you to will this, will also enable you to accomplish it, to the glory of his holy name, and to everlasting salvation of you all, through Jesus Christ. Amen.

This is followed by the call to confession and the confession itself in the form of prayer:

Humble yourselves, then, before the Lord your God, confess to him, with broken and contrite hearts, all your sins and pray with me:

Most Just and Merciful God, we poor men confess not only that we have been conceived and born in sins, but that we have often offended against thy holy commandments and grievously transgressed them. But as Jesus Christ has come into the world to save sinners, we pray, O faithful God and Father, that, for Christ's sake thou wouldst forgive all our sins, receive us into thy grace, and grant us everlasting life. Grant us also, Heavenly Father, heartfelt repentance, firm faith, true godliness of life, and steadfastness, even unto the end, through Jesus Christ. Amen.

Last there comes the absolution, conditional in form, befitting public confession. The minister exercises the office of the keys, according to the authority of Christ in Scripture. It is dependent on confession and made effective by repentance in faith, not by priestly mediation:

Upon this, your confession and prayer to God, as a minister of Jesus Christ, and in accordance with his Word in John, the twentieth chapter, "Whosoever sins ye remit, they are remitted unto them; and whosoever sins ye retain, they are retained," I declare unto all who are penitent the forgiveness of all their sins, in the name of the Father, and of the Son, and of the Holy Ghost. But unto the impenitent, their sins are retained, until they amend, for which may God grant them grace, through Jesus Christ, in whose name we pray: "Our Father who art in heaven," etc.[73]

This public order has an admirable solemnity and directness. Its dignified and concentrated expression can bear repeating without going stale. It warns worshipers of the responsibility to examine themselves, thereby holding before them the full seriousness of the binding key while lifting the spirit with the promise of divine help and the mercy of the loosing key. The old Dutch order reflects the ideal that Mann sought to defend against Schmucker in his *Plea for the Augsburg Confession*. With this ideal Jacobs fully agreed.

73. Jacobs, *History of the Evangelical Lutheran Church*, 40-41.

CHAPTER V

Emergence of an Opposing Tradition

The "Original Sin Moment"

In its issue of February 15, 1950, *The Lutheran,* the denominational magazine of the United Lutheran Church in America (ULCA), announced that a new "motion picture" entitled *The Difference* was now available through "synodical film distributors" and would be shown in congregations over the course of the next two months.[1] The purpose of the film was to recruit high school students to Lutheran schools of higher education and to launch an ambitious stewardship campaign to support the fourteen colleges and nine seminaries associated with the church. *The Difference* was no small enterprise. It was a forty-five-minute drama, produced by Cathedral Films of Hollywood using professional actors. The script was prepared under the direction of Henry Endress (1914-1981), executive secretary of the ULCA stewardship office and executive secretary of the Lutheran Layman's Movement.[2]

As a propaganda device to recruit students and raise money, *The Difference* defies the usual expectations. Instead of singing the praises of the idyllic campuses of particular Lutheran colleges connected to the ULCA, the film invents a generic school, using nondescript buildings

---

1. Henry Endress, "Explaining 'The Difference,'" *The Lutheran* 32.20 (February 15, 1950): 12-17.

2. *The Difference* was only one of many films that Endress produced. His *Martin Luther* (1952) received two Oscar nominations and was seen by millions across the globe. See William O. Avery, *Empowered Laity: The Story of the Lutheran Laity Movement* (Minneapolis: Augsburg Fortress, 1997) 71.

and grounds as a backdrop to the story. The film was shot in various locations around Los Angeles (including a local community college), none of which had any Lutheran association. Neither Martin Luther himself nor the term "Lutheran" figure in the film in any significant way. The focus instead is on what it means to be a "Christian" and to attend a "Christian" college. The biggest surprise is the plot. The film tells the fictional story of "Paul Reed," who, we are told at the very beginning of the film, does not want to go to a Christian college but does so at the wish of his widowed mother. We also learn that Paul's uncle, "William Saunders," who pays his nephew's bills and has a place reserved for him in the management of the family's manufacturing business, has no interest in things Christian. While he accedes to his sister's desire for her son to be educated at a Christian college, Saunders warns Paul not to be softened by religion. Saunders is a tough, "dog-eat-dog" businessman who rules his employees with an iron fist. This is not a promising scenario for a movie interested in the recruitment of young people from Luther League.

When Paul arrives at the college his attitude gets him into trouble right from the start. Faithful students and teachers try to show Paul that he can be both a Christian and a businessman, but it does no good. Lest one think that the students are all faithful and sure of their vocation, there is a minor plot involving "Don White," a student planning to go into the ministry but who is plagued by doubts, even to the point of failing to show up one evening at chapel when he is scheduled to preach. Life is complicated.

Before the first twenty minutes of the film are over, Paul is expelled from the college and is struggling to find his way. His "dog-eat-dog" uncle puts him on the assembly line to teach him a lesson. One day at work, Paul witnesses his uncle firing a long-time employee for being absent because of his sick wife. Shocked by this brutal act, Paul begins to rethink the course of his life. He does this in neither church nor the churchly environment of a Christian college, but on the assembly line, that is, in the "real world." When Paul returns to school, he is ready to listen. He is especially moved by the witness of an international scholarship student from India, "Chitta Ranjan," whose story of growing up an "untouchable" and coming to Christ because of the kindness of Christian doctors who cared for him when he was deathly ill as a boy, is the emotional highpoint of the film. Chitta proclaims that the love of Christians is grounded in the atoning sacrifice of Christ who died even for someone who is untouchable. There are more trials and tribulations Paul must undergo (including an attack of appendicitis that lands him in the hospital), but by the end he commits himself to Christ. At his graduation, he confronts his uncle, telling him that he will not work for the firm unless changes are made.

The Difference is a remarkable film. I have shown it to many classes of seminary students over the years as a representative artifact of the church of their grandparents' generation. The students laugh at much that is old-fashioned — the style of dress, the way male-female relationships are depicted, the stilted language — but within a few minutes they are taken in by the drama. They realize that this is a story about becoming a Christian, not about being a Lutheran, that grace results from struggle, not comfort, that life is shaped by the challenge and threat of sin. They admire the awareness of what we call today the "global church" in the figure of Chitta Ranjan. They are surprised by the socially aware criticism of harsh aspects of the business world. *The Difference* is not a glossy commercial for Lutheran colleges, but a forthright invitation to discipleship, to live life seriously as vocation in obedience to Christ.

Living life seriously was an issue much on the mind of the generations to which *The Difference* was addressed. In 1950 both parents and older children finishing high school age had faced the Great Depression and World War II. Many had to live their lives, like Paul Reed, without a father. People were ready to settle down, buy homes in the suburbs, and raise families. People did these things together in large numbers. The migration to the suburbs in the 1950s was the second largest migration of twentieth-century America, only exceeded by the migration from Europe to America in the two decades after 1900. The post-war generation also went to church. Every denomination increased its numbers. In 1940 less than half of adults belonged to institutional churches; by 1960 the number had risen to 65%. "The result," writes Andrew Finstuen, "was an astounding renewal within Protestantism, the twentieth-century equivalent of the First and Second Great Awakenings."[3]

The 1950s are often characterized as a period of repression and con-

---

3. Andrew S. Finstuen, *Original Sin and Everyday Protestants: The Theology of Reinhold Niebuhr, Billy Graham, and Paul Tillich in an Age of Anxiety* (Chapel Hill: The University of North Carolina Press, 2009) 13.

formity in which "suburbanization" became the dominant force. Suburban religion has been subject to scathing criticism, one critic asserting that "the homogenized suburbanite . . . likes his religion, unlike his martinis, diluted."[4] Popular books of the time such as Norman Vincent Peale's *The Power of Positive Thinking* (1952) are commonly scorned by academics and intellectuals as typical of the era. Gibson Winter (1916-2002) made the ultimate case for contempt in *The Suburban Captivity of the Church* (1962), a landmark book that influenced a generation of mainline church leaders.

This criticism is a distortion of the period. The post-war generation was not only conformist; it also worried about the dangers of conformity and the toll it takes on personal identity. David Riesman in *The Lonely Crowd* (1950) warned about the dangers of being "other directed" and thus losing identity. Movies such as *The Best Years of Our Lives* (1946) and *The Man in the Gray Flannel Suit* (1955), based on a popular novel, dealt with the psychological scars of returning veterans. The meaning of life was much on the minds of men and women who had sacrificed so much.

So was the transcendent. Reflection on things divine took place against the sober backdrop of the Cold War and the threat of nuclear annihilation. It also produced what Finstuen calls an "original sin moment" in American culture in which the general public, across a broad range, was ready to hear a stern message about the predicament of a world mired in sin and standing under the judgment of God.[5] Important figures such as Reinhold Niebuhr (1892-1971) and Paul Tillich (1886-1965) became widely known. *The Saturday Evening Post* with its long-running "Adventures of the Mind" series and *Time* magazine, presided over by Henry Luce (1898-1967), the son of Presbyterian missionaries to China, were notable for the literate and thoughtful way they engaged prominent Christian intellectuals and brought their ideas to the attention of the general public. Niebuhr made the cover of *Time* in March 1948, Tillich in March 1959. Tillich's work of existential Christian psychology, *The Courage to Be,* was a bestseller in 1952. The great revivalist preacher Billy Graham was beginning his extraordinary career. Original sin was his core theological belief. "Religion," writes Niebuhr,

4. Stanley Rowland, "Suburbia Buys Religion," *Nation* (July 28, 1956), quoted in Finstuen, *Original Sin and Everyday Protestants,* 27.

5. See Finstuen, *Original Sin and Everyday Protestants,* 1-67.

"is not simply as is generally supposed an inherently virtuous human quest for God. It is merely a final battle ground between God and man's self-esteem."[6] At mid-century, a surprising number of ordinary Christians — Catholic, evangelical, or mainline — could identify with this idea: Christianity as self-examination and repentance. In its own modest way, the ULCA recruitment film, *The Difference*, tapped into this remarkable "original sin moment" in American culture.

Worship as Repentance

A movie like *The Difference* would be unthinkable today in most Lutheran quarters or in mainline Protestantism generally. A church college in today's world would want to make an individual presentation to students. It would not want to be lumped together with all other schools of the denomination, let alone be represented by the generic idea of a fictional Lutheran school. The assertion that conversion to Christ is the center of the educational enterprise, which is so central to the plot of *The Difference*, would be wholeheartedly rejected. The fact is that church colleges long ago loosened their denominational ties.

The Difference does not represent the church today. But it represented the church of its day. That faith is a struggle, that sin is ever present, and that commitment to Christ entails amendment of life: these were precepts that Lutheran clergy and laity shared over half a century ago. These precepts were undergirded and reinforced not only by the preaching and teaching of Lutherans but also by worship. In making the film, Henry Endress, an official of the ULCA, could also rely on the rich resources of Lutheran liturgical practice to teach people the basics of the faith, especially confession and absolution, that exercise blessed by repetition week after week, month after month, year after year. Confession and absolution taught that faith requires self-examination, repentance, and the commitment to change.

For the wisdom and depth of this liturgical heritage, the ULCA was indebted to leaders such as William Julius Mann, who, in his debate with Samuel Simon Schmucker, defended confession and absolution as essential to Lutheran identity in America. Mann put the issue plainly. Confes-

---

6. Reinhold Niebuhr, *The Nature and Destiny of Man*, 2 vols. (New York: Scribner, 1941-1943) 1:200.

sion and absolution are grounded in scriptural mandate: "We all know how urgently the Gospel enjoins us to beware of an unworthy participation of the body and blood of Christ." "Examine the self," commands St. Paul, "lest one eat unto damnation." For this reason, "the Church could not do better than institute a particular service, preparatory to the celebration of the Lord's Supper."[7] Mann argued that while the practice of private confession is part of authentic Lutheran tradition, the use of a public order of confession is most fitting for the American religious environment. This became the consensus position for the denominations that would eventually make up the ULCA, and it became the practice for the majority of Lutheran denominations in America.

Mann spoke eloquently as to the purpose of this public order. It is to provide the occasion "to move the hearts of men, to preach to them repentance, and to warn them of a portentous responsibility. And all those who are lingering after the comfort of forgiveness of sins can there, at the same time, hear the blessed word of pardon, pronounced according to the command of Christ."[8] The presiding minister is "the duly appointed officer" of the congregation, whose office is to proclaim in the name of Christ, "the good tidings of forgiveness to the penitent, and the awful wrath of God to the impenitent and to the hypocrite."[9] This is the office of the keys, both binding and loosing.

The "Order for Public Confession Preparatory to The Holy Communion" in the *Common Service Book and Hymnal of the Lutheran Church* (1917), authorized by the General Synod, the General Council, and the United Synod in the South, is the preeminent example of such a service.[10] It is biblically anchored and grounded in Lutheran theology and liturgical practice. It is modeled after orders for public confession then already in use. It is serious, elevated in expression while at the same time plainspoken, the type of service that can bear repetition across the years of a person's life and go deep in the soul. By 1950 it had been in use for an entire generation.

The Public Order for Confession was originally prepared as part of

7. W. J. Mann, *A Plea for the Augsburg Confession* (Philadelphia: Lindsay & Blakiston, 1856) 22.

8. Mann, *Plea,* 23.

9. Mann, *Plea,* 24.

10. *Common Service Book of the Lutheran Church* (Philadelphia and Columbia: The Lutheran Publication Society, The General Council Publication Board, the Lutheran Board of Publication, 1917) 264-69. See Appendix I.

the *Church Book,* a remarkable achievement of Lutheran liturgical scholarship in the nineteenth century put together by a distinguished committee under the leadership of Beale M. Schmucker (1827-1888) of the General Council, son of Samuel Simon Schmucker, George U. Wenner (1844-1934), representing the General Synod, and Edward T. Horn (1850-1915) of the General Synod South. These men assembled a Lutheran liturgical order of service based on their assessment of the consensus of sixteenth-century practice. The order was as follows:

     I. Introit
    II. Kyrie
   III. Gloria in Excelsis
   IV. Collect
    V. Epistle
   VI. Alleluia
  VII. Gospel
 VIII. Creed
   IX. Sermon
    X. General Prayer
   XI. Preface
  XII. Sanctus and Hosanna
 XIII. Exhortation to Communicants
 XIV. Lord's Prayer and Words of Institution *or* Words of Institution and Lord's Prayer
  XV. Agnus Dei
 XVI. Distribution
XVII. Collect of Thanksgiving
XVIII. Benediction[11]

Notable is the exhortation to communicants, common to sixteenth-century Lutheran worship. The exhortation served to guard the Table and call worshipers to repentance. After much debate, the three leaders decided to include a public order for confession and absolution as well as a private order. Public orders were not common in the sixteenth century since private confession was legally mandated in most Lutheran territories. But a public order had become common in much of Ameri-

---

11. This list is from E. T. Horn, "The Lutheran Sources of the Common Service," *Quarterly Review of the Evangelical Lutheran Church* 21 (1891): 244.

can Lutheran liturgical practice and had received an eloquent defense by William Julius Mann.[12]

The rubrics for the public order instruct that it should be used as a "Vesper Service" scheduled for "the afternoon or evening of the Friday or Saturday preceding the Holy Communion" for those "who purpose to commune." Essential portions of it (the exhortation, the confession, and the absolution) can also be employed to precede the communion service itself on Sunday morning. The order opens dramatically with a plea for deliverance ("Make haste, O God, to deliver me," Psalm 70:1) and the acknowledgement that a "broken spirit" is a sacrifice to God that he will not despise, "a broken and contrite heart" (Psalm 51:17). The full text of Psalm 51, the great penitential psalm that tradition ascribes to David after his sin with Bathsheba, follows to be sung or said. It is the plea of a person of contrite heart who in shame is willing to engage in the examination of the self by facing up to sins committed and confessing one's essential nature: "Behold I was shapen in inquity: and in sin did my mother conceive me" (v. 5). Despite sin, faith and trust lead the sinner to turn to God, as David did, believing that the God of the Bible is not a remote, absolute deity of arbitrary power, but a God who is known in concrete acts of grace, caring for his people. As Luther says in his commentary on the psalm (1532),

> The people of Israel did not have a God who was viewed "absolutely," to use the expression the way inexperienced monks rise into heaven with their speculations and think about God as He is in Himself. From this absolute God everyone should flee who does not want to perish, because human nature and the absolute God . . . are the bitterest enemies. Human weakness cannot help being crushed by such majesty, as Scripture reminds us over and over. Let no one, therefore, interpret David as speaking with the absolute God. He is speaking with God as He is dressed and clothed in His Word and promises, so that from the name "God" we cannot exclude Christ whom God promised to Adam and the other patriarchs. We must take hold of this God, not naked but clothed and revealed in His Word; otherwise certain despair will crush us.[13]

12. For both the private order for confession and absolution and the public order, see *Church Book for the Use of Evangelical Lutheran Congregations* (Philadelphia: General Council's Publication Board, 1893) 364-73.

13. *LW* 12:312.

There then follows the Lesson, a list of thirteen possible texts, four from the Old Testament. They concern confession of sin (e.g., 1 John 1:8: "If we say we have no sin, we deceive ourselves and the truth is not in us"), but also include the reading of the Ten Commandments (Exodus 20:1-17) and St. Paul's admonition to examine oneself (1 Corinthians 11:23-29). These may be used for a preparatory address or sermon.

After a hymn comes the exhortation to communicants. It opens by reminding the hearers of St. Paul's command to self-examination and instructs them that the Lord's Supper is for the repentant who desire to turn from their sinful ways: "For this Holy Sacrament hath been instituted for the special comfort and strengthening of those who humbly confess their sins, and who hunger and thirst after righteousness." The penitent sinner is to eat the bread and drink the cup in faith: "Therefore whoso eateth of this Bread and drinketh of this Cup, firmly believing the words of Christ, dwelleth in Christ, and Christ in Him, and hath eternal life."

After the familiar prayer imploring God to "cleanse the thoughts of our hearts by the inspiration of Thy Holy Spirit," there follows the confession proper. This is the examination or *Verhör* in brief form that emphasizes for communicants what Wilhelm Julius Mann called "the portentous responsibility" of faith, exhorting them to have the "earnest desire" to be delivered from sin and the "earnest purpose" to obey God and "strive daily after holiness of heart and life":

THE CONFESSION

I ASK you in the presence of Almighty God, Who searcheth the heart:

DO you truly acknowledge, confess, and lament that you are by nature sinful, and that by omitting to do good and by doing evil you have in thought, word and deed, grieved and offended your God and Saviour, and thereby justly deserved His condemnation?

If this be the sincere confession of your hearts, declare it by saying: Yes.

Answer: Yes.

DO you truly believe that Jesus Christ came into the world to save sinners, and that all who believe on His Name receive the forgiveness of sins? Do you, therefore, earnestly desire to be delivered from all your sins, and are you confident that it is the gracious will of your Heavenly Father, for Christ's Sake, to forgive your sins and to cleanse you from all unrighteousness?

If so, confess it by saying: Yes.

Answer: Yes.

IS it your earnest purpose, henceforth, to be obedient to the Holy Spirit, so as to hate and forsake all manner of sin, to live as in God's presence, and to strive daily after holiness of heart and life? If so, answer: Yes.

Answer: Yes.

Let us humbly kneel, and make confession unto God, imploring His forgiveness through Jesus Christ our Lord.

¶Then shall all kneel, and say:

O GOD, our Heavenly Father, I confess unto Thee that I have grievously sinned against Thee in many ways; not only by outward transgression, but also by secret thoughts and desires, which I cannot fully understand, but which are all known unto Thee. I do earnestly repent, and am heartily sorry for these my offences, and I beseech Thee of Thy great goodness to have mercy upon me, and for the sake of Thy dear Son Jesus Christ, our Lord, to forgive my sins, and graciously to help my infirmities. Amen.

After the examination, the minister pronounces the absolution. It is conditional in form, giving full statement to both the loosing and binding keys:

THE ABSOLUTION

ALMIGHTY God, our Heavenly Father, hath had mercy upon us, and for the sake of the sufferings, death and resurrection of His dear Son Jesus Christ, our Lord, forgiveth us all our sins. As a Minister of the Church of Christ, and by His authority, I therefore declare unto you who do truly repent and believe in Him, the entire forgiveness of all your sins: In the Name of the Father, and of the Son, and of the Holy Ghost.

On the other hand, by the same authority, I declare unto the impenitent and unbelieving, that so long as they continue in their impenitence, God hath not forgiven their sins, and will assuredly visit their iniquities upon them, if they turn not from their evil ways, and come to true repentance and faith in Christ, ere the day of grace be ended.

The service concludes with the Lord's Prayer and a Collect for Peace, a peace "that the world cannot give" and through which the believers' "hearts may be set to obey Thy commandments."

This order for public confession fulfills the purpose of worship as argued in this book: *to call Christians to repentance, to warn them to be under no illusion as to who they are and how far they fall short when they stand before God and holy things, to teach them to worship God in humility, to feed them the Bread of Life, and to make them ready to give testimony to Christ in word and deed.* It is austere and uncompromising in calling Christians to explicit faith and discipleship, the latter understood as striving for holiness of life. This calls to mind the moral fervor of the early church. In faith and discipleship are the benefits of the Sacrament of the Altar received. Without faith and the thirst for righteousness, the communicant eats unto judgment. There is in this service no "cheap grace" of the formalistic assurance of forgiveness, no avoidance of the issue of "subjective holiness" that marks the church-type morphology. No one would label the ULCA a denomination that taught one-time conversion theology. That the sinner will fall into sin again, even a converted sinner such as "Paul Reed" in *The Difference,* was not a matter for debate. In good Lutheran fashion, the individual Christian was understood as *simul iustus et peccator:* "at the same time sinner and saved." A strictly evangelical theology of conversion had been rejected when Schmucker's attempt at reform failed to gain consensus.

Thus, the *Common Service Book and Hymnal* reflects not American evangelicalism, but the broad stream of traditional Lutheran teaching in America at the end of the nineteenth century. The Order for Public Confession is a scripted liturgical service. It calls worshipers to repentance not as a one-time event, like conversion at a revival meeting.

Rather, the service witnesses to grace as an experience of blessed repetition in which the divine promise to forgive those who truly repent and believe is offered each time that the liturgy of confession and absolution takes place. Though the sinner falls into sin again and again, betraying Christ, the promise of the Lord is that he will set the Table again and again so that the believer who opens her heart may receive forgiveness through the body and blood of the Lord. While Lutheran morphology may have deep-seated sectarian elements, challenging the individual believer to amendment of life and calling to mind the eschatological consciousness of the early church, it never finally abandons the ambition of the medieval and modern "church type" to embrace all people. Liturgical repetition of a public order of confession and absolution is the sign of this openness. But it is also the case that the act of worship is meant to change the worshiper, not symbolically, not *ex opere operato,* but in heart and action. This is what the Order for Public Confession in the *Common Service Book and Hymnal* sought to accomplish. Change in heart and action is how Paul Reed becomes a Christian in *The Difference.* The lesson of the movie is the lesson of the ULCA's own officially sanctioned worship. *Lex orandi, lex credendi:* "as we worship, so we believe."

The Morphology of American Lutheranism at Mid-Twentieth Century

Lutheranism in America at mid-twentieth century appeared to the culture at large as having an intriguing combination of rigor and openness. It is no surprise that Lutherans took part in the denominational growth of the post-war period. Indeed, they prospered, bringing together a spirit for evangelical outreach with a sober understanding of the "original sin moment." In April 1958 the President of the ULCA in America, Franklin Clark Fry (1900-1968), made the cover of *Time,* which called him "Mr. Protestant": "perhaps the most influential leader of world Protestantism." Lutherans in the United States numbered nearly 7,400,000; they had gained a remarkable 2,000,000 members in the ten years between 1948 and 1958. "The Lutheran Hour" was the best known denominational radio broadcast on the air. "This Is the Life" was the biggest-budget religious telecast in the country. All this activity was going on even though Lutherans were divided into seventeen separate synodical organizations.[14] "What do the Lutheran converts find in their new churches?" asked *Time:* "They find above all two things still relatively unchanged — liturgy and theology."[15] Worship grounded in a theology of repentance was a powerful instrument for witness and an engine for growth. Writing in 1961, perhaps with the cover story from *Time* in mind, distinguished American church historian Winthrop S. Hudson ventured the opinion that "the final prospect for a vigorous renewal of Protestant life and witness rests with the Lutheran churches." He noted their ability to grow in the post-war period and their coalescing into three major bodies, the Missouri Synod, the American Lutheran Church (ALC), and the ULCA, which would lead the way to the formation of the Lutheran Church in America (LCA) the following year. Their ethnic insularity, he claimed, protected them from "theological erosion" and kept them in "continuity with a historic Christian tradition." In this regard, Hudson observed:

> Among the assets immediately at hand among the Lutherans are a confessional tradition, a surviving liturgical structure, and a sense of continuity which, however much may be the product of cultural factors, may make it easier for them than for most Protestant denominations to recover the "integrity of church membership" without which Protestants are ill-equipped to participate effectively in the dialogue of a pluralistic society.[16]

The way church membership is understood in *The Difference* is a prime example of how this integrity was defended and pursued as a goal.

As the decade of the 1950s came to an end, eight Lutheran church bodies endorsed a new shared worship book: *Service Book and Hymnal,* published in 1958, the same year that Franklin Clark Fry made the cover of *Time.* The *Service Book and Hymnal* carried the churches through the mergers that created the ALC in 1960 and the LCA in 1962 and would serve as the official worship book of the two denominations until 1978. While there are controversial elements in the *Service Book and Hymnal* that depart from traditional Lutheran liturgical practice, such as the "Prayer of Thanksgiving," for the most part Lutheranism's "surviving

14. "The New Lutheran," *Time,* April 7, 1958, 60.

15. "The New Lutheran," 59.

16. Winthrop S. Hudson, *American Protestantism* (Chicago: University of Chicago Press, 1961) 176.

liturgical structure" as Winthrop Hudson called it, is maintained. Worship as repentance is the presumed practice. This is most clear in the public order of confession and absolution that the *Service Book and Hymnal* takes over from the *Common Service Book and Hymnal*.[17]

The liturgical revisions to the public order of confession and absolution in the *Service Book and Hymnal* were for the most part minor. The exhortation to communicants reads differently but has the same theological intent and content. In the confession, the second question, which in the *Common Service Book and Hymnal* speaks of belief in Jesus Christ as the basis for forgiveness and questions the earnestness of the penitent's desire to be delivered from sin, is shortened to the assertion that the believer must trust in the mercy of Christ. The third question, which in the *Common Service Book and Hymnal* asks the penitent to pledge "earnest purpose" in being obedient to the Holy Spirit, hate sin, and seek holiness of life, is replaced. In the *Service Book and Hymnal*, the penitent is simply asked to promise to forgive others and serve God. These changes in the *Service Book and Hymnal* make the public confession less particular in its demands on faith and action, but not by much. The conditional absolution and the final collect remain the same; both are pointed and forceful. The order holds a less prominent place in the *Service Book and Hymnal* than in the *Common Service Book and Hymnal* of 1917, reflecting the fact that separate preparatory services for Holy Communion were falling into disuse.[18] The *Service Book and Hymnal* describes the order as fitting for "a specially appointed preparatory service" such as Wednesday and Friday of Holy Week.

As to theology, there is no doubt in either of these orders that the benefits of the sacrament are bestowed to penitents in repentance and faith and that they, in turn, are called to amendment of life. The impenitent eat unto judgment. This is made especially clear in the conditionality of the absolution.

That a broad range of Lutheran churches in America beyond the

---

17. *Service Book and Hymnal* (Minneapolis and Philadelphia: Augsburg Publishing House and Board of Publication Lutheran Church in America, 1958) 249-52. For a full text of this service, see Appendix II.

18. My colleague at Luther Seminary, Roy Harrisville, who grew up in a Lutheran parsonage of the Norwegian Evangelical Lutheran Church, told me that a preparatory service for Sunday Communion held on Friday evenings four times a year was his father's practice until 1938. The elder Harrisville was then called to a new parish where the preparatory service was no longer held, and he accepted the new practice without protest.

ULCA could embrace this service in 1958 is no surprise. This is the Lutheran liturgical tradition at work. A perusal of Lutheran denominational service books, besides the *Common Service Book and Hymnal,* that precede the *Service Book and Hymnal* demonstrates a strong basic consensus among Lutherans concerning the function and meaning of public confession and absolution and especially the conditionality of public absolution. To take but two examples: in *The Hymnal and Order of Service* (1925) of the Augustana Synod, after worshipers in prayer declare themselves to be "poor miserable sinners, conceived and born in sin," that they have sinned against God, deserve "eternal condemnation," but seek divine mercy, the minister proclaims:

> If this be your sincere confession, and if with penitent hearts you earnestly desire the forgiveness of your sins for the sake of Jesus Christ, God according to his promise forgiveth you all your sins; and I, by the authority of God's Word and by the commandment of our Lord Jesus Christ, announce to you that God, through his grace hath forgiven all your sins: In the name of the Father, and of the Son, and of the Holy Ghost. Amen.[19]

In the *Altar Book* of the United Norwegian Lutheran Church, the absolution is less direct in that it is addressed in the third person. Forgiveness is not from the ordained minister, but from the words of Scripture, Mark 16:16. The absolution reads in part: "To them that believe on His Name, He giveth the power to become the sons of God and hath

---

19. *The Hymnal and Order of Service* (Rock Island: Augustana Book Concern, 1925) 594. The Augustana hymnal, 1925 edition, is especially beloved by those shaped by it in their formative years as members of the Augustana Lutheran Church. Arland Hultgren, Professor Emeritus of New Testament at Luther Seminary, states: "When persons with memories of the Augustana Lutheran Church are asked what to them is most memorable about it, they often give the quick reply, 'the liturgy.'" He goes on to quote notables in the denomination who agree with this sentiment, including Herbert Chilstrom, former bishop of the Evangelical Lutheran Church in America, and Conrad Bergendoff (1895-1997), distinguished theologian and church leader ("The Significance of the Augustana Liturgy for Faith," *Lutheran Quarterly* 24 [2010]: 1). Of the 1925 hymnal, Hultgren observes: "It had provided the liturgy for Augustana people during dramatic and changing times in North American history and culture which affected the church's self-understanding: the Great Depression, World War II, the boom in church membership in the 1950s, the planting and construction of new churches throughout the land, mobility of members, a diminution of Swedishness in the congregations, and a huge transformation of what it meant to be a part of the larger Lutheran family" (p. 6).

promised them His Holy Spirit. He that believeth and is baptized shall be saved."[20] Absolution depends on faith. In this the Swedes and the Norwegians, along with the Germans, agreed. All these liturgical practices fit well with the "original sin moment" of American culture in the post-war period.

But profound change in Lutheran liturgical practice was coming: nothing less than the emergence of an opposing tradition. Ironically, the signs of change appeared just as the sobriety and austerity of traditional Lutheran theology and liturgy, the latter embodied in the Common Service, had reached their apogee of influence in broader American culture.

Worship as Ritual Participation in the Divine

In 1947, as American Lutheranism stood on the threshold of a decade of rapid growth, Luther D. Reed (1873-1972) of Lutheran Seminary at Philadelphia published the first edition of his *magnum opus, The Lutheran Liturgy*. It was a broad-scaled interpretation and defense of the *Common Service Book and Hymnal* of 1917. Reed had served on the committee that put the book together. He also at the time led the Joint Commission on Worship started in 1945, whose task it was to spearhead the creation of a new pan-Lutheran hymnal. That hymnal would become the *Service Book and Hymnal* of 1958. Reed was a wide-ranging liturgical scholar. He knew Lutheran liturgical practice and stood in the tradition of Krauth, Mann, and Jacobs. He decried "extreme practices, whether individualistic or ritualistic."[21] He was also open to ecumenical influence: English hymnody, the Oxford Movement, and the modern liturgical renewal movement, which involved both Protestants and Roman Catholics but was dominated by Catholic scholarship.

It is the influence of the liturgical renewal movement that appears in a curious but significant passage in which Reed analyzes the confession of sins in the brief order for confession at the beginning of the service in the *Common Service Book and Hymnal*.[22] Reed calls confession of

---

20. *Altar Book with Scripture Lessons and Collects,* edition of 1915 (Minneapolis: Augsburg Publishing House, 1929) 10.

21. Luther D. Reed, *The Lutheran Liturgy,* 1st ed. (Philadelphia: Fortress, 1947) viii.

22. See Appendix III.

sins "a helpful preparation for each day's worship" in which the worshiper seeks "purification of spirit" by turning to God "in penitence and prayer" in order to receive "assurance of mercy and grace." As to the reason for confession Reed mentions in passing the admonition in the *Didache* to confess sin before receiving the Lord's Supper "that your sacrifices may be holy,"[23] but makes no other reference to the penitential and disciplinarian literature in the early church that defined confession of sins and its significance, nor to St. Paul's admonition to examine oneself that accompanies his recital of the Words of Institution. Instead Reed grounds the confession of sins in that section at the beginning of the Roman mass known as the *Confiteor* ("I confess"), the origin of which he dates to the eleventh century. The *Confiteor* was adopted by the Synod of Ravenna (1314) and authorized in the Missal of Pius V (1504-1572) in 1570.[24] Confession of sins is thus in Reed's view a medieval development. It was taken over by the Reformers because they "appreciated the spiritual values in a preparatory confession," although they adapted the practice of confession in their own way apart from the Roman rite. Further, Reed cites approvingly the Roman Catholic scholar Pius Parsch (1884-1954) in asserting that over against the medieval church and the Reformation, the early church displayed no excessive preoccupation with sin; in Parsch's words: "'the primitive Church' considered itself 'a holy people'" that did not "possess the clearly defined consciousness of sin of medieval and modern times. It did not, therefore, see the need for a special rite of purification."[25]

These astounding assertions have no basis in the historical record. As we have seen, "holiness" in the early church was not a formal mark applied to Christians automatically and without distinction; rather, it was a moral imperative, incumbent on believers and enforced by the strict discipline of the office of the keys. To be a "holy assembly," the church had to be made up of "those who live in accordance with righteousness."[26] Early liturgical practice allowed a single repentance for post-baptismal sins of a serious nature, no more. There was little room

23. Reed, *The Lutheran Liturgy*, 245-46.

24. Reed, *The Lutheran Liturgy*, 245.

25. Pius Parsch, *The Liturgy of the Mass*, tr. F. C. Eckhoff (St. Louis: Herder, 1936) 65-66, quoted in Reed, *The Lutheran Liturgy*, 256-57.

26. Hippolytus of Rome, *Exposition of Daniel* 1.17.7, translated and quoted in Pelikan, *The Emergence of the Catholic Tradition (100-600)* (Chicago: University of Chicago Press, 1971) 157.

for maneuver: "Nowhere in the West can the status of the penitent be twice assumed in a human life."[27] This harsh rule was taught in *The Shepherd of Hermas;* it was affirmed by Tertullian, St. Jerome, and the Third Council of Toledo in 589, among others. If one sought comfort in the sacramental life, believing that its benefits were bestowed by simply the act of participation, St. Augustine warned

> . . . that few share in the inheritance of God, while many partake in its outward signs; that few are united in holiness of life, and in the gift of love shed abroad in our hearts by the Holy Spirit who is given to us, which is a hidden spring that no stranger can approach; and that many join in the solemnity of the sacrament, which he that eats and drinks unworthily eats and drinks judgment to himself, while he who neglects to eat it shall not have life in him, [John 6:54] and so shall never reach eternal life. . . . [T]he good are called few as compared with the multitude of the evil, but that as scattered over the world there are very many growing among the tares, and mixed with the chaff, till the day of harvest and of purging.[28]

This statement reflects the fierce eschatological consciousness of the ancient church that shaped early Christian worship. It is not made by an obscure figure, but by the greatest theologian of his age.

Over against this harsh standard, the Middle Ages, beginning with the Irish, represents not "the clearly defined consciousness of sin" — which was in place from the beginning — but the promise that the sinner can come before God in repentance repeatedly throughout life and be absolved, a teaching that the medieval church and the Reformers embraced. What separates the medieval church and the Reformation from the early church is the relaxation of discipline; what they share with the early church is consciousness of the power and danger of sin. Like the early church, the Middle Ages and the Reformation taught in no uncertain terms that worship is grounded in repentance.

How did Parsch come to his strange misreading of the early church? The answer is the liturgical renewal movement of which Parsch was an early proponent. This movement, which traced its intellectual and

27. Oscar Daniel Watkins, *A History of Penance,* 2 vols. (New York: Burt Franklin, 1961) 1:481.

28. *NPNF* 4:205 (*Contra Faustum* 13.16).

theological roots back to German Romanticism and Idealism, taught that the liturgy of the mass, developed over the course of the history of the church, is the focus and essence of Christian worship and the act of God.[29] The inspiration for this assertion involves several interlocking intellectual and theological ideas.

The first is the notion of historical development itself, not an easy concept for the Catholic Church, which grounded its authority in the ancient notion of truth as unchanging: *ecclesia semper eadem* — the church is always the same. The problem of the historicity of the church as it affected the Roman Church was taken up in the nineteenth century in the Catholic Tübingen School by such figures as Johann Sebastian Drey (1777-1833) and Johann Adam Möhler (1796-1838). Also important was John Henry Newman (1801-1890) of the Oxford Movement, especially after his conversion to the Roman Church. Focusing on the concepts of dogma and tradition as ideal forms of revelation was a way by which Catholic theology could embrace the fact of historical change in the church while denying that such change is anything but unchanging truth disclosing itself as a living reality and unfolding over time to reveal the richness of the content of divine revelation. In the famous metaphor of Newman, the church is a river that cannot be known if one looks only at its source: one must take in the river as a whole "when its bed has become deep and broad and full."[30]

On the basis of this hermeneutic, revelation was reconceived. Instead of understanding it as most pure and authentic at its origin, "the faith which was once for all delivered to the saints" (Jude 3), it was now understood as undergoing a process of development and increase. The beginning is but the "seed"; history is the full flower. Thus, it is possible to take a text in its final developed form, such as the Roman rite of 1570, and trace back the elements that make it up piece-by-piece. Historical research concentrates on "the assemblage of texts and gestures" that appear over the centuries and that are finally formulated in the official text and actions of the mass. This final product is conceived as intentional and divinely directed:

29. André Haquin, "The Liturgical Movement and Catholic Ritual Revision," *The Oxford History of Christian Worship* (New York: Oxford, 2006) 696-720; Hans-Christoph Schmidt-Lauber, "Liturgiewissenschaft/Liturgik," and "Liturgische Bewegungen," *TRE* 21:383-406.

30. John Henry Cardinal Newman, *An Essay on the Development of Christian Doctrine*, 2nd ed. (Westminster: Christian Classics, 1968) 40.

... we see the Church's self-understanding (and thus Tradition) unfolding before our eyes. The liturgy permits us to overhear the
Church interpreting her own faith in the best way she knows
how. . . . The liturgy is the poetry of the Church, and just as poetry
is language at its most intensely expressive, so in the liturgy we hear
the Church's voice at its most eloquent.[31]

This hermeneutic became standard practice in the liturgical renewal
movement among both Catholic and Protestant scholars. It is the
method of Parsch's *The Liturgy of the Mass* of 1936 and was also employed
in two other influential studies of the time, one preceding Parsch, the
other following: Hans Lietzmann (1875-1942), *Mass and Lord's Supper: A
Study in the History of the Liturgy* (1926), and Gregory Dix (1901-1952), *The
Shape of the Liturgy* (1945).[32]

The second fundamental idea driving the liturgical renewal movement is the notion of "the liturgy" as the basis of liturgical studies.
Leitourgia in the New Testament and early church meant "service" as in
service to the neighbor.[33] In Eastern Christianity the notion of service
became attached to what came to be considered as the highest form of
service or duty for a Christian: the obligation of the Eucharist. *Hē
leitourgia* thus meant the service of the Lord's Supper. In the sixteenth
century the term enters Latin usage through the influence of By-
zantine texts and slowly begins to take on the meaning familiar today.
This change of meaning took time. Up through the early nineteenth
century in Germany, the common terms for worship were *cultus Dei* and
Gottesdienst. But by the 1830s "liturgy" became the dominant usage
among Catholic theologians, as in Franz Xavier Schmid, *Liturgik der
christkatholische Religion* (1832) and *Liturgik als Wissenschaft* (1836). Among
Catholic scholars, "the liturgy" (in the singular) comes to mean the
Tridentine Roman rite (1570) as the ideal and essence of Christian worship, the ultimate measure of Christian identity and proclamation.[34]

In this regard, the purpose of liturgical studies as a scholarly disci-

---

31. Aiden Nichols, *The Shape of Catholic Theology* (Collegeville: Liturgical, 1991) 183-84.

32. Hans Lietzmann, *Mass and the Lord's Supper: A Study in the History of the Liturgy,* tr.
Dorothea H. G. Reeve (Leiden: E. J. Brill, 1979), and the "Introduction and Further In-
quiry" by Robert Douglas Richardson in the same volume; Gregory Dix, *The Shape of the
Liturgy* (Westminster: Dacre, 1945).

33. On the following see Nichols, *Shape of Catholic Theology,* 182.

34. Schmidt-Lauber, "Liturgiewissenschaft/Liturgik," 383-84.

pline was to explain how liturgy, of whatever confessional persuasion, functions in Christian communities. Friedrich Schleiermacher (1768-1834) is most important in the initial development of liturgical studies. In his *Brief Outline on the Study of Theology* (1830) he argues that the analysis of Christian worship is a branch of practical theology. The purpose of such analysis is to assess how "religious self-consciousness" is thought and communicated in the local congregation.[35] The language of worship "is compounded of elements pertaining to both prose and poetry"[36] so as to be attractive, carry the weight of the doctrine of the community, and have an eloquence and literary beauty that can stand up to constant repetition, week after week, year after year. The language of worship is of crucial importance even in a Protestant community that considers the sermon the central act of Christian worship. The problem with preaching is that it is "something rather uncertain and accidental": its quality week to week cannot be guaranteed. In any event the study of preaching is the province of "homiletics."[37] These are simple ideas to be sure. But they are the basic stuff of liturgical studies. They inform the concept of "morphology" in this study.

There remains one more feature of the liturgical renewal movement to be described. It is the most important of all; for it is the movement's fundamental theological presupposition: the understanding of worship as ritual participation in the divine. Here the influence of Georg Friedrich Wilhelm Hegel (1770-1831) can be seen at work, even though it is rarely acknowledged. In his *Lectures on the Philosophy of Religion,* published posthumously in 1832, and his *Lectures on the Philosophy of History,* published in 1837, Hegel claimed that the communal life of the church is "the continual recapitulation of the divine history of Christ" and that this "is especially evident in its cultus and its sacraments."[38] Although a Protestant, in fact a Lutheran, Hegel accepted the doctrine of the mass

---

35. Friedrich Schleiermacher, *Brief Outline on the Study of Theology,* tr. Terrence N. Tice (Richmond: John Knox, 1966) 98 (§280). See Schmidt-Lauber, "Liturgiewissenschaft/ Liturgik," 387.

36. Schleiermacher, *Brief Outline,* 99 (§282).

37. Schleiermacher, *Brief Outline,* (§§284-85).

38. Stephen D. Crites, "The Gospel According to Hegel," *Journal of Religion* 46 (1966): 259. G. W. F. Hegel, *Christian Religion: Lectures on the Philosophy of Religion Part III,* ed. and tr. Peter C. Hodgson (Missoula: Scholars, 1979) 256-76. In what follows I am indebted to Crites's argument; also Emil L. Fackenheim, *The Religious Dimensions in Hegel's Thought* (Bloomington: University of Indiana Press, 1967).

as the perpetual sacrifice of Christ as an appropriate expression of the "Spirit" revealing itself in and through the community of faith in the Middle Ages. The cultus "[entails] an eternal repetition of the life, passion, and resurrection of Christ in the members of the community."[39] For Hegel, the initiative for representing divine truth in history passes over to Luther and the Reformation. This claim, of course, Catholics reject. But the idea of the "cultus" that re-presents Christ and makes Christ its own, was taken up by Catholic theology in the liturgical renewal movement. Catholic theologians, beginning in the Romantic era, employed it as a chief means to defend the Roman Church as the true church of history — indeed, as nothing less than the continuation of the Incarnation and participant in the atonement. What the Tübingen School and Newman saw in the concept of "dogma" as the defining element of Roman identity, Hegel ascribed specifically to the sacrifice of the mass. For Hegel this claim about the meaning and significance of the mass was not only historical. It is not simply the case that the doctrine of the mass was a fitting representation of the gospel in the Middle Ages. Rather, in his view the mass was an instance of the universal function of cultus as a channel of the divine to all of human experience.

This claim on Hegel's part requires fuller explanation. For Hegel human history is a tightly knit ritual drama centered in the Bible and the church. In Hegel's opinion, history has a definite plot whose meaning is revealed in certain central occurrences by which the seemingly endless variety may be organized and interpreted. These central occurrences are symbolized or "re-presented" in the biblical narrative: the fall, the *kairos* of the Incarnation, the atonement, and the rise of the "Spiritual Community." In this regard, the mass as sacrifice is a crucial element in the divine-human drama. The drama began when *Adam* ate of the fruit of the tree. The Lord declares: "Behold, the man is become as one of us, to know good and evil" (Genesis 3:22 KJV). For Hegel, this is the symbolic representation in story of humanity leaving animal existence and coming into full consciousness. "The apple of knowledge," writes Stephen Crites, "which kills the happy ape in the garden brings life to man, with his pain, his self-seeking, his evil — and his destiny of self-conscious reconciliation with God."[40] The plot of history is the reconciliation of God and humanity. It is accomplished in the Second

---

39. Crites, "Gospel According to Hegel," 268-69.
40. Crites, "Gospel According to Hegel," 251-52.

Adam as God and Man come together in Christ and his atoning death. Christ passes over into the Spiritual Community which is his Body. Christ becomes church. In the cultus or worship of the church, as interpreted by medieval Catholic doctrine, reconciliation through the atoning death of Christ becomes the event of the mass. Through the church and the mass, reconciliation becomes the actualized possession of the people of God, who symbolize the journey of corporate humanity through history. In what Crites calls "Hegel's scrambled version of Reformation theology,"[41] Luther's objection to the mass is in essence the rejection of the externality of the ritual representation of Christ; that is, "Christ as a particular being apart from the congregation." What Luther wants, or perhaps better, what Luther's theology effects as it plays itself out in Lutheran identity is that reconciliation through Christ as Spirit becomes the inner possession of the believer.[42]

The understanding of the mass as the realization of the atoning sacrifice of Christ in the community and thus the possession of the community is the fundamental claim of the liturgical renewal movement. It undergirds all of the movement's analyses of liturgical particularities. The movement claims to be inspired and grounded by scholarly work in comparative religion and the history of religion, and indeed it is. But those disciplines, as they developed in Germany in the nineteenth century, were deeply beholden to Hegelian ideas and influence. Hegel's categories served as a rich and suggestive intellectual template from which to pursue the philosophical and theological constants in human religious experience, whether pagan or Christian, especially as these play themselves out in the rituals of worship. These rituals are the heart of religion; they are the "mysteries" through which the divine manifests itself again and again.

Odo Casel (1886-1948) is "the theologian of the mysteries" who more than any other stamped his mark on the German liturgical movement."[43] Here is his description of what the mass is and does as a representation of universal ritual participation in the divine:

> In the mystery cult the epiphany goes on and on in worship; the saving, healing act of God is performed over and over. Worship is

41. Crites, "Gospel According to Hegel," 259.
42. Crites, "Gospel According to Hegel," 259.
43. Haquin, "Liturgical Movement," 701.

the means of making it real once more, and thus of breaking through to the spring of salvation. The members of the cult present again and again in ritual, symbolic fashion, that primeval act; in holy words and rites of priest and faithful the reality is there once more. . . . Thereby they win a share in the new life of God; they enter his chorus, they become gods. The mysteries' way, therefore, is the way of ritual action as sharing in the god's acts; its aim is union with the godhead, share in his life.[44]

Worship as repentance is grounded in confession of sins and receives the assurance of mercy in faith. Worship as ritualized participation in the divine is a different path to God:

But our union with God is not established simply by faith in his message, but by effectual contact with his redemptive acts. The saving activity by which the church continues the work of Christ does not consist solely in the Word as preached, but in the Word as sacramentally efficacious. So, in our assembly, the reading and preaching of the Word is followed by the eucharistic celebration, in which the mystery of Christ's redemptive work is sacramentally renewed, so that we can take part in it.[45]

This type of conceptuality and the way it is expressed is romantic, soft-grained, and somewhat sentimental. It is also vague; all mysticism is. The literalism of the biblical narrative and creed are made secondary to symbol and ritual transcending time and space. One begins to wonder what the objective referent is for all this theologizing.

In any event, these three characteristics of the liturgical movement are evident in *The Liturgy of the Mass* by Pius Parsch: a historical interest in "the assemblage of texts and gestures" that creates the Roman rite over time; the assumption that the Roman rite is "the liturgy," the ideal and essence of Christian worship, the ultimate measure of Christian identity and proclamation for all time; and the understanding of worship as ritual participation in the divine. In this regard, he ignores

44. Odo Casel, *The Mystery of Christian Worship and Other Writings* (Westminster, MD: Newman, 1962) 53. I am indebted to Oliver K. Olson for pointing me to key representative texts and quotations of the liturgical movement. See his *Reclaiming the Lutheran Liturgical Heritage* (Minneapolis: Reclaim Resources, 2007) 43-50.

45. Charles Davis, *Liturgy and Doctrine: The Doctrinal Basis of the Liturgical Movement* (New York: Sheed and Ward, 1960), 69-70.

those sources, so prominent in the early church, that witness to worship as repentance. He quotes the Words of Institution from 1 Corinthians 11, but stops at verse 26, ignoring St. Paul's command to examine oneself.[46] He makes no reference to Pliny's letter to Emperor Trajan, even though it is the earliest description of Christian worship we have from a non-Christian source. It does not serve his purpose of providing words or actions that appear in the mass. That the *Didache* grounds Christian behavior in the Ten Commandments, as does the description of Christian worship in Pliny's letter, is of no interest to Parsch. Rather his sole focus is the rubrics for worship that are recorded in chapters 9 and 10 of the ancient text. Contained in these rubrics is the warning that guards the Table: "You must not let anyone eat or drink of your Eucharist except those baptized in the Lord's name. For in reference to this, the Lord said, 'Do not give what is sacred to dogs' [Mt. 7.6]."[47] Of this passage, Parsch merely says: "The confession of sins before the Eucharistic celebration resembles the Confiteor of our Mass."[48] In Parsch's historical method, if the confession of sins cannot be directly related to the mass, it does not exist, or does not yet exist. In a later chapter, Parsch brings up the text of the *Didache* again, quoting from chapter 14: "On the day of the Lord you shall assemble, break bread, and celebrate the Eucharist; but first confess your sins, that your sacrifice may be holy." It is here that he makes the observation so convincing to Luther D. Reed: "In later sources describing the ancient Christian Mass, we find nothing about a rite of contrition. The primitive Church considered itself 'a holy people'; nor did it possess the clearly defined consciousness of sin of medieval and modern times. It did not therefore see the need for a special rite of purification."[49] Grace and mercy is ritual participation in the divine. This is the wisdom of the early church. What the early church had to say about sin and discipleship in relation to the sacraments is, in the view of Parsch, irrelevant. All that counts is the power and effect of the words and actions of "the liturgy."

While Parsch's argument may have been convincing to Reed, who was a full-fledged participant in the liturgical renewal movement and

46. Parsch, *Liturgy of the Mass,* 21.

47. Cyril C. Richardson, *Early Christian Fathers* (New York: Touchstone, 1996) 175 (*Didache* 9.5).

48. Parsch, *Liturgy of the Mass,* 27.

49. Parsch, *Liturgy of the Mass,* 65-66.

whose own theology displays the characteristics of the movement described above, it did have its skeptics at the time. One of them was no less than the Vicar of Christ. In 1947, the same year that Reed's first edition of *The Lutheran Liturgy* was published, Pope Pius XII (1876-1958) expressed reservations. While he gave thanks for "the remarkably widespread revival of scholarly interest in the sacred liturgy," he goes on to say: "duty obliges Us to give serious attention to this 'revival' as it is advocated in some quarters, and to take proper steps to preserve it at the outset from excess or outright perversion."[50] Chief among these excesses was the neglect of confession of sins, which he considered essential for reception of the Sacrament of the Altar. His criticism demonstrates his awareness of the great catholic consensus concerning worship as repentance. It is well worth quoting in full:

> It is an unquestionable fact that the work of our redemption is continued, and that its fruits are imparted to us, during the celebration of the liturgy, notable in the august sacrifice of the altar. Christ acts each day to save us, in the sacraments and in His holy sacrifice. By means of them He is constantly atoning for the sins of mankind, constantly consecrating it to God. Sacraments and sacrifice do, then, possess that "objective" power to make us really and personally sharers in the divine life of Jesus Christ. Not from any ability of our own, but by the power of God. . . .
>
> But though the principles set forth above are excellent, it must be plain to everyone that the conclusions drawn from them respecting two sorts of piety are false, insidious and quite pernicious.
>
> Very truly, the sacraments and the sacrifice of the altar, being Christ's own actions, must be held to be capable in themselves of conveying and dispensing grace from the divine Head to the members of the Mystical Body. But if they are to produce their proper effect, it is absolutely necessary that our hearts be properly disposed to receive them. Hence the warning of Paul the Apostle with reference to holy communion, "But let a man first prove himself; and then let him eat of this bread and drink of the chalice." This explains why the Church in a brief and significant phrase calls the various acts of mortification, especially those practiced during the season of Lent, "the Christian army's defenses." They represent, in

50. *Mediator Dei* (November 20, 1947) §§4, 7 (http://www.vatican.va/holy_father/pius _xii/encyclicals/documents/hf_p-xii_enc_20111947_mediator-dei_en.html).

fact, the personal effort and activity of members who desire, as grace urges and aids them, to join forces with their Captain — "that we may discover . . . in our Captain," to borrow St. Augustine's words, "the fountain of grace itself." But observe that these members are alive, endowed and equipped with an intelligence and will of their own. It follows that they are strictly required to put their own lips to the fountain, imbibe and absorb for themselves the life-giving water, and rid themselves personally of anything that might hinder its nutritive effect in their souls. Emphatically, therefore, the work of redemption, which in itself is independent of our will, requires a serious interior effort on our part if we are to achieve eternal salvation.[51]

Examination of oneself and worship as repentance: these are the central ideas that Pius XII witnesses to in these paragraphs of his encyclical, the very same ideas that are given witness in the Lutheran liturgical tradition. Even if one wants to parse carefully what the Pope asserts concerning people "equipped with an intelligence and will of their own," the basic demand challenging the worshiper is no different from Luther's exhortation to communicants of 1525; nor is it different from the formulation of exhortation to communicants found in the classical version of *The Book of Common Prayer* (1662).[52] Long before the

51. *Mediator Dei* §§29-32.
52. The exhortation in the *Book of Common Prayer* (London: Collins, 1968, pp. 246-47) reads:

> Dearly beloved in the Lord, ye that mind to come to the holy Communion of the Body and Blood of our Saviour Christ, must consider how Saint Paul exhorteth all persons diligently to try and examine themselves, before they presume to eat of that Bread, and drink of that Cup. For as the benefit is great, if with a true penitent heart and lively faith we receive that holy Sacrament; (for then we spiritually eat the flesh of Christ, and drink his blood; then we dwell in Christ, and Christ in us; we are one with Christ, and Christ with us;) so is the danger great, if we receive the same unworthily. For then we are guilty of the Body and Blood of Christ our Saviour; we eat and drink our own damnation, not considering the Lord's Body; we kindle God's wrath against us; we provoke him to plague us with divers diseases, and sundry kinds of death. judge therefore yourselves, brethren, that ye be not judged of the Lord; repent you truly for your sins past; have a lively and stedfast faith in Christ our Saviour; amend your lives, and be in perfect charity with all men; so shall ye be meet partakers of those holy mysteries. And above all things ye must give most humble and hearty thanks to God, the Father, the Son, and the Holy Ghost, for the redemption of the world by the death and pas-

contemporary ecumenical movement made its emergence, worship as repentance was the shared, ecumenical practice of Christians, even when they were most divided.

Pius XII also raised concern about the vagueness of the liturgical movement. What, he asked, is the objective christological referent of modern faith as conceived by this school of thought? "It is perfectly clear," he declares, "how much modern writers are wanting in the genuine and true liturgical spirit who, deceived by the illusion of a higher mysticism, dare to assert that attention should be paid not to the historic Christ but to a 'pneumatic' or glorified Christ."[53]

The Attack on "Penitential Piety"

Pope Pius XII was succeeded by Pope John XXIII (1881-1963) who gave permission for Vatican II. John XXIII inspired the Roman church to embrace the most thoroughgoing reform since the Council of Trent. Among the victors of this reform was the liturgical renewal movement, which understood worship as ritual participation in the divine. Holiness was conferred on the church as "the whole people of God" by liturgical declaration and action. According to Wolfhart Pannenberg, one of the Protestant aficionados of the liturgical renewal movement, this development entails a sea-change in religious practice and sensibility. The church has moved from "penitential piety" to "eucharistic piety."[54] Penitential piety is "guilt consciousness," a hangover of the Middle Ages

---

sion of our Saviour Christ, both God and man; who did humble himself, even to the death upon the Cross, for us, miserable sinners, who lay in darkness and the shadow of death; that he might make us the children of God, and exalt us to everlasting life. And to the end that we should alway remember the exceeding great love of our Master, and only Saviour, Jesus Christ, thus dying for us, and the innumerable benefits which by his precious blood-shedding he hath obtained to us; he hath instituted and ordained holy mysteries, as pledges of his love, and for a continual remembrance of his death, to our great and endless comfort. To him therefore, with the Father and the Holy Ghost, let us give (as we are most bounden) continual thanks; submitting ourselves wholly to his holy will and pleasure, and studying to serve him in true holiness and righteousness all the days of our life. *Amen.*

53. *Mediator Dei* §162.
54. Wolfhart Pannenberg, *Christian Spirituality* (Philadelphia: Westminister, 1983) 31.

and the Reformation, two periods in the church that are deeply and de-
structively intertwined:

> The Reformation . . . developed from theological reflection on the
> sacramental institution of penance in the medieval church and its
> problems. By replacing the absolution of the priest with the prom-
> ise of God and of Christ himself, the Reformation overcame the
> need for mediation of medieval Christianity and achieved a new im-
> mediacy to God and Christ. At the same time — and by the same
> step — the meaning of penitence was extended far beyond that par-
> ticular sacramental act so as to permeate every aspect of Christian
> existence. The penitential mentality became ubiquitous.[55]

The penitential mindset of guilt consciousness is a bad thing in
Pannenberg's view. It makes the church captive to an outmoded morality that is suspicious of joy and sensual pleasure. Evangelicalism or
"Revivalist movements," as he calls them, are beset by the penitential
mentality. They demand "moral conversion" which is "an unnatural
imposition on our lives"[56] and the enemy of "a lively Christian spirituality."[57] The modern world means "the secularist emancipation of everyday life from God."[58] It has brought with it "a more optimistic anthropology."[59] Individualism, let alone moralistic individualism, is
giving way to new corporate ideals of existence: "the rise of socialism
. . . Western youth movements and the counterculture." "Traditional
social structures like the family . . . are losing ground." Humanity is
seeking "more authentically human forms of community and social
life."[60]

To this new way of being in the world, the Christian church, once it
releases itself from the shackles of repression, can speak a powerful
word: "We must never forget," says Pannenberg, "that baptized Christians are, in principle, liberated from the power of sin."[61] The church
serves the world not by inducing guilt, but rather by being a symbolical

---

55. Pannenberg, *Christian Spirituality,* 22-23.
56. Pannenberg, *Christian Spirituality,* 26.
57. Pannenberg, *Christian Spirituality,* 22, 26.
58. Pannenberg, *Christian Spirituality,* 26.
59. Pannenberg, *Christian Spirituality,* 24.
60. Pannenberg, *Christian Spirituality,* 33.
61. Pannenberg, *Christian Spirituality,* 27.

entity in which "worship is in the center." The church is the liturgy; liturgy is the church: "The worship of the Christian community anticipates and symbolically celebrates the praise of God's glory that will be consummated in the eschatological renewal of all creation in the new Jerusalem."[62]

Pride of place in worship is given to the Eucharist. This is "eucharistic piety": *"The Eucharist, not the sermon, is in the center of the church's life."*[63] The Eucharist does not require the confession of sins and absolution. This is a misreading of Paul in 1 Corinthians and of the witness of the early church, which, Pannenberg claims, assumed that it was a holy people. The obsession with penance, he asserts, begins with the influence of Celtic Christianity (!).[64] The distortion of the faith caused by this obsession takes different forms in Roman Catholicism, Calvinism, and Lutheranism.[65] What needs to be recovered is the understanding that "forgiveness of sins is exhibited in the Eucharist itself."[66] The Eucharist is God's being in the world through his people. It is the act of salvation when it is performed. This is how the church is a "symbol," or, to use Hegelian language, a "representation" *(Vorstellung).* The church does not need to preach, and it does not need to make converts in the manner of sectarians. All it has to do is be in the world. "The Christian church," asserts Pannenberg, "is a symbolic community" that represents "the community of all human beings in a society of perfect justice and peace, the global village, the kingdom of God."[67] We belong to God by ritual participation in which holiness is not earned, but bestowed.

Pannenberg's argument has won converts to the liturgical renewal movement. "Pannenberg's description of the epochal shift in Christian piety summed up the reorientation of my own liturgical piety," writes Thomas H. Schattauer of Wartburg Seminary in a volume of essays by worship professors of Lutheran seminaries in the United States and Canada.[68] "The focus of worship shifted from matters of personal sal-

---

62. Pannenberg, *Christian Spirituality,* 36.

63. Pannenberg, *Christian Spirituality,* 40.

64. See Pannenberg, *Christian Spirituality,* 16-17.

65. Pannenberg, *Christian Spirituality,* 40-41.

66. Pannenberg, *Christian Spirituality,* 41.

67. Pannenberg, *Christian Spirituality,* 35.

68. Thomas H. Schattauer, ed., *Inside Out: Worship in an Age of Mission* (Minneapolis: Fortress, 1999) 9.

vation and devotion to matters of the liturgical assembly's significance 'for the life of the world.'" Schattauer testifies to his own change: "Whereas my former liturgical piety was penitential, individual, retrospective, and institutional, the newly emerging piety was eucharistic, communal, prospective, and symbolic."[69]

The Limitations of Eucharistic Piety

Pannenberg's argument for the liturgical renewal movement as "eucharistic piety" is important not only because it has been influential, but also because it is representative of the basic ideas that have motivated the movement from the beginning. The argument has at least three serious weaknesses. First, Pannenberg gets the history wrong, blaming an unhealthy consciousness of sin on the Middle Ages and the Reformation and exempting the early church. He claims that early Christians understood baptism as the forgiveness of sins "once and for all," that the discipline of forgiving post-baptismal sins one time and one time only was an exception, and that it was the Irish who imposed the idea that converted Christians live "under the power of sin."[70] This turns the actual history of the church on the matter of penance upside down. Misreading the early church on the matter of sin and holiness and ascribing preoccupation with sin to the Middle Ages and the Reformation is a common feature of the liturgical movement. It is the key mistake, the chronic error, on which not only the theology but also the ecumenical claims of the movement are based.

Second, to assert that the Christian church is the ideal community on earth, symbolic of the "global village," is patently false. Sin and alienation beset the church as they do all human communities. Liturgy does not inoculate the church. This claim would appear bizarre to any non-Christian, whether that person is a believer in another religion or an atheist; it would be unconvincing to anyone committed to the separation of church and state who wishes to ground the state on a secular basis; and, lest we forget, it would be rejected by Martin Luther, who attacked the very idea of "Christendom": "for the world and the masses are and always will be un-Christian, even if they are all baptized and

---

69. Schattauer, ed., *Inside Out*, 9.
70. Pannenberg, *Christian Spirituality*, 16-17.

Christian in name."[71] Pannenberg's defense of eucharistic piety is grounded in a vague, sentimental, Rousseau-like vision of utopian existence in which people seek freedom from guilt, alienation, and conventional morality. It was a social vision that came on the scene in the 1960s after "the original sin moment" of the post-war years ended. In some quarters, such as mainline seminaries and college religion departments, this vision continues to dominate. In this cultural milieu, the idea of worship as ritual participation in the divine, with its gauzy romanticism and mysticism, is ready-made. Eucharistic piety is a church-type theology of an especially extreme form. The question of subjective holiness is cast aside, the masses are embraced, and the church is the organ of redemption because of what it possesses — in this case, the Eucharist. And its redeeming work serves not only its members, but the entire world, whether they accept or not. Pannenberg collapses the history and life of the church into the performance of the liturgy.

Third, and perhaps worst of all, there is something delusional about making the claim that the Christian community of the church type, grounded in eucharistic piety, is the ultimate symbol of God in the world. If the church type symbolizes anything it is decline. The Roman church post–Vatican II is rocked by scandal in Europe and America. There is a widespread sense that Catholicism lost its moorings in the 1960s. The territorial church in Europe is empty of worshipers; mainline Protestants in America have been losing members for over four decades. The last time mainline denominations experienced growth was during "the original sin moment." The future of the church belongs not to the liturgical movement, but to Christians of the sect type, especially evangelicals and Pentecostals in the Global South, movements that practice the very "penitential piety" Pannenberg decries.

Despite these weaknesses of Pannenberg's argument, weaknesses that reflect problems in the liturgical renewal movement as a whole, the movement dominates the understanding of worship in the Evangelical Lutheran Church in America (ELCA) and other mainline Protestant denominations. It is taught in seminaries to the exclusion of any other perspective. It has become in fact a rigid, controlling orthodoxy. The liturgical renewal movement is the basis on which the *Service Book and Hymnal* of 1958 removed the exhortation to communicants from the Communion service and embedded the Words of Institution in the

71. *LW* 45:91.

"Prayer of Thanksgiving," thus returning a central element of the Roman mass to Lutheran worship, the eucharistic prayer.[72] Luther wanted no part of the canon of the mass or eucharistic prayer:

> mass and prayer, sacrament and work, testament and sacrifice —
> must not be confused; for the one comes from God to us through
> the ministrations of a priest and demands our faith, the other proceeds from our faith to God through the priest and demands his
> hearing. The former descends, the latter ascends.[73]

Such an objection makes no difference when worship is conceived as ritual participation in the divine. In this conception, ascending is essential to what worship does. The eucharistic prayer is much more clearly evident in the *Lutheran Book of Worship* (1978), where, despite much controversy, including the calling of a conference to debate the matter, the so-called *epiclesis* or prayer calling on the Holy Spirit was added.[74]

The liturgical renewal movement's distrust of penitential piety is clearly evident in the *Lutheran Book of Worship* and *Evangelical Lutheran Worship* (2006). In both hymnals, confession and absolution are optional instead of mandated in the communion service. The *Lutheran Book of Worship* has unconditional absolutions in the public orders for confession as the preferred option. In *Evangelical Lutheran Worship,* an unconditional absolution is the only option. In neither book is there a

72. *Service Book and Hymnal,* 34.

73. *LW* 36:56. Olson, *Reclaiming the Lutheran Liturgical Heritage,* 33.

74. "Send now we pray, your Holy Spirit, the spirit of our Lord and of his resurrection, that we who receive the Lord's body and blood may live to the praise of your glory and receive our inheritance with all your saints in light." *Manual on the Liturgy: Lutheran Book of Worship* (Minneapolis: Augsburg Publishing House, 1979) 70. The conference, A Theological Symposium on Liturgy, met in October 1974. It included representatives of the Inter-Lutheran Commission on Worship preparing the hymnal and scholars and officials from the American Lutheran Church, the Lutheran Church in America, and the Missouri Synod. The result was that the eucharistic prayer with the *epiclesis* was made optional rather than mandated and that the hymnal includes the option of simply reading the Words of Institution by themselves apart from being embedded in prayer, though the latter is traditional Lutheran liturgical practice. These same options continue in *Evangelical Lutheran Worship* (Minneapolis: Augsburg Fortress, 2006). On the debate over the eucharistic prayer in the 1970s, see Oliver K. Olson, "Contemporary Trends Viewed from the Perspective of Classical Lutheran Theology," *Lutheran Quarterly,* old series 26 (1974): 110-57; Olson, *Reclaiming the Lutheran Liturgical Heritage,* 7-8.

full statement of the binding key, which might induce guilt or fear, emotions shunned under the new regime of liturgical theology and practice.[75]

In this trend toward unconditional absolution in public confession, contemporary Lutheran confessional theology is also at work. The Osiandrian theme of absolution as the impartation of grace alone, the position of extreme absolutionism, which was taken up by the Norwegian Synod in the nineteenth century, has now become, in some quarters, a theological principle. For Osiander, a true or unconditional absolution could only be proclaimed in the disciplined context of private confession between pastor and parishioner. What is now claimed is that an unconditional absolution must be spoken at all times, whether in private confession (a rare practice in the ELCA) or public worship. This development in the theological understanding of absolution in effect eliminates the binding key. This would satisfy neither Luther nor Osiander. In the evolution of Lutheran confessional theology it has more to do with Peter Laurentius Larsen and Ulrik Vilhelm Koren, central figures of the old Norwegian Synod in the nineteenth century, than with the central thrust of the Reformation in the sixteenth century or the Lutheran liturgical tradition generally.

The liturgical renewal movement is also the reason for the curious alternative to confession and absolution, the "Thanksgiving for Baptism" in *Evangelical Lutheran Worship*. The purpose of this contrived addition to the liturgy presumably is to assure worshipers "that baptized Christians are, in principle, liberated from the power of sin"[76] and to banish any leftover "guilt consciousness" of penitential piety that might interfere with worship as celebration. Because of the liturgical renewal movement and its eucharistic piety, the largest Lutheran denomination in the United States has turned its back on the liturgical tradition of historic Lutheranism. Worship as repentance has been re-

---

75. See the *Lutheran Book of Worship*, where conditionality in the absolution makes its last appearance. It is expressed in the mildest form possible in the second option of the brief order for confession and forgiveness: "In the mercy of almighty God, Jesus Christ was given to die for you, and for his sake God forgives you all your sins, To those who believe in Jesus Christ he gives the power to become the children of God and bestows on them the Holy Spirit." The binding key is in four words: "To those who believe . . ." (77). In the "Corporate Confession and Forgiveness," the absolution is unconditional (see pp. 193-95).

76. Pannenberg, *Christian Spirituality*, 27.

placed by worship as ritual participation in the divine. This is not development of the tradition but opposition to the tradition.

From the Altar to the Confessional

In a letter to priests written in 2009, Pope Benedict XVI calls for renewal among clergy and laity. He notes the scandals that have plagued the church. The situation is critical. To bring renewal, priests must lead the people of the church "from the altar to the confessional." "Priests ought never to be resigned to empty confessionals or the apparent indifference of the faithful to this sacrament." "The sacrament of Penance," says the Pope, is "an inherent demand of the Eucharistic presence."[77] This recalls the warning that Pius XII gave to the liturgical movement to heed the warning of St. Paul to examine oneself. To receive the gifts of the altar "it is absolutely necessary that our hearts be properly disposed to receive them."[78] The phrase "from the altar to the confessional" in Pope Benedict's letter is most intriguing. There is no doubt that the church has the "altar," that is, the Sacrament of the Altar. It proclaims Christ as present. It encourages frequent communion. But in the exuberance and excess that has followed Vatican II the great gift of the altar is in danger of being taken for granted. The grace of God is the privilege of repentant believers, not the possession of the conventionally baptized. The way to the altar is through the confessional. To go forward to reform a broken church, the church must go back to the roots of its penitential practice, to the great catholic consensus of worship as repentance.

77. "Letter of His Holiness Pope Benedict XVI Proclaiming a Year for Priests on the 150th Anniversary of the 'Dies Natalis' of the Curé of Ars" (June 16, 2009, http://www .vatican.va/holy_father/benedict_xvi/letters/2009/documents/hf_ben-xvi_let_20090616 _anno-sacerdotale_en.html).

78. *Mediator Dei* §31. This is also the warning of *Sacra Tridentina* (1905), a decree of the Congregation of the Holy Council approved by Pope Pius X (1835-1914) encouraging more frequent communion among the laity. Inviting the faithful to the Lord's Table, the decree nevertheless reminded them of the imperative to repent: "Although it is especially fitting that those who receive Communion frequently or daily should be free from venial sins, at least from such as are fully deliberate, and from any affection thereto, nevertheless, it is sufficient that they be free from mortal sin, with the purpose of never sinning in the future; and if they have this sincere purpose . . . daily communicants should gradually free themselves even from venial sins, and from all affection thereto" (§3).

Pope Benedict is right. Worship must be grounded in repentance. If any church should understand this, it is the Catholic Church, whose priests in Europe and America, in shockingly large numbers, find themselves mired in shame and dishonor. Pannenberg may dismiss "guilt consciousness" as a relic of the past. But this consciousness is precisely what the church needs in an antinomian and scandal-plagued age. It can be affirmed by Catholic and Protestant alike. It is the true ecumenical basis for understanding the liturgical traditions of the church. Above all, it is a divine mandate. When Jesus announced that "The time is fulfilled and the kingdom of God is at hand" (Mark 1:15), he was proclaiming his own presence in the world. He is the "altar" of God and through him we offer up our sacrifice of praise (Hebrews 13:10, 15). But he also gives his people two imperatives: "repent" and "believe" (Mark 1:15). These imperatives of Jesus the preacher of the kingdom of God point to the "confessional." The church does not supersede the kingdom or replace it. If the confessional is ignored, the church loses its way.

What is true for the Roman Church in its time of crisis is true for the Lutheran church and other mainline denominations in their time of crisis. Lutherans are a long way from the 1950s, when they were a church on the move, confident and eager in their mission. Now American Lutheranism is in steep decline, divided and contentious. It participates not in the divine, but in the self-absorption of contemporary American culture. The war cry of our age, says psychologist Bernie Zilbergeld (1939-2002), is, "I DESERVE. . . . I deserve love. I deserve to be trusted. I deserve freedom. I deserve friendship. I deserve respect. I deserve sexual pleasure. I deserve happiness."[79] This war cry is the motive force of much of what is taught in the mainline church about personal ethics, pastoral care, and even the gospel itself. Many would like to make Luther the precursor of the modern liberator who teaches a gospel of self-fulfillment in which the "law" becomes that which restricts us and the "gospel" that which releases us from any encumbrance, who binds the conscience not to Scripture but to oneself, who endorses, as it were, a new type of "happy exchange" *(fröhliche Wechsel):* not that between the sins of believers and the innocence of Christ, as Luther describes it in *The Freedom of the Christian* (1520), but rather that between the ego and the id.

79. Bernie Zilbergeld, *The Shrinking of America: Myths of Psychological Change* (New York: Little, Brown, 1983) 41.

Did Luther show the way to the pursuit of this type of personal happiness? No, he did not. Yes, he knew that salvation is a gift from God that we cannot earn on our own. But he also knew that for the Christian life is the struggle of the spirit against the flesh lest the old Adam gain the upper hand and bury us in the wages of sin:

> If you are a Christian, you must learn that you will undoubtedly feel all kinds of trials and evil inclinations in your flesh. For if faith is present, a hundred more evil thoughts and a hundred more new trials come than were there before. Only see to it that you are a man and do not let yourself be taken captive by them. Resist constantly and say: "I will not! I will not!" . . . [A] true Christian life is never at rest.[80]

There is more monk than American in this claim. If this is not understood, then one fails to comprehend the fundamentals of Luther's ethics.

Luther knew how powerful old Adam truly is. He knew how far we have truly fallen. The true self is a "furious and untamed beast"[81] who "does not want God be God" because he or she wants to be God alone.[82] It is this self who crucifies Christ because, as St. John tells us, "we love darkness and hate the light" (John 3:19-20). Luther discovered this in his own life. By his fame and notoriety, he brought it to the consciousness of the West in a new way.

It is very hard to face up to the ugliness of the true self, to take the journey that Luther took into the dark night of the soul. This culture, including the culture of the academy, resists it. But if we take the journey or God forces us to take the journey, we may find that we are able to hear the gospel in the ideal form that the confessions claim is possible — the gospel "purely preached," telling us that God is not done with us yet — "Father, forgive them," says Jesus, "for they know not what they do" (Luke 23:34).

This is the pure gospel that Luther discovered. And he was not alone at the time. The great artist Hieronymus Bosch (1450-1516) anticipates what Luther discovers in his great painting "Christ Carrying the Cross" (see the frontispiece of this book). The sneering, grinning, hateful faces

80. *LW* 30:71.
81. *LW* 26:308.
82. *LW* 31:10.

you see in this painting are your face and my face. Christ knows this; he knows who we are. And still he carries his cross.

Georg Spalatin (1484-1545), Luther's friend, had a friend who feared death so much that he was obsessed by it. Spalatin pleaded with Luther to send his friend a word of comfort. Luther did so. He wrote, in the year 1519, "A Sermon on Preparing to Die" in which he says that in this word of Christ on the cross, "Father, forgive them, for they know not what they do," Christ "intercedes for his enemies, for their sin, death, and hell . . . [so] we hold to Christ and firmly believe our sin, death, and hell are overcome in him and no longer able to harm us."[83] We do not participate in the atonement; it is the work of Christ alone done on our behalf. But we must prepare to receive it in and through confession of sins. The church cannot "let the people go on in their public sins, without any renewal or reformation of their lives." To do so is to "truly fail to understand the faith and Christ."[84] This is why the binding and loosing of sins are essential. To go forward, Lutherans and other Christians must go back to the roots of the liturgical tradition in the Reformation that built upon the heritage of Scripture and the early church. Worship life must recover gravity and seriousness of purpose through worship as repentance. This is the catholic consensus.

83. *LW* 42:108.
84. *LW* 41:147.

The Order for Public Confession,
Common Service Book (1917)

Preparatory to The Holy Communion

¶The Order for Public Confession is a Vesper Service, and should be appointed for the afternoon or evening of the Friday or Saturday preceding the Holy Communion, when all who purpose to commune should be present.

¶When the Confessional Service immediately precedes The Service, the Order shall begin with the words: In the Name of the Father, and of the Son, and of the Holy Ghost. Amen. Then shall follow: The Exhortation, the Confession, the Absolution and the New Testament Benediction. The Service shall begin with the Introit for the Day.

¶A Hymn of Invocation of the Holy Ghost, *or another suitable Hymn may be sung.*

¶*The* Versicles *with the* Gloria Patri *shall be sung or said, the Congregation standing until the end of the* Psalm.

The Versicle

MAKE haste, O God, to deliver me.
Make haste to help me, O Lord.

The sacrifices of God are a broken spirit.

A broken and a contrite heart, O God, Thou wilt not despise.
 Glory be to the Father, and to the Son, and to the Holy Ghost:
As it was in the beginning, is now, and ever shall be,
 world without end. Amen.

¶Then shall be sung or said this Psalm:

The Psalm

HAVE mercy upon me, O God, according to Thy loving kindness: according unto the multitude of Thy tender mercies, blot out my transgressions.

Wash me thoroughly from mine iniquity: and cleanse me from my sin.

For I acknowledge my transgressions: and my sin is ever before me.

Against Thee, Thee only, have I sinned, and done this evil in Thy sight: that Thou mightest be justified when Thou speakest, and be clear when Thou judgest.

Behold, I was shapen in iniquity: and in sin did my mother conceive me.

Behold, Thou desirest truth in the inward parts: and in the hidden part Thou shalt make me to know wisdom.

Purge me with hyssop, and I shall be clean: wash me, and I shall be whiter than snow.

Make me to hear joy and gladness: that the bones which Thou hast broken may rejoice.

Hide Thy face from my sins: and blot out all mine iniquities.

Create in me a clean heart, O God: and renew a right spirit within me.

Cast me not away from Thy presence: and take not Thy Holy Spirit from me.

Restore unto me the joy of Thy salvation: and uphold me with Thy free Spirit.

Then will I teach transgressors Thy ways: and sinners shall be converted unto Thee.

O Lord, open Thou my lips: and my mouth shall show forth Thy praise.

GLORY be to the Father, and to the Son, and to the Holy Ghost;

As it was in the beginning, is now, and ever shall be: world without end. Amen.

Then shall one or more of the following
Lessons of Holy Scripture *be read:*

The Lesson

Exodus 20:1-17.
Daniel 9:4-9, 17-19.
Isaiah 57:14-21.
Isaiah 1:11-18.
1 John 1:5-9.
1 Corinthians 11:23-29.
John 20:19-23.

Matthew 11:25-30.
Mark 12:28-31.
Luke 13:1-9.
Luke 15:1-2, 11-31.
John 13:1-17.
Matthew 5:21-29.

¶*Then may follow an Address or Sermon,*
after which shall be sung a Hymn.

The Hymn

¶*Then shall the Congregation stand,*
and the Minister shall say the following Exhortation

Exhortation

DEARLY Beloved! Forasmuch as we purpose to come to the Holy Supper of our Lord Jesus Christ, it becometh us diligently to examine ourselves, as St. Paul exhorteth us. For this Holy Sacrament hath been instituted for the special comfort and strengthening of those who humbly confess their sins, and who hunger and thirst after righteousness.

But if we thus examine ourselves, we shall find in us nothing but sin and death, from which we can in no wise set ourselves free. Therefore our Lord Jesus Christ hath had mercy upon us, and hath taken upon Himself our nature, so that He might fulfill for us the whole will and law of God, and for us and for our deliverance suffer death and all that we by our sins have deserved. And to the end that we should the more confidently believe this, and be strengthened by our faith in cheerful obedience to His will, He hath instituted the Holy Sacrament of His Supper, in which He giveth us His Body to eat, and His Blood to drink.

Therefore whoso eateth of this Bread and drinketh of this Cup, firmly believing the words of Christ, dwelleth in Christ, and Christ in Him, and hath eternal life.

We should also do this in remembrance of Him, showing His death, that He was delivered for our offences, and raised again for our justification, and, rendering unto Him most hearty thanks for the same, take up our cross and follow Him; and, according to His commandment, love one another even as He hath loved us. For we are all one body, even as we are all partakers of this one Bread, and drink of this one Cup.

Let us pray.

ALMIGHTY God, unto Whom all hearts are open, all desires known, and from Whom no secrets are hid: Cleanse the thoughts of our hearts by the inspiration of Thy Holy Spirit, that we may perfectly love Thee, and worthily magnify Thy holy Name; through Jesus Christ, Thy Son, our Lord. Amen.

¶ *Then shall the Minister begin the* Confession *as here followeth:*

The Confession

I ASK you in the presence of Almighty God, Who searcheth the heart:

DO you truly acknowledge, confess, and lament that you are by nature sinful, and that by omitting to do good and by doing evil you have in thought, word and deed, grieved and offended your God and Saviour, and thereby justly deserved His condemnation?

If this be the sincere confession of your hearts, declare it by saying: Yes.

Answer. Yes.

DO you truly believe that Jesus Christ came into the world to save sinners, and that all who believe on His Name receive the forgiveness of sins? Do you, therefore, earnestly desire to be delivered from all your sins, and are you confident that it is the gracious will of your Heavenly Father, for Christ's Sake, to forgive your sins and to cleanse you from all unrighteousness?

If so, confess it by saying: Yes.

Answer. Yes.

IS it your earnest purpose, henceforth, to be obedient to the Holy Spirit, so as to hate and forsake all manner of sin, to live as in God's presence, and to strive daily after holiness of heart and life? If so, answer: Yes.

Answer. Yes.

Let us humbly kneel, and make confession unto God, imploring His forgiveness through Jesus Christ our Lord.

¶*Then shall all kneel, and say:*

O GOD, our Heavenly Father, I confess unto Thee that I have grievously sinned against Thee in many ways; not only by outward transgression, but also by secret thoughts and desires, which I cannot fully understand, but which are all known unto Thee. I do earnestly repent, and am heartily sorry for these my offences, and I beseech Thee of Thy great goodness to have mercy upon me, and for the sake of Thy dear Son Jesus Christ, our Lord, to forgive my sins, and graciously to help my infirmities. Amen.

The Order for Public Confession

¶*Then shall the Minister rise and say the* Absolution. *The Congregation shall remain kneeling until after the* Benediction.

The Absolution

ALMIGHTY God, our Heavenly Father, hath had mercy upon us, and for the sake of the sufferings, death and resurrection of His dear Son Jesus Christ, our Lord, forgiveth us all our sins. As a Minister of the Church of Christ, and by His authority, I therefore declare unto you who do truly repent and believe in Him, the entire forgiveness of all your sins: In the Name of the Father, and of the Son, and of the Holy Ghost.

On the other hand, by the same authority, I declare unto the impenitent and unbelieving, that so long as they continue in their impenitence, God bath not forgiven their sins, and will assuredly visit their iniquities upon them, if they turn not from their evil ways, and come to true repentance and faith in Christ, ere the day of grace be ended.

¶*Then shall the Minister kneel, and all shall say the* Lord's Prayer.

The Prayer

OUR Father, Who art in heaven; Hallowed be Thy Name; Thy kingdom come; Thy will be done on earth, as it is in heaven; Give us this day our daily bread; And forgive us our trespasses, as we forgive those who trespass against us; And lead us not into temptation; But deliver us from evil; For thine is the kingdom, and the power, and the glory, for ever and ever. Amen.

¶*Then shall the Minister say the* Collect for the Day *except when* The Service *immediately* follows *this Order.*

(After the Collects.)

Amen.

¶*Then may other suitable Collects be said, and after them the* Collect for Peace.

The Lord will give strength unto His people.

The Lord will bless His people with peace.

The Collect for Peace

O GOD, from Whom all holy desires, all good counsels, and all just works do proceed: Give unto Thy servants that peace, which the world cannot give; that our hearts may be set to obey Thy commandments, and also that by Thee, we, being defended from the fear of our enemies, may pass our time in rest and quietness; through the merits of Jesus Christ, our Saviour, Who liveth and reigneth with Thee, and the Holy Ghost, ever One God, world without end.

¶ *The Minister shall rise and say the* Benediction.

THE Grace of our Lord Jesus Christ, and the Love of God, and the Communion of the Holy Ghost, be with you all.

AMEN

The Order for Public Confession,
Service Book and Hymnal (1958)

The Order for Public Confession
for a Specially Appointed Preparatory Service

❡*This Order is provided for use when a Service of Preparation for Holy Communion is held on a day before the administration of the Sacrament. It is specially appropriate as the Vesper Office on Wednesday and Friday in Holy Week.*

❡*A Hymn of Invocation of the Holy Ghost, or another suitable Hymn may be sung.*

❡*The Versicles with the Gloria Patri shall be sung or said, the Congregation standing until the end of the Psalm.*

> MAKE haste, O God, to deliver me.
>   R. Make haste to help me, O Lord.
> I said, I will confess my transgressions unto the Lord.
>   R. And thou forgavest the iniquity of my sin.
> GLORY be to the Father, and to the Son, and to the Holy Ghost:
>   R. As it was in the beginning, is now, and ever shall be,
>   world without end. Amen.

❡*Then shall be sung or said this Psalm:*

PSALM 51. *Miserere mei, Deus, secundum.*

HAVE mercy upon me, O God, according to thy lovingkindness: according unto the multitude of thy tender mercies, blot out my transgressions.

Wash me thoroughly from mine iniquity: and cleanse me from my sin.

For I acknowledge my transgressions: and my sin is ever before me.

Against thee, thee only, have I sinned, and done this evil in thy sight: that thou mightest be justified when thou speakest, and be clear when thou judgest.

Behold, I was shapen in iniquity: and in sin did my mother conceive me.

Behold, thou desirest truth in the inward parts: and in the hidden part thou shalt make me to know wisdom.

Purge me with hyssop, and I shall be clean: wash me, and I shall be whiter than snow.

Make me to hear joy and gladness: that the bones which thou hast broken may rejoice.

Hide thy face from my sins: and blot out all mine iniquities.

Create in me a clean heart, O God: and renew a right spirit within me.

Cast me not away from thy presence: and take not thy holy spirit from me.

Restore unto me the joy of thy salvation: and uphold me with thy free spirit.

Then will I teach transgressors thy ways: and sinners shall be converted unto thee.

Deliver me from bloodguiltiness, O God, thou God of my salvation: and my tongue shall sing aloud of thy righteousness.

O Lord, open thou my lips: and my mouth shall show forth thy praise.

For thou desirest not sacrifice, else would I give it: thou delightest not in burnt offering.

The sacrifices of God are a broken spirit: a broken and a contrite heart, O God, thou wilt not despise.

Do good in thy good pleasure unto Zion: build thou the walls of Jerusalem.

Then shalt thou be pleased with the sacrifices of righteousness, with burnt offering and whole burnt offering: then shall they offer bullocks upon thine altar.

GLORY be to the Father, and to the Son, and to the Holy Ghost:

As it was in the beginning, is now, and ever shall be, world without end.

Amen.

¶*Then shall be read one or more of the following Lessons:*

Exodus 20:1-17	Matthew 11:25-30
Daniel 9:4-9, 17-19	Mark 12:28-31
Isaiah 57:14-21	Luke 13:1-9
Isaiah 1:11-18	Luke 15:1, 2, 11-31
1 John 1:5-9	John 13:1-17
1 Corinthians 11:23-29	John 20:19-23

¶*A Hymn may be sung after the Lesson.*

¶*Then may follow an Address or Sermon,*
after which may be sung a Hymn.

THE EXHORTATION

¶*Then shall the Congregation rise,*
and the Minister shall read the following Exhortation:

DEARLY Beloved: The Holy Supper of our Lord Jesus Christ hath been instituted for the special comfort and strengthening of those who humbly confess their sins, and who hunger and thirst after righteousness. Forasmuch as we intend to come to the Lord's Table, it becometh us diligently to examine ourselves as St. Paul exhorteth us.

We find, when we do this, that we are under the dominion of sin and death. To save us from death, make us children of God and exalt us to ever-lasting life, our Lord Jesus Christ had mercy on us, took our nature upon him, and himself became obedient unto death.

In order that we should believe this with greater confidence and be strengthened in cheerful obedience to his will, he hath instituted the Sacrament of the Altar in which he giveth us his Body and his Blood to eat and to drink. Who-ever eateth this Bread and drinketh this Cup, firmly believing the words of Christ, liveth in Christ and Christ in him, and hath eternal life.

We should also do this in remembrance of him, showing his death, that he was delivered for our offences and raised again for our justification. For all that he hath done we are bound to give him most hearty thanks, to take up our cross and follow him, and as he gave commandment, to love one another as he hath loved us. For as we are all partakers of this one Bread and drink of this one Cup, so are we all one body in him.

⁋*Then shall the Minister say:*

Let us pray.

ALMIGHTY God, unto whom all hearts are open, all desires known, and from whom no secrets are hid: Cleanse the thoughts of our hearts by the inspiration of thy Holy Spirit, that we may perfectly love thee, and worthily magnify thy holy Name; through Jesus Christ, thy Son, our Lord. *Amen.*

⁋*Then may the Minister conduct the Examination of Conscience, saying as follows:*

I ASK you, in the presence of God, who searcheth the heart:

DO you confess that you are by nature a most unworthy sinner, and that you have grievously offended against him, in thought, word, and deed, and have merited only his wrath and condemnation?

Answer: I do so confess.

DO you trust entirely in the mercy of God in Jesus Christ?

Answer: I do so trust.

DO you promise heartily to forgive others, as you believe that God forgives you, and to serve him henceforth in newness of life, to the glory of his holy Name?

Answer: I do so promise.

¶*Then shall the Minister begin the Confession, saying:*

Let us humbly kneel, and make confession unto God, imploring his forgiveness through Jesus Christ our Lord.

¶*Then shall all kneel and say:*

O God, our heavenly Father, I confess unto thee that I have grievously sinned against thee in many ways; not only by outward transgressions, but also by secret thoughts and desires which I cannot fully understand, but which are all known unto thee. I do earnestly repent, and am heartily sorry for these my offences, and I beseech thee of thy great goodness to have mercy upon me, and for the sake of thy dear Son, Jesus Christ our Lord, to forgive my sins, and graciously to help my infirmities. Amen.

¶*Then shall the Minister rise and say the Absolution. The Congregation shall remain kneeling until after the Benediction. Where customary, the Minister may lay his hand on the heads of the penitents as he says the Absolution.*

ALMIGHTY God, our heavenly Father, hath had mercy upon us, and for the sake of the sufferings, death, and resurrection of his dear Son, Jesus Christ our Lord, forgiveth us all our sins. As a Minister of the

Church of Christ, and by his authority, I therefore declare unto you who do truly repent and believe in him, the entire forgiveness of all your sins: In the Name of the Father, and of the Son, and of the Holy Ghost. *Amen.*

¶*Here the Minister may also say:*

ON the other hand, by the same authority, I declare unto the impenitent and unbelieving, that so long as they continue in their impenitence, God hath not forgiven their sins, and will assuredly visit their iniquities upon them, if they turn not from their evil ways, and come to true repentance and faith in Christ, ere the day of grace be ended.

¶*Then shall the Minister kneel, and all shall say the Lord's Prayer.*

OUR Father, who art in heaven, . . .

¶*Then shall the Minister say the Collect for the Day. Other suitable collects may then be said, and after them the Collect for Peace.*

The Lord will give strength unto his people.

R. The Lord will bless his people with peace.

O GOD, from whom all holy desires, all good counsels, and all just works do proceed: Give unto thy servants that peace which the world cannot give; that our hearts may be set to obey thy commandments, and also that by thee, we, being defended from the fear of our enemies, may pass our time in rest and quietness; through the merits of Jesus Christ our Saviour, who liveth and reigneth with thee and the Holy Ghost, one God, world without end. *Amen.*

¶*The Minister shall rise and say the Benediction.*

THE Grace of our Lord Jesus Christ, and the Love of God, and the Communion of the Holy Ghost, be with you all. *Amen.*

Invocation and Brief Order for Confession, *Service Book and Hymnal* (1958)

THE SERVICE

¶*The General Rubrics contain directions additional to those which appear in the Services.*

¶*The Congregation shall rise. The Minister shall sing or say:*

IN the Name of the Father, and of the Son, and of the Holy Ghost.

¶*The Congregation shall sing or say:*

Amen.

THE CONFESSION OF SINS

¶*The minister shall say:*

BELOVED in the Lord! Let us draw near with a true heart, and confess our sins unto God our Father, beseeching him, in the Name of our Lord Jesus Christ, to grant us forgiveness.

¶*The Minister and Congregation may kneel.*

¶*They shall sing or say:*

Our help is in the Name of the Lord.
  Response. Who made heaven and earth.
I said, I will confess my transgressions unto the Lord.
  Response. And thou forgavest the iniquity of my sin.

⁋Then shall the Minister say:

ALMIGHTY God, our Maker and Redeemer, we poor sinners confess unto thee, that we are by nature sinful and unclean, and that we have sinned against thee by thought, word, and deed. Wherefore we flee for refuge to thine infinite mercy, seeking and imploring thy grace, for the sake of our Lord Jesus Christ.

⁋The Congregation shall say with the Minister:

O MOST merciful God, who hast given thine only-begotten Son to die for us, have mercy upon us, and for his sake grant us remission of all our sins; and by thy Holy Spirit increase in us true knowledge of thee and of thy will, and true obedience to thy Word, that by thy grace we may come to everlasting life; through Jesus Christ our Lord. Amen.

⁋Then the Minister, standing, and facing the Congregation, shall say:

ALMIGHTY God, our heavenly Father, hath had mercy upon us, and hath given his only Son to die for us, and for his sake forgiveth us all our sins. To them that believe on his Name, he giveth power to become the sons of God, and bestoweth upon them his Holy Spirit. He that believeth, and is baptized, shall be saved. Grant this, O Lord, unto us all.

⁋Or, he may say:

THE Almighty and merciful God grant unto you, being penitent, pardon and remission of all your sins, time for amendment of life, and the grace and comfort of his Holy Spirit.

⁋The Congregation shall sing or say:

Amen.

186

Index of Names

Ambrose, 66
Anselm, 59
Anthony of Egypt, 58
Aquinas, 59, 60n.10
Asbury, F., 107
Augustine, 48n.44, 50-53, 59, 71, 151
Avery, W. O., 134n.2

Bach, J. S., 3, 4
Barth, K., 26-27, 31, 121n.44
Baur, F. C., 68
Bellarmine, R. C., 64, 96-97
Benedict XVI, 168-69
Berardino, A. di, 37n.13, 66n.25
Bonhoeffer, D., 19-20, 25-26, 31
Booth, I., 20n.14
Bosch, H., 170
Bourke, D., 27n.30, 48n.44
Brecht, M., 69
Brohm, T. J., 125
Bromiley, G. W., 27n.29
Buber, M., 16, 64

Cahill, T., 57n.4
Callistus I, 49, 50
Calvin, J., 3
Carothers, J. E., 21, 22n.17
Casel, O., 156, 157n.44
Cassian, J., 48

Chadwick, H., 37n.14
Chilstrom, H., 148n.19
Clement of Alexandria, 66
Columba, 10, 56
Conkin, P. K., 105n.7, 106n.8, 107n.10
Crites, S. D., 154n.38, 155-56
Cyprian, 50

Davis, C., 157n.45
Decius, Emperor, 50
Demetrias, 47
Deutscher, K., 13n.1
Dickinson, E., 15
Diocletian, Emperor, 50
Dix, G., 37n.14, 153
Donatus, 50
Dostoevsky, F., 38, 39n.18
Drey, J. S., 152
Duffy, E., 65n.21

Elert, W., xn.5, 7
Endress, H., 134, 138
Evagrius of Pontus, 48

Fackenheim, E. L., 154n.38
Fagerberg, H., 124n.60
Fairweather, A. M., 60n.8, 63n.16
Fairweather, E., 59n.6
Finke, R., 28